DOUBLE AGENT

THE EDDIE CHAPMAN STORY

FRANK OWEN
WITH A NEW PREFACE BY STEVE CHADDE

Double Agent: The Eddie Chapman Story

Frank Owen

with a new Preface by Steve Chadde

Preface copyright © 2014 by Steve W. Chadde
Printed in the United States of America.

ISBN: 979-8869063472

Originally published in 1954 as *The Eddie Chapman Story* by Julian Messner, Inc.,
New York. The original book is now in the public domain.

TYPEFACE: Clifford 10/12.5

PREFACE

DOUBLE AGENT: THE EDDIE CHAPMAN STORY chronicles the early life and war time adventures of Eddie Chapman, a British citizen who was first recruited by the Nazis as a spy but who later became a double agent for the Allies.

Born in 1914, and brought up in Sunderland, Chapman found work in the shipyards there. He then served in the Coldstream Guards until the mid-1930s, when he went AWOL and embarked on a second 'career' as a safecracker. He was a member of a "jelly gang", which specialised in robbing safes by blowing them open using the explosive gelignite. He enjoyed some success until 1939, when the police discovered him trying to blow open a safe in Glasgow.

While awaiting trial, he broke out of jail and made his way to Jersey where he was arrested. He was about to be returned to Scotland when the Germans occupied the Channel Islands.

By the start of 1939, however, he was being hunted by the police and fled to Jersey. He was caught by the Jersey police in February 1939 after burgling a nightclub and was sentenced to two years' imprisonment, with an extra year added after an attempted escape in September 1939. He remained in prison after the Germans invaded the Channel Islands in July 1940, and was finally released in October 1941.

Life on the occupied Channel Islands was harsh, and Chapman sought a way to return to Britain. He volunteered his services to the Germans as a spy and was eventually accepted by the German secret service, the Abwehr. The Abwehr was in a desperate position; it was getting only very low-quality intelligence out of Britain from its network of spies there. (In fact, though the Abwehr was unaware of this, MI5 had already caught almost all of the German spies in the UK and recruited several of them as double agents.)

The Abwehr saw Chapman as an ideal candidate for a spy. He claimed to be hostile to the British state, not least because he was still wanted by the police for his crimes on the UK mainland (throughout his life, Chapman maintained that he offered to help the Germans so that he could return to Britain). His connections with the criminal underworld offered the possibility that he could recruit additional agents for the Germans, and his expertise with explosives would enable him to carry out acts of sabotage. In particular, the Germans wanted him to attack the De Havilland aircraft factory in Hertfordshire, which made the much-feared Mosquito bomber.

After a year's training in German-occupied France, Chapman was dropped by parachute into a field in Cambridgeshire on 16 December 1942. Instead of disappearing into the criminal underworld, as his German handlers intended, he promptly turned himself in to the police and MI5. His arrival was expected; unknown to him or the Germans, the British had cracked the Germans' secret codes and knew in advance when agent *"Fritzchen"* ("little Fritz"), the Germans' codename for Chapman, would be dropped into the UK.

Chapman was taken to a secret MI5 detention centre in west London known as Camp 020. He was interrogated by the formidable Lt Col Robin "Tin Eye" Stephens, who owed his nickname to the steel-rimmed monocle which he always wore. Chapman was fully willing to cooperate: he told his interrogators everything about his time in occupied France and the mission that the Germans had given him. He even volunteered to work for the British against the Germans. Although Chapman's criminal past was troubling, Stephens concluded:

"In our opinion, Chapman should be used to the fullest extent... he genuinely means to work for the British against the Germans. By his courage and resourcefulness he is ideally fitted to be an agent."

Eddie Chapman thus became Agent ZigZag, one of the most important British double agents of the Second World War (his code name of ZigZag was in acknowledgement of his rather erratic personal life). MI5 decided to re-infiltrate Chapman into Germany and obtain more information about the Abwehr. Under the supervision of an MI5 officer, Chapman made radio contact with the Germans and informed them that he was preparing to carry out his sabotage mission at the De Havilland factory. He was sent to the factory at Hatfield, along with an MI5 minder, to work out a plan of attack so that he could tell his German controllers later what he had done.

The "attack" itself was one of the most remarkable deception operations of the Second World War. During the night of January 29–30, 1943, an elaborate system of camouflage was installed at the De Havilland factory to make it appear to German reconnaissance aircraft that a very large bomb had exploded inside the factory's power plant. Bomb-damaged transformers were created out of wood and papier-mache, and buildings were disguised with tarpaulins and corrugated iron sheets painted to appear from the air as if they were the half-demolished remains of walls and roofs. Rubble and debris was spread around the power plant, to make it appear as if it had been thrown there by an explosion. Separately, MI5 arranged for a fake story to be planted in the Daily Express reporting "an explosion at a factory on the outskirts of London."

The ruse was a complete success, even deceiving the factory's own staff. Chapman radioed the Germans to inform them of the successful "demolition" of the factory's power plant. The Abwehr was delighted with Chapman's work. In March 1943 he returned via neutral Portugal to Germany and travelled on to an Abwehr safe house in German-occupied Norway. To his amazement, he was awarded Germany's highest honour, the Iron Cross, in recognition of his work for the Abwehr. He was, and remains, the only British citizen ever to have been awarded this medal. However, Nicholas Booth suggests that as the Iron Cross was only ever given to military personnel, Chapman's "Iron Cross" may instead have been a War Merit Cross 2nd Class, or *Kriegsverdienstkreuz*.

Chapman was inducted into the German Army as an *oberleutnant* or first lieutenant. Chapman was also rewarded with 110,000 Reichsmarks and his own yacht. An MI5 officer wrote in an assessment "the Germans came to love Chapman... but although he went cynically through all the forms, he did not reciprocate. Chapman loved himself, loved adventure, and loved his country, probably in that order."

Chapman returned to Britain in June 1944 and survived the war, later publishing an account of his exploits in three books: *The Eddie Chapman Story* (1953), *Free Agent: The Further Adventures of Eddie Chapman* (1955) and *The Real Eddie Chapman Story* (1966).

On the romance front, Chapman had two fiancées at the same time, each in opposing war zones. He was betrothed to Freda Stevenson in England when he met Dagmar Lahlum in Norway. Stevenson was being financially assisted through MI5, and Lahlum was being treated by von Grunen. He abandoned both women after the war to marry his former pre-war lover Betty Farmer whom he had hurriedly left at the Hotel de la Plage in 1938. He and Farmer later had a daughter Suzanne in 1954.

In 1967 Chapman lived in Italy and went into business as an antiquarian. Chapman and his wife later set up a health farm (Shenley Lodge, Shenley, Herts) and owned a castle in Ireland. After the war Chapman remained friends with Baron Stefan von Grunen, his Abwehr handler (also known as von Gröning, wartime alias Doctor Graumann), who by then had fallen on hard times. Von Grunen later attended the wedding of Eddie Chapman's daughter.

Chapman passed away, age 83, on December 11, 1997 from heart failure. Betty, his wife of 50 years, recalled that Eddie said "it was better to live one day as a tiger than a whole life as a lamb."

UNCOMMON VALOR SERIES

Double Agent: The Eddie Chapman Story is part of a series entitled *Uncommon Valor,* taken from the quote by Admiral Chester W. Nimitz, U.S. Navy: "Uncommon valor was a common virtue," referring to the hard-won victory by U.S. Marines on Iwo Jima. The intent of the series is to keep alive a number of largely forgotten books, written by or about men and women who survived extreme hardship and deprivation during immensely trying historical times.

Steve W. Chadde
SERIES EDITOR

The elder Eddie Chapman.

CONTENTS

PUBLISHER'S NOTE

WHEN EDDIE CHAPMAN decided to publish his unique experiences during World War II he meant to tell the truth, and nothing but the truth. But as soon as the manuscript was completed—with Frank Owen's assistance— the censors of the British War Office stepped in and performed a major piece of editorial surgery, eliminating its most important parts and thus automatically, though unintentionally, misrepresenting the author's role in the events he described.

Their authority for gutting the book was the Official Secrets Act, a formidable law that forbids any person who is, or was, associated with British Intelligence ever to discuss or publicize details of that association. Eddie Chapman was an undercover agent for British Intelligence.

Now, there are good reasons for this law. In its long and unequaled history, British Intelligence has had occasion time and again to use with devastating success on many different enemies, under many different circumstances, the same tactics, the same forms of deception. British intelligence wants the lid kept tightly closed on its box of tricks, and the Official Secrets Act is designed to provide such protection.

To Chapman, this meant that he emerged from the pages of his first-person story as a Nazi spy, which he was not. The best he could hope for was that an astute public would read the truth between the lines.

In order to give American readers a complete, and also a fairer, account of Chapman's adventures, the publishers commissioned George Voigt, London correspondent of Time magazine, to ferret out and fill in the censored facts. In order to protect Chapman and Owen from prosecution for violation of the Official Secrets Act, it was necessary to publish Mr. Voigt's contribution in the third person, so as to differentiate the censored facts from that part of the story that Chapman was allowed to tell.

In its present form, the book constitutes the only complete version of the Eddie Chapman story ever likely to be told.

Eddie and Betty Chapman, 1950s. Betty initially turned down Eddie's offer of marriage but then realised 'life would be more interesting with him than without him.'

DOUBLE AGENT
The Eddie Chapman Story

Eddie Chapman, 1950s.

FOREWORD

IT was around Christmas, 1944, and I was back in England on a mission from Admiral Mountbatten's Southeast Asia Command. I was sitting at home in Westminster, waiting for a call to tell me that I was booked on a courier plane for Washington.

The telephone rang. My wife answered it. She turned to me: "It's a chap called Eddie."

I was busy working on some papers. I said:

"I know lots of Eddies, but just now I don't want to see any of them."

My wife went back to the phone, and then returned. She said: "He says you'll know him. He owes you £20."

I leaped for the phone. There was only one Eddie I knew who owed me £20.

Seven years before, at the time of the Spanish Civil War, a beautiful Russian woman I knew asked me to try to obtain some news of her lover, who was fighting in Spain. I had just come back from beleaguered Madrid, and I suppose she imagined I could help her, but I couldn't. The man was killed in the battle of Teruel, as we learned later.

One night soon afterwards, she rang me up in tears, and asked to see me. I met her in a nightclub off Piccadilly. She told me that they were bringing the body of her lover to Paris for burial, and that she had to make the journey to see him for the last time. Could I lend her the fare? There was a plane leaving the next morning.

It was around midnight, and it was Saturday. I said:

"Well, the fare is £7. Here is a tenner."

"But Frank," she murmured reproachfully, "how am I to get back!"

We drank another bottle of champagne, and I induced Milly, the owner of "The Bag O' Nails," to cash a check for £20 that I could give to Lydia. A few more words, and she was gone.

I do not know if she ever saw her dead lover again—but I heard a week later that she had acquired a live one. His name was Eddie Chapman. That was the last I heard of my £20.

So I had stored Eddie in my memory. I had met him several times in the West End, in one or another of those now almost legendary nightclubs of the Roaring Thirties—"Frisco's," or "Smoky Joe's," or "The Nest," or "The Bag O' Nails"—or all of them. I knew his trade. He was a safecracker. My pal from Scotland Yard, who also had an occasional drink with Eddie, assured me that he was one of the best in the business. This admirable copper and his Flying Squad colleagues were waiting to pin about seven years' penal servitude on Eddie as soon as they got the chance.

I seized the phone.

"Eddie! Where are you?"

"In the pub right opposite your flat. Come on over!"

"Don't you move! I'll be there!"

In "The Westminster Arms" I asked him: "Where did you drop in from?"

"Berlin. Would you like a check or £20 in cash?"

He pulled out a fat roll of banknotes. It must have contained several hundred pounds.

"Come now, Eddie, you shouldn't walk around with all that stuff loose. Put it in a bank, boy!"

"In a bank?" cried Eddie. "That'd be the place! Why, someone might pinch it!" Then, seriously: "Honestly, I'm really worried about where I can park it."

I asked him: "How much have you got?"

"About eight thousand quid."

"Where did you get it?"

"Hitler!"

A big laugh. Then Eddie said, "I mean it."

He began to tell me his story. I said "Drink up! We'll go over the road to my place and talk. I'll take the money now, by the way!"

We went back home, and sat up all night while he talked. A few weeks later when I was back in Burma I found time on the Chinese frontier to set his story down in the form of notes.

Eddie is six feet tall and well-proportioned, with a wire and whipcord body. He has the erect bearing of the Guardsman he once was. He has good looks, a quick brain, high spirits and a certain desperate quality which makes him attractive to men and dangerous to women. He was about thirty-two when I met him again (1944).

The story he told me begins before the war. However, I will have to go back still further in order to present the man against his proper background. Not that it is true to say that Eddie is the product of his environment. It seems to me that most things do not happen to Eddie— Eddie is the factor that causes them to happen. All this man's adventures, which read like a thriller, have come about because of his own personality.

The narrative which follows has been set down as nearly as possible in Eddie's own words. It is his own story—or as much of it as I am allowed to tell.

FRANK OWEN.

1

ON THE RUN

MY FAMILY came from Berwick-on-Tweed. They belonged to the sea. Some were masters, others were pilots, but most of them were marine engineers. My father was a chief engineer, and so was his brother— and there, but for the grace of God, go I.

We lived in a village in the north of England, amid the woods. It was marred only by heaps of slag thrown up by the mines. I was given my first lessons at the village school. It was dirty and the teachers were all women. I regularly ducked school, and instead walked two miles to the Derwent river where I would strip and swim in its shady reaches.

I was pretty good at most sports, and having no interest in any lessons (though I read what pleased my fancy) I became captain of the football and cricket teams. My father, the engineer, had decided that his son was to be an engineer, too—his universe revolved around an engine.

Things were going badly at home. The great depression of 1929 was hitting the northeast of England. Seafaring folk of all branches were out of work. Men who had studied for years for an exacting profession were suddenly thrown on the scrap heap, or on the beaches. Father, who had experience at every type of marine engineering, was glad to take a fitter's job.

His pay was two pounds eighteen shillings a week, less insurance. On this, my mother had to keep the whole family going. The job was not even permanent, and often the Old Man would bring home only his dole money. Piece by piece our small family treasures were sold. Father's gold watch, his personal mementoes, bits of furniture. Then the greatest sacrifice of all, the piano.

Our home was four miles from the sea, and mother realized that we children must have fresh air. My sister and brother would be packed into the pram, and mother and I took turns pushing it to Roker, which was the nearest sandy beach. She had not enough money to pay for the tram fare.

The next family venture was to manage a pub. It was small and smelly, and for customers relied on the men who worked in the dockyard, and a few fishermen. At the age of thirteen I was drawing their pints of beer and serving them spirits. It was against the law, but nobody gave a damn.

On Saturday and Sunday mornings I had to sweep the sawdust from the floors, empty the spittoons, and clean the brasses. Serving was fun, and I learned to cuss as only dockhands can. I learned boxing, too, from a well-known local bruiser who was always drunk. I went fishing with the fishermen. I listened to their wild stories of women and drink. All very dirty, and interesting.

On my fourteenth birthday I left school and set forth to earn an honest living. Earning a *decent* honest living is by no means an easy business.

The trade of motor mechanic was chosen for me. A local garage hired me to serve petrol and clean the cars; my wages, six shillings per week. Four nights of the week I worked till near midnight. For this I was paid time and a half. Sundays I worked for double time. Arriving home fagged out at night, I would fall into bed to be awakened next morning by mother at six A.M. telling me it was time to start again. I hated it.

My health grew so bad from lack of sleep that I had to leave the garage and go to work in an office at a shipyard, where one of my uncles happened to be timekeeper. My job was to write out pay checks and time cards. I would start at seven in the morning and finish at six in the evening. My wage was once more six shillings a week. I loathed this job, too.

From there I went to the Sunder Forge and Electrical Engineering Co., to serve an apprenticeship as an electrical engineer. I began in the test room working on electrical sea plants. My wages obstinately remained six shillings per week. Night school from six to nine occupied four nights of the week. One day I got mixed up in a fight with a fellow apprentice and knocked him around so badly that he was in hospital for several weeks. Mother had to pay my wages to him as compensation.

◆ ◆ ◆

In 1930, unemployment hit Sunderland like a sledgehammer. I was working only one week in three, and had to go on the dole. I was one of three million. Well-to-do people who know nothing about the dole talk most (and most ignorantly) about it. They regard it as a kind of charity; it is not.

In order to get my pittance of six shillings a week I had to go to a school called the Dole School. This was a government institution which was supposed to give men instruction in their trade. I was given a large piece of rough metal and a bad file, and told to file the metal straight. I was taught nothing that could assist me in any way in advancing the knowledge of my trade. It was not even useful to me when I later became a master cracker of safes, and a gangster.

Without telling my parents I had already given up going for my dole. I reckoned that it was a waste of time. Instead, packing sandwiches and taking my bicycle, I would leave home at seven in the morning, ride to a lonely part of the beach, and swim and laze around till evening. The problem was how to get six shillings a week to take home. To some extent I solved it by collecting empty beer and lemonade bottles from the shore, taking them back to the various shops and raking in the penny or twopence.

Now I began to ask myself, "Why work, either?" I could earn enough without work, so I stopped working, and basked in the sunlight, loafing, looking at the sky, feeling the soft wind, kicking the warm sand.

One Sunday I took my kid brother to the beach. We stretched naked on a quiet part of the shore, when suddenly there came a choking cry for help. I jumped up. My brother excitedly pointed to the figure of a man struggling about fifty yards from the shore.

I rushed into the water, grabbed the sinking body, and somehow managed to bring him back. As I staggered into the shallows with the man hanging around me a number of people collected on the beach. I suddenly became aware of my nakedness, turned the half-drowned victim over to another man who had waded in to help, and shamefacedly returned to the sea. My brother by this time had put on his shirt and shorts, and walked out into the sea with a bathing suit.

While the man was being attended to, we slipped quietly away. I did not want a thrashing for not attending church, so I swore my brother to secrecy. Next day the local paper carried headlines of the rescue, and the man who had taken over once I went back into the water claimed all the credit. That day I learned a good deal about human nature. But someone who had seen the incident wrote to the editor. I was traced, and without warning an invitation came for me to go to the Town Hall. The Mayor of Sunderland presented me with a certificate from the Royal Humane Society. What was worse, mother found out that I had skipped church and I got into trouble again.

Now calamity caught up with me. It was the custom of the electrical company to send a report to the parents informing them of the progress of the apprentice during the year. One evening, after a long cycle ride in the country, I arrived home and saw my report lying on the table. It had been opened. My absences for long periods were noted, and there were questions about the reason. I was frightened at being found out. I rushed into the larder and grabbed a loaf of bread. On the table near the report lay sixpence. I took it, and, jumping on my bicycle, I rode away from home.

2

THE BIG CITY

I HAD NEVER been out of the northeast of England. I had nowhere to go, but Dick Whittington is a hero in every boy's library. This Sunderland lad, too, had a vision of London, the great city paved with gold; London, where men quickly made large fortunes. I pedaled faster and faster, on and on.

But now it was winter, and slush lay on the road. Soon it was dark. I lit my lamp and pushed on toward London until I was too tired to ride. I found a haystack, ate my bread, buried myself in the snug warmth, and fell asleep.

When I awoke it was morning, and someone else was sleeping on the other side of the rick. He was a miner going to Doncaster to seek work in the pits. I told him I was bound for London, so we agreed to go part of the journey together. The snow came down again and it became bitterly cold. My hands were blue and I was hungry. That night we slept in a hostel. The beds were full of bugs. While there someone stole my gloves. I missed them next morning but said nothing. We begged food all along the road to Doncaster. I found the plain working folk extraordinarily kind to a couple of tramps in need of something to eat. We were never refused at any cottage.

My mate had relatives in Doncaster, and we stayed at their house for the night. We got hot food and a hot bath. In the bathroom, I found out who had pinched my gloves. My mate had finished his bath, and had gone into the bedroom to dress. He had left his jacket hanging behind the bathroom door and I noticed the gloves sticking out of a pocket. Without saying a word to him, I simply took them and put them back into my own pocket. I had learned that it is unnecessary to comment on certain things.

Next morning my mate intended to apply for a job in the mines, and I decided to go along with him. I had no money, and so I thought that if I worked for a few weeks it would help me on my way to London. At the pithead we saw a foreman who asked me if I had any previous experience. I said, "No." I got no job. My mate had better luck.

It was a terrible winter, and now the prospect of the long ride to London had become so forbidding that my courage failed me. I felt ashamed, but I was whipped.

It was a nightmare journey back. No sleep, no money, no food, for I was too miserable to ask—just pedaling up the Great North road in defeat. Once I fell off my bicycle, I was so tired. I crawled to a house. The kind woman on the doorstep gave me a meal and a shilling, "for the road, sonny."

At last I reached home. It was three o'clock on a misty morning. How long it had taken me I could not remember. I knocked timidly at the door, then louder. A window opened, mother's cough sounded, then her voice: "Who's that?" Then she rushed downstairs, opened the door, took me in her arms and sobbed as though her heart would break.

I went back to work, and for a few months everything was normal. The other apprentices knew of my escapade, and jeered at me. I got into fights.

It was no good trying to settle down. I was soon determined to be off to London. Shortly after my seventeenth birthday, I went to the local Army Recruiting Office and joined the Coldstream Guards.

I was six feet tall, lean, and pretty tough, so faking my age was easy. The first intimation my parents had was the notice for my departure to Caterham. They were astounded, but father talked sense to me. "Now that you have made your bed you must lie in it. It won't hurt you, if you don't let it."

I was given a ticket to London costing thirty shillings, which was two weeks' pay (from the time I had taken the King's Shilling), and off I went.

◆ ◆ ◆

At Caterham a picket waited for me at the door. He was standing so stiffly at attention that he looked as though he had a ramrod stuck up his spine. I asked him for the guardroom. Without moving his head or looking at me, he answered, "Straight ahead, first left." I followed the directions and found myself face to face with a huge corporal of the Grenadier Guards.

"What do you want?" he roared. I told him. He asked me for my papers, examined them, then bellowed:

"Picket!"

As though by magic the picket appeared.

'Take this man to Reception," bellowed the corporal, as though the other man were two hundred yards away. "Very good, Corporal," the picket bawled back.

I will never forget that rush from the guardroom to the Reception. The picket walked so fast that I had to trot to keep up. His gait was peculiar. Chin tucked in, head up, shoulders back, he flung his arms so high that they passed shoulder height, and his legs were stiff as if he walked on stilts. I had never before seen such extraordinary walking. I soon learned that this was the natural thing to do at Caterham. It still seems bloody nonsense to me.

At Reception I was shown into the presence of another corporal—a nice old fellow with a large mustache and an immense belly. He looked at me, grunted, "Huh, rookie," then spat indifferently into the fire. He told me that my barrackroom was upstairs and that the other rookies there would tell me what to do.

I found that these chaps were a mixed crew. One was from a public school (his father was colonel of a famous regiment), another resembled a bundle of rags, a third was a farm laborer, a fourth a clerk. They showed me how to make my bed. Lying on army biscuits (mattresses) was not comfortable, but I slept.

Next morning at six o'clock I heard a bugle. At once the other lads leaped out of bed and started dressing. One of them shook me, and said:

"You'd better get up! If Corporal comes in and catches you in bed—brother, he'll give you hell." I was still dog tired, and told him sleepily to go away. I dozed off again, and was awakened by the clank of buckets and the swish of scrubbing floors. The boys were scouring the barrackroom.

The door opened, and in came the corporal.

I watched him from beneath the sheets. At first he did not notice me. He inspected the floor, snarled at the men, stamped over to the window, then turned—and caught sight of the occupied bed! He let out one astonished yell, rubbed his eyes as if he was seeing an apparition, then pounced on me. I fell on the floor, the bed went up in the air, the pillows hit me from every angle.

"Get —— dressed!" the corporal roared, with a flood of curses, "and get a —— bucket of water." I obliged. The corporal then made me scrub the whole barrackroom as well as the stairs.

For breakfast we had a plateful of cold meat and some porridge. The corporal ate with his hands and shoveled the food down his throat. This belching, bellowing block of humanity was too much for the public schoolboy. He pushed his food to one side. "What! Not hungry?" said the corporal, and grabbing the meal from the plate, wolfed it down.

◆ ◆ ◆

I enjoyed life at the Guards depot. It has probably not changed.

The training is good, but it is tough. In charge of the barrackroom is a man called "Trained Soldier." You must address him in this manner, "Yes, Trained Soldier. No, Trained Soldier." Above him is a sergeant who rules your life. He is master of the squad, and captain of your fate. Your destiny in the Guards is in his hands, and heaven has no part in it.

At seven you have breakfast, at nine you do your first parade—and what a parade! As soon as the roll call is finished you are marched off to drill. The sergeant shouts, "Left, right, left, right," as fast as he can, and you march to his tune, taking care always to swing your arms at shoulder height. Sometimes, when a squad has made a lot of mistakes, the sergeant makes the men hold their rifles above their heads, or at arm's length, then gives them a double marching time with knees raised.

When drill is over, gymnasium takes its place, with an hour for double-time drill. The favorite exercise is down on the hands, arms bend, arms stretch; this is repeated over and over again. When I had finished my training I could do it at least sixty times. Even now my muscles are as strong and flexible as tough cord. It helped me a lot in my future trade.

As I said, you get tough; continually marching and drilling and shouting makes you so. Shouting in the Guards is part of the training. For three weeks you shout.

One day during a drill parade, I turned left instead of right.

"You constipated blankety-blank crab," howled the sergeant and, seizing my rifle, he banged it on my toes, then shouted, "Do that again, and I'll ram this bloody rifle up your arse!"

One day while playing handball I smashed my kneecap, and was carried to the depot hospital. The medical orderly in attendance looked at it. "That's nothing," he pronounced and, producing a needle, sewed up the wound. It gave me hell. I could not move for two days, and I stayed in bed. When the doctor saw my knee he sent me to Millbank Hospital, where I was X-rayed and the patella found to be broken. I was in hospital for more than a month, and was then granted three weeks' sick leave.

In order to collect my clothes and money I had to travel back to the depot. My leg ached and I limped. The Irish sergeant on duty at the barracks gate, seeing me make my way slowly along the road, roared at me to get a move on and swing my arms. I tried, but could not make it fast enough. The sergeant ordered me to double fifty yards back and come in at double-quick marching time, otherwise I would be reported. I tried, but nearly collapsed. Luckily, my squad sergeant happened to be passing. He explained what was wrong with me, and I was allowed to hobble to my barrackroom.

The Trained Soldier in charge of our barrackroom was fond of boxing. When there was any punishing to be done, Trained Soldier would invite the culprit to put the gloves on, and then proceeded to thrash him.

One night, having by this time thoroughly recovered from my injury, I had neglected to polish a barrackroom bucket to its required brilliance. I was asked to fight with Trained Soldier. Now the usual procedure of this champion was to rush at his man and punch him till he knocked him out. He rushed at me now, but I side-stepped and left-hooked him, bringing the blood spurting from his nose. He turned and came at me wildly and completely wide open. I knocked him down. He got up, and I knocked him down again. This time he stayed down. When he came around he asked me where I had learned boxing. When I told him the name of the Sunderland fighter who had taught me, Trained Soldier said thoughtfully, "I wish we'd had him here before you." We became friends, and from then on, whenever anyone misbehaved, Trained Soldier called on me to dish out the punishment.

Unluckily for me, he decided to enter me for the Guards' boxing tournament. I got through the first few fights all right, and then was matched against a red-haired Irishman with a wallop like a triphammer. In the first round he came straight out of his comer, and landed a blow on my chin which put me down for the count. It took me two hours to come around and as many days before I could eat again. I have never been in a ring since.

When my training at the Guards depot was completed I was drafted to the Tower of London, where I received my first red tunic and bearskin. How proud I was when I put it on! But I could never quite lose a feeling of looking ridiculous. The refrain of the "Toy Drum Major" would continually run through my head: "All brand new in their coats of blue, 'twas a sight to thrill you through and through."

I found life agreeable at the Tower—guard duties twice a week, plus an occasional picket or two. Two or three times I did keys duty. Every night at twelve o'clock the Tower is locked up. The Beefeater places the keys on a velvet cushion which he carries. He has an escort with him. When he reaches your post you have to challenge him:

"Halt, who goes there?"

"The Keys," he bellows.

"Whose Keys?"

Then comes the pompous reply, "The King's Keys."

Bawling back as loudly as you can you give him the okay: "Pass the King's Keys, all's well."

Thereupon you present arms, and His Majesty's Keys are borne past. In time you come to like the ceremony.

While I was on duty in the Tower I was handed a telegram telling me that my mother had collapsed and had been taken to the Tuberculosis Hospital. When I reached Sunderland father told me the bad news. There was no hope; it was a question of a few days, perhaps even a few hours. I found her in a ward with twenty or thirty other patients, women of varying ages, and all doomed. As I entered, a bed was wheeled past me. I stepped aside.

The bed was gently wheeled into a corner by the window. A white blanket covered the still figure. It was my mother.

She looked happy and beautiful. Her cheeks were flushed. I took her in my arms and kissed her. The smell of ether and carbolic acid sickened me. I gave her the flowers I had brought. She clung to them as if they would give her health and life. She was proud of her son in his red tunic.

She introduced me to the nurse. "This is my son." She leaned back, talking about my childhood, our walks together, the ambitions she had for my future.

Then she grew silent, smiled, tried to say something, and a little froth came to her mouth. Her eyes froze and set—and she was dead.

◆ ◆ ◆

I went back to London. London fascinated me—the stir of the big city, the theatres, the pageants and royal processions at which I occasionally did guard duty in the streets.

Our battalion was transferred to Pirbright for a shooting course, and I was due for leave. I had ten or twelve pounds to my credit. I decided to spend it and my leave in London. I took a room and set out to enjoy myself. I went to the theatre, the cinemas, explored Soho and the Embankment.

I was drinking coffee in a Marble Arch café when I noticed a pretty dark-haired girl at a nearby table. She smiled, and I joined her. Up to this time I had had no girl friend, and I felt excited. We laughed and talked—she was amused by my North Country accent. She suggested a drink at her flat, and I accepted. Her place was utter luxury to me, a radio, a couch, soft lights, bathroom, cocktail bar. I stayed the night, and convinced myself that I was madly in love.

Leave came to an end and she begged me to stay. She cried, threatened suicide. I stayed. Being still young and naive, I did not inquire where she got her money. One day I found out: she had several men keeping her. Not only that, when she needed more money she got others. When I knew I felt sick. I left her. She followed me and when I refused to go back, she phoned Marlborough Street Police Station and said, "Here's one of your deserters."

I was court-martialed, and sentenced to ninety days in the "glass house." Thus, I was introduced to prison.

The glass house is no picnic. The first thing that happens there is that you receive a "jail crop"—all your hair is sheared to the scalp. All orders are carried out at double time, and so is drill. The diet is scanty, and equipment is cleaned with a lump of brick dust. For cell duty, you must clean rusty pans or buckets. The brutality exceeds that in prisons for civilians. Do not try to be funny in the glass house; it hurts.

During my imprisonment the authorities discovered that I had taken a flat in the West End and given a wild party to a number of more or less "well-known" people. I was informed that I would be discharged from the Army on completing my sentence. I found those ninety days were slow in passing, and I considered myself lucky that I did only three of them on bread and water.

3

OTHER PEOPLE'S MONEY

I WAS RELEASED from the glass house in June, 1933. I had three pounds in cash, a civilian suit, and a jail crop, also a railway ticket to Sunderland, the town of my enlistment. I remained in London, and went back to my old digs in Praed Street.

For some time I drifted around the West End, doing odd jobs here and there, until I got fixed up with an electrical company. But I had not enough experience to hold the job down. I tried my hand working as a film extra. During this period I met and mixed with all types of tricky people—racecourse crooks, touts, thieves, prostitutes. Pretty rapidly, the cellars of the West End became known to me. I did many things to keep from starving. Perhaps the first "borderline" tricks I got up to were conceived almost as jokes, or at any rate were thought "smart" in some circles. I pilfered a little; I did some betting; I even tried getting work occasionally, but lack of experience and that Army testimonial, which simply stated "Services no longer required," did not help me.

I drifted toward the rapids of serious crime, with the inevitable result. The detection of crime in London is not brilliant, but it is methodical and painstaking. Small slips are added up by Scotland Yard until there is sufficient evidence upon which a sound indictment can be based. Then you catch it for a lot of things you thought you had got away with. You sometimes catch it for other criminals' offenses, too. I "fell," and duly received nine months for a smash-and-grab job. This I served at Lewes. Lewes is a good enough place to do time in. The prisoner either makes baskets or mats. I made mats.

Nearing the end of his sentence in this prison was a man who became my closest pal. His name was Freddie. A cool, selfpossessed, determined character if ever there was one, he was doing three years for post-office robbery and safecracking. I was attracted to him from the moment we met.

When my time was up, I sought out Freddie in London and we went into partnership. He was the prince of all safecrackers. Scotland Yard considered him the most dangerous man in this line of crime in London.

Our first job was a hundred percent successful. We went up to the north of England and robbed a large furrier's establishment at Harrogate.

Arriving by car, we parked it in a suitable spot, then clambered over a high wall. We found ourselves looking at some formidable iron grilles. After half an hour's sawing, we cut through a couple of bars; then with the aid of a jemmy the window was raised. Now we were in the basement. Tiptoeing upstairs, we found ourselves in the store. The wardrobes stood all round, and light fell through a glass door. Gently, we forced the wardrobe doors. Nothing at first except clothes. Then we came to one—I think it was the seventh we had forced—which was full of furs. Lucky seven!

We took some beautiful mink coats off the hangers. According to the labels their prices ranged from £.350 to £450. In all we collected five minks, two silver-fox capes and some other capes—ermine, stone marten, etc.

After we had parceled the coats we forced the office door open. Inside was a safe, and it was here that Freddie gave me his next lesson, this time in the art of safecracking.

It was a small safe. With the aid of a screwdriver he found the "joint" at the back, levered it up, and got a jemmy inside.

Then, by using a little force, he snapped the rivets one by one. Next, he pulled off the back, exposing the asbestos. This was quickly cleared away and the back of the "tin," which is the safe proper, was in view. This was now broken through, and there we found the money, all neatly done up in bags ready for the bank, or for us: about £.200.

We finished the job and got away. As we drove back to London, it started snowing and turned bitterly cold. We decided not to drive into town in the early hours of the morning because of the danger of being stopped and searched by police cars, which may check any vehicle that seems suspicious at that hour. Instead, we planned to drive the car up a quiet country lane and wait there for daybreak. We took all the mink coats out of the boxes and swathed ourselves in them, then fell fast asleep, wrapped in hundreds of pounds of luxury.

♦   ♦   ♦

Life was easy for me now. I had a car, plenty of money, and a flat in the West End. Nightclubs had always had a fascination for me and I was now a regular visitor to several in Soho. "The Nest," in Kingley Street, was a favorite haunt of mine at this time—the Negro music appealed to me and so did the girls. "Smoky Joe's" and the "Hell" clubs in Gerrard Street, "El Gaucho" and the "Shim Sham" all knew me well.

In our own world Freddie and I now began to operate a type of robbery which was then unfamiliar in England. We were blowing safes open with gelignite. We certainly supplied Fleet Street with some exciting headlines. So new was this method of ours that the press suggested that we were Americans, and this theory was supported by the fact that traces of chewing gum were often found near the blown-up safes. In fact, we simply used chewing gum to keep the gelignite explosive in place. Scotland Yard did us the "honor" of forming a special "Gelignite Squad."

Then Freddie and I quarreled, and I began a new partnership with a Burmese boy, Nickie, whose father had been a judge in Burma. Nickie was without nerves and made an excellent accomplice. All went well until one day I left my flat behind the Burlington Arcade and decided to pay a working visit to Scotland. Edinburgh was selected for the scene of operations, and the Co-operative Stores was to be our target for the night.

We booked at an hotel, and the next night broke into the store. I made ready to blow open the two large safes. Nickie and another boy, Phil, were keeping watch through the shutters. Peter, my chauffeur, was sitting in the car on the opposite side of the street waiting for a signal to step on the gas in order to dim the noise of the explosion. All was going well, and I went to open the glass skylight for our getaway. It was jammed. In a fit of temper, I smashed it in. Crash! A policeman, doing his rounds, flashed his torch through the glass door.

Nickie shrank back from the revealing beam, but his foot caught against a pile of canned preserves near the door. They fell with a hellish clatter. At that moment a squad car happened to be passing. Instantly there was a general uproar, whistles blowing, horns hooting, policemen shouting, and car engines "revving."

We moved out fast. We got out over the high wall which enclosed the Co-op Stores, but when we dropped onto the railway track Phil broke his ankle. I jumped at a passing freight train, which was running at about 12 m.p.h., and clung to the buffers. Nickie also got away. Peter had managed to drive the car off unobserved, and the three of us met back at the hotel. But Phil had been caught. There was nothing left for the rest of us but to bolt for England. We settled the hotel bill at 3 A.M., a form of honesty that did not pay, and left Edinburgh in haste. We got as far as Scotch Corner when a police car headed us off. I sprang over a wall at the roadside into some fern, but tripped and fell, and the cops grabbed me. When they found dozens of sticks of gelignite in the back of our car they realized that they were on to something pretty hot. We were driven back to Scotland in handcuffs.

The four of us were in Edinburgh Prison awaiting trial. But my lawyer got on to the fact of the local rivalry which existed between the Scottish and English police. He applied for fourteen days' bail for me, and astonishingly it was granted, though for me alone. I left for London, and sent money from there to get my friends out of jail. (In Scotland, the actual cash must be deposited; there is no surety.)

When the boys arrived in London they had a quick conference. Phil had decided not to join them. They resolved to jump bail and leave England, but not until they had made some quick money.

A man I knew said that if we could reach Monte Carlo he could get us on a boat for South America.

Swiftly, we organized robberies. A series of explosions shook the property structure of the city. Scotland Yard raked the underworld, raiding every nightclub and dive in the Squalid Square Mile. The cops knew exactly whom they were looking for; there was no mistaking the pattern of the artists at work. We faced twelve years' penal servitude apiece if we stayed in the country another forty-eight hours.

We had no passports. I and my girl friend, Peter and Nickie hopped on a plane for the Channel Isles, intending to go from there to the south of France. At the De la Plage Hotel, Jersey, we gave out that we were film people. It seemed to satisfy the management.

Then occurred one of those things that policemen dream of. They were put on the scent—by a bottle of scent posted by one of the gang to his girl in England. The fool signed his name, and the postmark did the rest.

One Sunday, in April, 1939, we were having lunch in a ground- floor room when suddenly the door was flung open and in rushed brown-hatted detectives of the Jersey police force. There was a melodramatic scene. I jumped straight through the window and ran up the hill, where I hid in an empty school building, and the police passed by. I found a mackintosh and put it on, then coolly walked back into town.

I went to a not so sweet-smelling boarding house. Telling the landlady that I was an engineer on one of the boats in the harbor, I booked a room and climbed into a hard bed. I did not greatly like my landlady, and would like her still less before long.

Next morning, on going out to explore, I found myself practically next door to the police station. I watched the police going in and out. Just opposite was a newspaper shop and outside it the contents' bills read:

"Amazing Scene in Jersey Hotel."

I walked over and bought a newspaper. Staring me in the face was a photograph of myself, and a vivid account of the events of the previous day.

I went back to my digs, got into bed and waited for nightfall. Then I paid a "business" visit to the office of the Casino, where, over and above my other activities, I drank a bottle of champagne—a piece of bravado and folly.

By now I was tired, and my brain was not working too well. Maybe it was the champagne; these indulgences should never be mixed with working hours. I resolved to return to my digs to sleep. It was a mistake—my second—and I paid for it. I entered my room and went to bed. Suddenly, at about 2 A.M., the door burst open and the police walked in. "We think you are Eddie Chapman," said the officer in charge, "and we think Scotland Yard wants you." They made no mistake this time. Before my eyes were fully open the handcuffs were on my wrists.

I was taken to the St. Helier police station. Luckily for me I had committed a crime against Jersey law, and therefore I would be tried in Jersey. In England, of course, I was wanted for other offenses. On the way to the police station, therefore, I thought it best to inform the detectives that they might want me themselves.

The Jersey trial was interesting. The whole court rose to say the Lord's Prayer in French: *"Notre père qui est aux cieux,"* etc. You are not allowed to plead for yourself in the Channel Isles, and must have a lawyer. The Attorney General is decidedly the power behind justice. He overawes his younger and less able opponents. He conducts the prosecution and demands the sentence.

I got two years. It is the maximum sentence that can be served in a Jersey jail.

4

ON THE INSIDE, LOOKING OUT

J ERSEY PRISON is old-fashioned. It is only twenty years since the treadmill was abolished. The place is small, having cells for only sixty inmates, but the prison is never full. The buildings are of granite and look impressive from the outside. It is extremely chilly in winter for those inside.

The prison staff consisted of about a dozen wardens, a chief warden and a governor; at most times the staff was more numerous than the prisoners. The administration was run by a prison board of five. Religion was in the hands of a chaplain assisted by an organist. The only work done there in my time was stone- breaking, a task that holds limited interest. I was given a small hammer and a large chunk of stone. I sat in a cell alone and broke the chunk into chips. These were afterwards used on Jersey buildings. We had no exercise, and the silent system was in force.

My fellow-prisoners were nearly all short-time men, Irish potato diggers or Jersey natives in for drunkenness or wife- beating. During my sentence some of the local characters came back to prison ten, twelve, and even, in one instance, sixteen times, but only for a few days, or at most a month. The routine was monotonous; reading was the only relaxation. The library had about two hundred books, and before my time was half through I had read all of them. I read Tennyson's poems, many of which I learned by heart. H. G. Wells' *The Outline of History* made a great impression upon me. Wells' support of Darwin and his condemnation of the blindness of the clergy found an instant sympathizer in myself.

I had been in prison three months when I resolved to escape. My work had by now been changed. My duties were gardening and cleaning the offices. One day, while I was sweeping the garden path, I picked up an old airways timetable. After studying it, I reckoned that with two hours clear I could catch the departing plane for England. I chose Wednesday for my D-Day. There was a suitable plane that day, and also it was the prison governor's day off—an important part of my plan.

My duties took me into the governor's house. He and his wife and family were sometimes out for the whole day. The warden in charge would give me a job to do. He would then sit smoking or drinking tea, while he kept a neglectful eye on me. This Wednesday afternoon he dozed in the June sun. I strolled past him into the house. I had observed that the governor's son, a lad of eighteen, was of my own build. I went upstairs into his bedroom and chose a suit which I found on the bed. I put it on. Then I descended to the governor's study and took the thirteen pounds in petty cash in his open desk drawer. I climbed out onto the roof.

As I made my way along the roof I was seen by some nurses in the adjoining hospital. They stared at me, and pointed. I took a piece of string out of my pocket and began measuring the slates. I heard their laughter at mistaking me for an escaping convict. When they went away, I scrambled along the slates to the end of the roof and dropped over the edge into the courtyard below. I passed into the street to the nearest kiosk, and telephoned the airways booking center for a seat on the 3:30 plane. "Sorry," they said, "the plane left at 3:10. You must have seen an old timetable. A pity, too, because the plane was almost empty."

I went to a café and ordered coffee and a packet of cigarettes. There was nothing to be done until dark, so I drifted into a pub and started drinking. Presently I met a couple of girls and we went off together for some dinner and a dance. I got on very well with the tall one, who said I reminded her of somebody she'd seen somewhere, which was probably true. "You will hear of me again," I assured her.

I made my way to a quarry. In a quarry you generally find the explosives which I needed, and obtained. On leaving I saw an empty car standing by the roadside, and decided to borrow it. I was forcing the ignition when I felt a violent blow on the head. The owner had come back with the girl he had been necking with in the woods. I knocked him down, and the girl ran off screaming. I left the car and hurried into town. I had to get under cover quickly, and preferably in the Town Hall where I could also get on with the necessary job.

A hue and cry had already been raised for the escaped convict who had pinched the governor's son's suit. Under a street lamp a man shouted: "That's him!" I bolted around the comer into the dark. I ran toward the seashore. There I found a locked bungalow. I broke in, got myself some food, and went to sleep. The absent owner was a fat man, so that I could not change into his suit. His fisherman's hat was the right size, though.

Next day I was sitting in a café eating bananas and cream when the waitress gossiped: "I see by the paper that terrible man's escaped again."

"Let's have the paper," I said. My face was all over the pages.

As I walked along the beach I noticed that four men were standing on the cliff watching, two of them in uniform. Some kids were kicking a football about and I joined them as casually as I could. Presently the men came down and approached me. "You're Eddie Chapman," said the leader. "Try and take me," I yelled, starting to fight. They took me back to the cooler where the governor roared: "Take that suit off him!" I was shoved into a cell, in my shirt.

Next day, I appeared in court in my prison garb. I asked to be sent to England for trial. Once again the Attorney General prosecuted. He did not propose to gratify my wish. He asked the court for a sentence of twelve months, to run after I had served my other sentence.

This meant that I would do three years instead of two. Now, the law of Jersey was that no man must do more than two years in the local prison. However, by some special pleading, the Attorney General convinced the court that this prisoner would not be doing three years, but two years and one year. At school I had been taught that two and one make three, but that apparently is not so in the Jersey criminal courts, at any rate not when the Attorney General is practicing arithmetic.

◆ ◆ ◆

I began my new term in Jersey prison with three months' solitary confinement. I had not been out of this very long before I qualified for further punishment. I had picked up a gimlet and hacksaw, left by a local carpenter who had been working in the prison. On Sunday my meal was given me at 4 P.M. and I was locked in for the night. As soon as the warden had gone I got busy cutting out the lock. I had spent about three hours on the job and had practically completed it when—clang!—the iron gate at the end of the corridor opened and the governor marched in. He was accompanied by the chief constable and a Scotland Yard man who had come over to the island to talk to me. The key was turned in the cell door— and the lock promptly fell out. The governor spluttered with rage and humiliation in front of his visitor. I got another three months' solitary.

When this punishment was over I was ordered to crack stone again. I simply sat down and said "No." I just did not give a damn what happened. I got another month. I went on a hunger strike. I told the governor, "If I could, I'd murder you. As I can't, you can murder me."

The governor got the wind up that I might really die. He appealed to me to eat, offering me parole. He wasn't a bad chap, I suppose. At any rate I changed my mind and agreed to take some beef tea. I was allowed to work in the garden again. The governor came rather to like me, I think, and one of the Jersey-born wardens taught me French.

I was still better off than my confederates, Nickie and Peter, who had been taken back to England, tried at the Old Bailey, and sentenced. I would have faced a similar fate. But, of course, something might easily happen! It did.

Suddenly events in Europe went far beyond the world of an outlaw such as I was. History had taken a hand in my unimportant destiny. The Danzig crisis piled up, and was over. Soviet Russia had made her uneasy truce with Nazi Germany. Dare Hitler next defy the democracies of the West? He took a gamble. Poland was invaded, and Britain declared war on Germany on September 3, 1939. The news was given to me by a warden who brought my bread and water.

The brief battle of Poland proved Hitler victorious. Stalin, with one eye on his new ally, Germany, promptly invaded Finland. A few months more, and the Norwegian campaign had also been brought to a violent close. Then the Panzer horde burst through the neutral screen of Holland and Belgium. Wardens in the prison vied with each other in saying that as soon as the Nazi armies came up against the impregnable Maginot Line of the French frontier they would smash themselves to pieces and the war would be over inside two months.

The usual silly tales were told—the Nazis possessed tanks made of compressed paper and wood. The British Tommy and the French Poilu were better equipped, better trained, and either one could outfight any three Germans. The Allied generals had all had World War I experience, their Nazi counterparts were new and incompetent. There were supposed to be thousands of British planes. Stories went around of British officers scorning the German menace and taking with them to France their tennis rackets, cricket bats, golf clubs and packs of hounds.

When the German attack was launched across the Low Countries I made a cheeky bid for freedom. I asked to be sent direct to the front as a trained soldier. I was curtly refused.

Soon came rumors of disaster—the Germans had broken through, the Allied armies were in retreat, split and shattered. At first, no one could believe it—not even, it seemed, the authorities putting out the news. The radio lied, the newspapers lied, everyone lied. The B.B.C. and Paris broadcasts played up some British local successes so much that at times the Jersey folk might have supposed we were advancing and winning. These reports—together with the more truthful accounts—were brought to the prisoners by the various wardens, although this was forbidden by the prison authorities. On the whole, we made out fairly well what was going on.

I recall one young warden bringing a map to my cell one day and, after studying our various retreats and listening to Allied propaganda, saying sarcastically, "If we advance much further we'll be fighting in the streets of London."

The atmosphere in the prison was depressing and apathetic, and it grew worse in those blazing June days when the truth could no longer be concealed. The Germans had smashed across the hinge of the Maginot Line. The King of the Belgians had asked for an armistice—and was labeled in the British Press as "King Quisling." Then the evacuation of the British army from Dunkirk began.

All the small boats from Jersey were ordered to take part in this job. The Seine was crossed by the German tanks, and Paris fell. At this, the people in Jersey lost all control of their own fate. Everybody was giving orders; nobody really knew what was going on. One day the military were going to defend the island at all costs; loud cheers. Next day they were gone. The rest of the population was trying to follow them, including the wardens. Naturally I, too, thought of only one thing—how to get abroad and away.

Now Britain stood alone, and her situation was desperate indeed. Every ton of shipping was needed. Only a few small vessels could be spared to try to evacuate the population of Jersey.

Children were piled into the holds of the ships. Queues miles long waited night and day for a chance to get on board. People swarmed into St. Helier from the outlying districts and left their motor cars for anyone who wanted them. Houses, furniture, farms, country estates were given away; shopkeepers offered their goods free to any passer-by. Confusion beyond belief reigned outside the prison walls. Inside, the normal routine continued.

The Governor of Jersey made a speech. He regretted leaving the island, but pressing duties called him elsewhere. The people of the island could have easily spared him earlier. Then, three days before Jersey was occupied, the Luftwaffe decided to bomb it. Over they came—the prisoners in the jail heard the bombs whistling down. We were locked in our cells as the crashes split the air. Nobody likes being bombed, but believe me, to be bombed in a locked cell with no chance either to fight or quit is even less attractive. An Irishman near me was howling out a prayer—"Oh, Mother Mary! Spare me, a miserable sinner!" He was certainly all of that. I think he was in for murder.

All the other prisoners were screaming to be let out. One was crying for his mother, another for his wife and children. I was tom between half-hoping a bomb would hit the prison (not my cell!) and give me another chance to escape, and hoping even more earnestly that the place would escape bombing altogether. There were no wardens. We heard later they were at the boats trying to get passage to England. Two of them managed it. I thought it was a shame that they did not all succeed. Why, I might have then made myself prison governor!

When the last evacuee ship had pulled out the rest of the jailers turned up once more and resumed the old routine, and we prisoners were put to work again. I really then saw the enemy for the first time. A Nazi plane droned over. As it came near I could see the swastikas on the wings. It was a strange sensation, standing there helpless, not knowing whether to dive for shelter under a wooden bed, or just stupidly gape. I gaped. The plane flew over the prison and the hospital, and then away into the distance. The faces of the wardens were white and strained. They had always been the masters of somebody else's fate. What would their own be now?

Next day, the Germans came over again. They flew low. The pilots fired a few machine gun bursts from their planes at the houses, and some people were killed. Then down fluttered leaflets. They contained an ultimatum: Surrender or else! All large houses and public buildings were ordered to show some white emblem.

The Acting Governor accepted the ultimatum. He really had no choice—he had no arms and no troops. Panic swept the prison. One warden was certain that the Germans would rape his wife; why, neither I nor anyone else could understand. Others felt the same. Some went home and talked of shooting their wives in order to spare them this fate. British propaganda had certainly done its work well.

Meantime, some of the bar and hotel keepers were working overtime pouring their stocks of beer down the gutters of the streets. Whiskey and gin bottles were smashed by the hundreds; anyone could get free cigarettes and household supplies. The streets and piers were full of derelict cars. Horses, sheep and cattle roamed the roads.

Next day the buildings in the town were festooned with white flags. Housewives hung tablecloths outside their windows. In the prison, a bed sheet was hoisted on the flagstaff, and another was laid out on the lawn. Jersey had surrendered.

That afternoon, a squadron of German bombers flew over "just in case." Then a fighter landed at the airport. Out got a young German officer with two noncoms. They walked into the town and ran up the German flag over the Town Hall. They cut the telephone connection at the post office with Great Britain.

German transport planes came in. They landed troops and guns. Barges followed with more troops. The townsfolk were terrified; the streets were deserted. When the first German seaborne regiments came ashore they brought with them a band. The stillness of the town was rudely broken by a catchy military march. Curious faces were pressed to the windows. Wives unlocked their bedroom doors; children crawled out from underneath the beds. The Germans were playing "Pack up your troubles in your old kitbag."

It amused me to hear the comments of the wardens—my only links with the outside world. One of them said to me, "The Germans are not at all bad chaps—they have brought cash with them —why, they pay for everything they buy in the shops."

The Germans certainly did buy everything. English dress materials and English suiting were what they all wanted. Every ounce of coffee, tea, chocolate they could lay their hands on also went quickly, and soon the shops were empty. Inside four months they had cleaned out the island, which was reputed to have had three years of supplies.

Some of the wardens would bring us stories of children being petted by the soldiers—how they gave them sweets, etc. A good impression was being built up. But another warden told me with indignation how he had seen a Jersey girl walking down the street with a German soldier—Jersey was not quite ready for that, and many of the citizens were scandalized. Then the number of these incidents grew. More and more girls were seen with Germans. They dined openly with them in restaurants, went swimming with them, entertained them, attended their concerts. They would stand outside the various hotels waiting for the smart young officers. Jersey had submitted.

Terror is a favorite German weapon; but terror does not necessarily mean naked force—you can scare a man to death by suggestion. In Jersey, the Germans did not need to clamp down an iron regime. Often, to impress the population they would stunt fly over the island—diving, twisting and zooming. The soldiers held practice exercises for the invasion of England. A warden described how he had seen troops with full kit marching up to their necks in water. This was before the British successfully bombarded their conglomeration of barges in the Channel ports.

When the Germans were blitzing England they would sometimes fly over Jersey. One day I counted more than two hundred planes. When the planes came back, there were only some forty or so, and they were flying in bad formation. This was not quite so good. But the Germans put out fantastic claims of the damage done in England. Many of the island people believed them.

◆ ◆ ◆

The only remote contact which we of the jail population had so far made with the conquerors had been to see their planes, and to hear their bombs. We were now to meet them.

One day I was squatting in what was known as the Stone Yard, splitting logs to make sticks for firewood. Suddenly, without warning, the door of the gate was unlocked, and the sentries shouted, "Attention!"

The governor walked in, followed by three German soldiers. One was a young *Oberleutnant* of the Security Police and the others were noncoms of the same corps. We prisoners all stood to attention. In turn, we were commanded to come forward for questioning. The interpreter, one of the noncoms, spoke dreadful English. The governor was asked to stand at the other end of the yard while the interrogation was in progress.

My turn came for questioning.

"What are you in for?" asked the interpreter.

"*Ich bin Verbrecker,*" I answered.

"*Ach, Sie sprechen Deutsch,*" interpolated the lieutenant.

"Yes, a little. I am in for safecracking, and for trying to escape."

He laughed a little. "Bad luck you did not get away with it—what's it like here?"

I told him it was monotonous, and the food was bad. I added, "Any chance of work?"

"Sorry," said the lieutenant, "not my line!"

After a few good-natured remarks the German officers left.

They made a full inspection of the prison, apparently searching for political prisoners, but as these had previously been removed to England they were out of luck. They had more success when they visited the local internment camp. There, several Italians and Germans were found who were released. This visit also had another significance. The Germans now took over the prison, and together with the post office and a few administrative buildings here and in Guernsey these were the only official buildings in the British Empire ever occupied by them. On the whole, they behaved pretty well. At the same time, it must be said that little was done to provoke them. The official attitude of the island authorities was one of complete submission.

Not everybody succumbed to German blarney, or brutality. A girl who was working as a waitress in a café was called upon to serve four German soldiers. She took the order and, on approaching the food lift, shouted down the shaft:

"Four dinners for four gangsters!"

One of the soldiers understood English and made a complaint to the military police; the girl was arrested and given a month's imprisonment. A special guard was sent to look after her.

When the order came in for the civil police to salute all Wehrmacht officers, and the prison followed suit, it dismayed several of the older wardens. They were, for the most part, ex-soldiers of the 1914-18 war, and bitterly resented this humiliation. At the beginning all of them took their war medals off their tunics, but later, as an act of resistance, they put them back on. I remember a fine old chap called Bill Carrier, an ex-professional footballer who had played for several first division teams in Britain. He hardly concealed his contempt for the Germans. When they came on a visit he would dourly touch his cap to their commander and just barely obey his orders. But as soon as the Nazi had turned his back he would wink at us and give the V- sign.

Islanders who were sent in for minor offenses against the Wehrmacht were usually under the control of the prison wardens. If, however, they got a sentence longer than two months, they were transferred to a prison in France. One young Irishman who came in had walked into a restaurant, ordered a meal and sat eating it with his hat on. This had not suited a German soldier, who got up from his chair and flung the Irishman's hat to the ground. The Irishman replied by punching the Jerry's head and flooring him. He got one month's hard labor.

◆ ◆ ◆

There were grimmer incidents.

Several French students tried to escape from France. They had taken a motorboat and set out for the coast of England. The motorboat broke down, and they had drifted ashore at Jersey. There were about a dozen of them ranging in age from fifteen to eighteen. The leader was a dark, merry-eyed boy, full of high spirits, the son of a French doctor. Their antics in prison cheered us up considerably. When first they arrived, they danced and shouted and sang. They drew caricatures of Hitler and Goering on the walls. They also felt very bitter toward the British prison officials who insisted on standing at attention and removing their hats when any of the German officers were talking to them. When they shouted "Attention!" to the French boys, the latter simply squatted.

Soon these boys grew terribly thin on our prison diet. This consisted of one pound of potatoes and six ounces of bread in the morning; one pound of potatoes and potato soup, and four ounces of bread for lunch;

and one pound of potatoes and six ounces of bread again for supper. This diet never varied. My own weight fell from 161 pounds to 131 pounds. Often I saw my new friends eating raw potatoes with the skins on to try to still their hunger. Several times I managed to steal extra potatoes and pass them on, a small service for which I was showered with gratitude. Eventually, the Frenchmen were tried before a German court-martial. The young leader with whom I had made friends was, with a comrade, sentenced to be shot; his other companions received sentences ranging from life to ten years' hard labor.

The young Frenchman died a soldier's death. When the executioners came for him, he shook hands and kissed all his friends goodby. They raised a hellish din and were brutally knocked down. When the two boys came to the place of execution they refused to have their eyes blindfolded. At the command to fire, they shouted with their last breath *"Vive la France!"* The Jersey people piled flowers on their graves. These were my first French friends. They taught me a new idea of France—and of Germany.

There was another set of fellow-prisoners, whom I and the others in Jersey prison liked a lot less. These were Germans. At one period, the enemy occupation forces started sending in their soldiers who were convicted of minor offenses. What partly reconciled us regulars to the newcomers was the trouble they caused the prison authorities. They cussed their British jailers soundly in German.

"Scheiss-Engländer," they would yell, *"Ihr könnt mich am Arsch lecken."* (Bloody Englishmen—you can kiss my backside.)

They refused to be locked up, and walked about the prison doing just as they pleased. The entire staff was terrified of them. At last a German military guard was put into the prison to keep discipline and protect the wardens.

My own term in prison was coming to an end. I had served two years and eight months of my sentence, and while I had been shut up in a cell a war had changed the pattern of the world. My own fate had not escaped the impact of these years. Nor had my own ideas remained the same. I had no money, no friends; but a plan of campaign was beginning to form in my brain.

Britain was my native land, and there, beleaguered as she was in 1941, life still seemed sweet. In London I had learned the things that I liked in life; a bad life no doubt, but I had enjoyed it. I wanted to go home even though punishment awaited me. Wait!

Perhaps I could somehow work that debt off. Was it perhaps possible for me to start again, to render some service to my own people that might enable me to go back and not be forever on the run?

It all sounds fine talk now, perhaps it was phony talk even then, and I don't pretend that there were no other motives in the plans I began to turn over in my mind. They did not occur to me, either, in one moment or in one mood. Months of solitary hours in prison had molded them. But anyway I began to make a plan. With the aid of some grammar books I had taught myself to read and write both French and German. Speaking was only a matter of practice. And then . . . ?

Early one morning in October, 1941, I shook hands with the wardens and walked out to freedom.

5

I JOIN THE GERMANS

A T THE prison gate a man met me. "Hullo, Eddie," he said. "I heard you were coming out. How about some breakfast?" He was the local bookmaker who had served a short term of imprisonment for some black-market offense.

I was surprised and pleased to see him. I went home with him and ate bacon and eggs for an hour. Sandy, as he was known on the island, became a good friend of mine. He gave me twenty pounds and a black-marketing job. That afternoon I set off to put my plan into action.

I went to see the Commandant of Jersey—Herr von Stülpnagel. Arriving at the Kommandantur, I was stopped by a sentry and asked about my business. I answered that I came to talk with the Commandant and that it was *"geheim"*—secret. The sentry directed me to the office of a German major. This bull-faced character asked me to sit down and tell him what it was all about. I said:

"I would like to join the German Secret Service."

Bull Face laughed good-naturedly, and asked me what qualifications I possessed.

"Were you ever in the I.R.A.?" he asked.

Thereupon I produced the various newspaper clippings of my case, and gave him a brief record of my history; and, what was more, an appreciation of my future if the British police should get hold of me.

The officer became interested, especially when I told him that I was bent on getting my revenge on society for the ills which I insisted it had done to me. There were some personal scores that I would give a lot to settle, I said. The major called in his secretary and, after warning him that *"alles ist streng geheim"* (all is strictly secret), and that he must not speak one word of the matter to anyone, he wrote down as much of my history as I could tell him, with an account of all the underworld connections I had in London. He made some comments himself, saying that I might possibly be good at sabotage. We then had a drink together, and the major gave me a cigar. He promised to let me know what would happen to my application.

Life in Jersey was easy enough for me. Sandy had a barber shop which was frankly a front for his black-market activities. When the Germans came into the shop I talked to them in German, and offered to buy any stocks of liquor or miscellaneous articles which they could obtain with occupation marks when on leave or relief in France. I doubled the price and sold the goods extremely well, and in time they were supplying nearly all the St. Helier pubs with black-market liquor. Cigarettes sold for seven and sixpence a packet, and were obtainable only on the black market. Ten packets of cigarettes were swapped for a pound of tea.

In order to further my fortunes with the Germans, I became friendly with them. Often I was invited to their brothel club, the "Belle Amie," in company with officers in various branches of the services.

One day I was riding my bicycle on the road when a dispatch rider, traveling at full speed, smashed into me. I was thrown some distance, but luckily got off with a few bruises and cuts. The motorcycle was also damaged, and you could have cut the air with the foul language of the rider. The police came, and my name and address were taken down. A few days later a military policeman came to my rooms and told me that I was to report to the Kommandantur. He thought it was on account of the accident.

When I arrived I was shown into a room where several officers of the Military Police were sitting. One of them said to me:

"Your name is Edward Chapman, and we have been warned that you are a dangerous man, and that you brought explosives to this island when you came here. Where are they?"

I protested that it was a lie. The officer let me go after giving me a warning that if I tried to do anything against the German occupation I would be shot. I wished him good morning and walked out, feeling alarmed.

I was much impressed by the discipline, politeness, and generally fine physique of the German soldier in Jersey in 1941. When one of them entered a restaurant he acknowledged his comrades either by giving the military salute or, if he belonged to the Hitler elite, stretching his arm and giving the full salute of the S.S. troops. Every soldier saluted in the German army. A *Gefreiter*, who was a noncom, saluted his junior officers and the officers of all branches of the German armed forces, whether they belonged to the Marine, the Luftwaffe, or simply the Todt Organization, or labor corps. This body was looked down upon by men of the regular fighting forces, despite all Hitler's attempts to glorify it.

The Germans naturally had control of the local Jersey newspaper, and a stream of virulent propaganda against Britain poured out from its presses. The cinemas mostly showed the same type of films. Later, in various parts of German-occupied Europe,

I saw only few films of this kind. The reason was simple: the German "master race" had enough fighting to do at the front without seeing it on the screen.

Wireless sets were allowed in Jersey, except in certain districts where "V" signs had been drawn on the walls and the Germans had confiscated the sets to punish their owners. Naturally, it was a source of comfort to me to hear the news from the B.B.C.

In Jersey, food rationing was not severe in that autumn of 1941 when I left the island—three quarters of a pound of meat and one pint of milk per day, plenty of potatoes and fresh vegetables. There was, however, a real shortage of clothing—no shoes, no suits, and little underwear. Liquor could be obtained only in the black market, and the police were soon hand in glove with its chief operators. Often they would stop me and ask if I could let them have cigarettes, or a bottle.

Some of the German marines who were passing to and from France would bring me cases of cognac. We swapped tea for it; a quarter of a pound of tea for a bottle of cognac. Naturally, I regulated my prices on the basis of useful services. If a special customer was temporarily out of funds he got the stuff for nothing.

One evening, I went to the "Belle Amie" in the company of a German captain. We drank three bottles of cognac. A curfew was in force and residents had to be at home by midnight. At 2 A.M. I left with my host. Outside the cabaret the island police arrested me. Some German marines tried to free me, and a free-for-all began. The Military Police joined in, and I was carted off to the local police station. My friend, the captain, telephoned to the Governor of the island, and I was released. A little while later I was not to be so lucky.

◆ ◆ ◆

The day arrived, one noontime while I was doing some black-marketing in Sandy's barber shop, when in came the Jersey police. They arrested me and a Jerseyman named Faramus, who was my assistant. They gave no explanation, but when we arrived at the police station a German guard, consisting of three men, was waiting to take over. They asked us where our clothes were, and escorted us to our homes. I packed my bag, and was told to take enough for a week. Faramus and I were then handcuffed together, driven to the harbor and put aboard a boat with an escort. An *Oberleutnant* warned us: "I will shoot you if you attempt to escape."

It was not the last time I would hear that ominous phrase.

We disembarked at Granville and were immediately put on a train for Paris. During the journey the guards did not speak to us. I made some jokes about them in English to Faramus in order to cheer him up because he was extremely frightened.

So was I, and I needed cheering up myself. I asked the officer why I had been arrested, but he replied without a smile, "You will find out later." Some French folk saw us sitting in the train.

"Anglais?" they asked.

"Yes," we shouted. The guards laughed, and the kindhearted French people threw some food in through the window. We were glad to get it.

At Paris we boarded a bus for St. Denis. None of the Germans spoke French, and I acted as interpreter, asking for directions. The Parisians looked at us with undisguised sympathy.

We arrived at the English internment camp at St. Denis, where the Germans put us in a punishment cell. The same night, after we had eaten, we were transferred to an old-fashioned fort which was being used as a camp for hostages and people held on suspicion of espionage. There Faramus and I were taken into the offices, stripped and searched by the noncoms. Then we were led to the building where the prisoners were housed. It was an old barracks, surrounded by thick barbed wire twelve feet high, and flooded by searchlights. At each end of the building stood a guard tower on which two machine guns were mounted, commanding a complete view of the prison.

There was a single entrance to the building through the barbed wire, and beside it stood another armed sentry. We were conducted to a room and locked in. Up till now no indication had been given to us as to our exact whereabouts, and the guardroom had refused all information. An electric light was burning in the room, which contained six or seven army bunks, complete with bedding. There was no heating.

Faramus and I sat down and started to discuss the situation. No charge had been made against either of us, and we were naturally anxious to know the reason for the elaborate precautions which had been taken by the Germans since our arrest. Faramus was despondent.

A light tap sounded on the door. A whisper came through the crack: *"Qui est là?"* I answered, "We are English. What is this place?" The voice answered, *"Le fort de Romainville. Aujourd'hui les sales Boches ont fusillé six hommes."* I was stunned. The voice then gave some hurried details about the camp, and ceased.

That night Faramus and I did not sleep well; in fact, we shook hands and said goodby in case the Germans should decide to shoot us too. When we awoke the sun was shining through our window. Somehow death seemed far away.

In the suburb of Romainville, tiny figures were going about their work. I opened the window and looked out. *"Bonjour, Monsieur"*—I twisted my neck. A pretty French girl was laughing at me from another room. A second blond head popped out. The girls' names were Suzy and Paulette, and I learned later that they were in jail on a charge of suspected espionage. They asked us if we had eaten. I said no. Suzy produced a piece of string; to one end she attached a stone and swung it until I was able to catch it. To the other end she attached a package of sandwiches. We carried on a mild flirtation for some time, and I began to feel that perhaps after all prison life had its compensations.

In the course of the morning the cell door opened and a couple of sets of overalls and pairs of sabots were flung in. Then, with other prisoners, we were marched out to chop wood. There were about twenty in the working party; half of them appeared to be Jews.

We had been working for half an hour when the German armed guards came to us—*"Achtung! Achtung!"* The officer in charge had a list of names with him. The prisoners jumped to attention.

I noticed the face of a Jew standing next to me—it was ashen. He trembled violently.

"What is wrong?" I whispered. The Jew answered:

"Those are the names of the people they are going to shoot." The German officer called out ten or twelve names. The owners fell out one by one, and stood waiting for their summons to the slaughter. In turn they were marched away, and shot; the rest continued chopping wood. The Germans executed these men because a commandant at Nantes had been assassinated by the French Underground. They were shot without trial. I do not think that they felt like heroes. They looked like sheep—foolish, senseless, stunned. And that was how I felt.

Life in the camp was easy—not too much work and, surprisingly, plenty of amusement. With a few of the brighter spirits Faramus and I soon had a more than reasonable share of entertainment.

The camp building was divided into two sections, male and female, by locked doors. About thirty women were held either as communists or espionage suspects. The men's exercise ground was divided from the women's by a stretch of barbed wire running down the center. My specialized knowledge helped me. I made, in time, some keys which enabled some of us to pass into the women's quarters. This meant tiptoeing past a sleeping guard—but he slept soundly. The girls were attractive, and welcomed a little male company. We enjoyed several parties with them. During the day they would cook meals in preparation for the evening's fun, and—strange are the ways even of a hostage prison—somehow they always had a bottle of wine or cognac.

The people in the prison were an interesting mixture. Kahn was a Jewish banker who had escaped from Germany with a million marks before war broke out. He was caught in Paris when the French army collapsed. He had an international reputation as a racing boat amateur. In prison, as a hobby, he painted portraits—the fellow painted everyone, including the guards. Then there was a Monsieur Karr, a red-headed Frenchman, also a Jew, who was reputed to have been a highly placed official in the French government. An announcer from Radio Paris was there because of his refusal to work for the Boche. Lutsch was a Swiss who professed privately to have worked for British intelligence. There was a French officer who had been working for the German Secret Service, but was now in prison suspected of double-dealing. Fresnay was a loyal Frenchman accused of smuggling British agents out of France. Then there was the inevitable Gestapo spy who reported all our movements to the camp commandant. He was called the Black Devil. There were also two diamond merchants from Amsterdam, a criminal from Alsace-Lorraine, who had served nearly all his life behind bars, and a nondescript collection of escaped prisoners of war.

One day the Black Devil reported our night excursions to the camp commandant, and a letter was found from Paulette addressed to me. The Black Devil showed it to the commandant. I was interrogated and denied the whole story. The commandant put me in the dungeon for a couple of days. It was so cold that I buried myself in gravel to keep warm. When I came out I learned that Paulette had received fourteen days in the punishment cell on bread and water.

I was furious, and stormed into the Black Devil's room. He was playing cards with some other "narks." I kicked over the table and punched him around the room. He had a beautiful black eye and a cut on his face. I then opened the window and tried to throw him out. The German guards rushed in and overpowered me with kicks and blows. For this escapade I was given one month's bread and water. While I was serving this sentence, other prisoners attacked the Black Devil. Some of them were beaten up and others punished by a bread-and-water diet. One good thing came out of the trouble: the Black Devil was plainly of no further use as an informer, so he was sent away from the camp, no doubt to continue his dirty work elsewhere.

An amusing thing happened while I was in solitary—I managed to pick the lock of my cell door and also of Paulette's, who was next door. One night we left the lights on and a sentry spotted them. Next day my cell was searched from top to bottom for implements. I hid what I had smuggled in inside a loaf of bread. It made me laugh inwardly to watch the Jerries levering up the floor boards and ripping the beds open to see if they could find anything when the answer lay on the table in front of them.

One day an Italian boy was put in a punishment cell for stealing bread. He was an amusing little fellow, full of schoolboy pranks. While in the cell, he leaned out between the bars to wave to me and the others in the courtyard. A shot rang out. A sentry had fired, hitting him squarely between the eyes.

Not long after this routine murder, I was called to the commandant's office and shown into a private room. I went with mixed feelings, recalling my last interview in Jersey. In the room sat a young man of about my own age. He gave me a cigarette.

"You are Edward Chapman?" he asked. I nodded.

"You are interested in joining the German Secret Service?" He was a tall, quiet, rather scholarly-looking man, with sharp blue eyes, and spoke excellent English. Later, I learned that he had been educated in England, and wore the boating tie of Southampton College. He called himself Thomas. Now, for the second time, a German intelligence officer took down all the details of my life. He seemed amused at my escapades in camp, which I told him freely. At the end of the interview I was no wiser than I had been before as to how my bluff was working.

◆　◆　◆

Events went on as usual in the prison camp—senseless brutalities mingled with incredible license. The food was filthy, the main meal being lunch which consisted of *getrocknetes Gemüse*—dried vegetables. When this mess was boiled, hundreds of small worms would float on top of it. The prisoners got rid of them by boiling this "soup" two or three times. There were stoves in every room, but there was no fuel. My gang went on foraging expeditions, smashing up beds and even pulling the rafters out of the roof to provide fuel. I still marvel at the things we got away with, in this as in many other matters.

All manner of theories were put forward in the prison camp as to where the Allies would land to liberate France—some wild, others made up of sound reasoning. There was a German guard in the camp who had himself been imprisoned for being a communist, but was released at the outbreak of the war. When the prisoners worked in his charge he passed on all the British radio news from the B.B.C. One night the British dropped pamphlets over Paris. I happened to be doing a job under him. He pointed to a piece of paper lying on the ground. I picked it up. It contained news and a speech by Winston Churchill. Naturally it made the rounds of the camp.

Then a wireless was brought down by one of the guards for repair, one of the boys in the camp being a radio engineer. He repaired it, and for some time we had British news. This was extremely difficult to get because of the interference set up by the Germans on the frequency which the British were using. Many Frenchmen missed the news for days for this reason.

When one was tuned in to a *Schwarzsender,* or illegal transmitter, as the Germans called the B.B.C., all that came through was a frightful wailing *doodle oodle, doodle oodle,* which could be clearly heard everywhere. Naturally most people preferred not to run such a risk.

In February, 1942, I was again summoned to the commandant's office. This time I met an attractive German-American woman accompanied by a young man. She was a brunette, with large brown eyes, a rosebud mouth, and well manicured hands. Her clothes must have come from Schiaparelli or Molyneux. Obviously she was the man's superior, for he treated her with deference. She asked all the questions. Her American accent was authentic, and she might have stepped down from a movie screen.

What work did I think I could do in England? Was I prepared to carry out sabotage? Was it for money or hatred of the British that I wanted to work against them? I told her that I was only interested in money and that I disliked the British, chiefly for their prisons and their police. I explained, as I had done before, that I was wanted by them on several criminal charges, and that if they ever caught up with me I would receive at least fifteen years. This seemed to satisfy her and her companion, and they left saying I would hear from them again.

In March, 1942, I had another visit from the man who called himself Thomas. He informed me that an important official was coming to see me. The official arrived, and I liked him the moment I saw him. He was a German monarchist, Baron von Grunen. He was six feet tall, and heavily built. But it was his expression that pleased me most. He had the benevolent air of a good man—a man of understanding and tolerance, a scholar and a philosopher. I react to people instinctively, without judgment. There in that room I met a man who was destined to become a friend, an adviser, and a fellow conspirator. At that moment he was a highly placed member of the German Secret Service.

We talked of my background. With the Baron was another rather tall German, who spoke English with a true Oxford accent. We all laughed when I told of my adventures in the punishment cell. They both chided the commandant, saying, "Don't regard this man as a German gentleman; he is simply a trained brute." I told them how this same brute had come to my cell one morning, drunk, and had drawn his revolver and, with a theatrical gesture, threatened to shoot me. The incident had been so farcical that I had invited him to go ahead. The commandant had glared, leveled the gun at me and then put it back in its holster.

Before von Grunen left, he told me not to worry and try to keep out of trouble, as I would be out of the place in a fortnight.

About this time the R.A.F. raided the Renault works in Paris, and from my window it appeared as if they made a thorough job of it. Paris, below me, looked beautiful, lit up by searchlights and tracer bullets. The staccato rattle of light flak was followed by the boom of heavy flak and bombs. When the raid was over, the whole city seemed aglow with flames.

At six A.M. on April 10, 1942, my punishment cell was opened. The guard handed me my civilian clothes and told me to get dressed and shaved. I came out of the cell and went downstairs, knocked on the door of Faramus, the boy who had been with me in Jersey, and said goodby. I told him that I was leaving and promised to try to send him some food. Then I bade everyone goodby. They all thought that I was en route for another prison.

At the Kommandantur I was given back my valuables and money. Thomas was waiting for me, innumerable documents were signed, and then, at last, I was free. Outside the gate stood a large car and we drove straight to the Gare du Nord. On the way, Thomas told me I was going to Nantes. He had brought plenty of cigarettes, but not having eaten for three days in the cell, I was hungry. We had a first-class compartment to ourselves. Thomas warned me to speak nothing but German. When the train was under way we went into the dining car to eat. Thomas had coached me to raise my right hand and say "Heil Hitler." Now, for the first time, I did this. I felt like a damned fool.

Several officers were dining, and they raised their right arms solemnly, and all murmured the holy words of the Nazi creed. Then we sat down and ate. Thomas had no appetite, but I was ravenous. I ate his meal as well as my own. A German captain sitting opposite me wished me *"Guten Appetit."* His comment was wasted. My appetite could have coped with all the food on that train.

Back again in our compartment, Thomas seemed embarrassed. Suddenly, like a guilty schoolboy forced to divulge some minor delinquency, he blurted out:

"Now you are among friends and we are going to help you, so please do not try anything silly like jumping out of the compartment or attempting to escape, because I am armed."

Saying this, he produced a minuscule automatic which didn't look as though it could have killed a rabbit. He replaced it in his pocket. I assured him that when life was becoming so interesting I had positively no intention of risking anything so final as ending it. Thomas said then:

"We are going to a French château at St. Joseph near the Loire river, just on the outskirts of Nantes. Don't try to investigate what is going on inside this château," he added. "You will be told everything you need to know by me or Herr von Grunen. From now on I am looking after all your interests. I shall be your teacher in many things. We will live together and I will be your friend."

The train arrived dead on time. During this period the Germans prided themselves on the efficiency of their services. Meeting us at Nantes station was a young man who looked like a prize fighter; he was introduced as Leo. Outside the station in a car was another German. Both these boys had lived in Alsace, both spoke perfect French and Flemish as well as Low German. We drove from the station to "La Bretonnière," the name of the château which was to be my home for the next few months.

6

THE MAKING OF A SPY

THE CHÂTEAU was small but lovely. It stood in a park surrounded by a high wall. There was an orchard, and vines grew in profusion. Outside the house someone had, with striking success, planted banana trees; with their broad green leaves they were an impressive sight. Sandy paths wound their way through the park.

It was a glorious spring day when I arrived and, after years in prison and months in a concentration camp, I felt suddenly calm and at one with the world. An Alsatian dog came toward me wagging her tail; she was followed by four mongrel pups, all of different colors. A cat had just had kittens. Two young geese floated by on the pond, followed by their doting parents.

Inside the château I was taken into a lounge and introduced to two more Germans. One was Herbert Vosch, who spoke English with a slight German accent. He was, as I learned later, to be my sabotage instructor. The other was Robert Keller, who turned out to be a radio operator. They offered me cigarettes and whiskey, and I turned to examine the comfortable room. Some French etchings were on the walls; a wireless on a mahogany sideboard was playing dance music. Yes, this was better than the last three years!

We talked politely for some minutes, then Thomas said, "Now that you are here we must give you a German name." I was teased by the others while several names were considered. Finally "Fritz Graumann" was chosen. Everyone in this unit, which was labeled by the German government *Dienststelle A.S.T.,* was known by a *nom de guerre.*

The German officers warned me to be on guard against the French servants. If they remarked on my English accent when I spoke French, I was told to say I was a German-American and had lived most of my life in the United States, but had never become naturalized. A three-course lunch followed, with a bottle of '27 Chateauneuf du Pape, and with our coffee we had a glass of Remy Martin. A cigar finished the meal. I began to feel that not all Germans were Huns.

Then I was taken to von Grunen. The Baron was upstairs in his bedroom, writing. He rose and shook my hand. "Glad to see you out, old man," he said. "Come and have a glass of really good brandy." He then gave me some cognac, and as I wanned up, so did the Baron.

"Now, Fritz," he began, "what you need is a long rest, plenty of sunshine, fresh air, walks, and good food. From now on, for a few days, do as you like. You are to consider yourself an entirely free man. The only thing is, if you want to go to town you must take someone with you. It is not possible for me, at the moment, to give you a military pass."

For some time we talked together. Then I left von Grunen to explore *Dienststelle A.S.T.*

The château consisted of eight bedrooms, dining rooms, a lounge, office and kitchen. Next to the building was a small gardener's house. This had been furnished, and was given to me.

Radio communication was carried on by three operators in a small bedroom on the top floor. A clothes cupboard, always kept locked when not in use, held the various wireless sets. There were sets for running off the mains; also, in case of a breakdown, sets which could be run off batteries. The transmission took place between Paris and Berlin, and also with some station in the south of France.

Another interesting part of *Dienststelle A.S.T.* was also in my little house—the laboratory which had been fitted downstairs. Around the walls stood various chemicals in sealed glass bottles, and on the small marble tables were scales with bowls for pulverizing crystals into powder.

For ten days I led a quiet life, sunbathing, walking, and eating good food. In the mornings, Thomas and I set out for a three or four-mile run. This was followed by a swim in the Loire, at this point forming one of the most beautiful reaches in Europe, with majestic châteaux placed on either bank.

During this period I had many conversations with Thomas. He was an authority on folk dancing and had scoured England, discovering and learning different dances. Often he would demonstrate some intricate movement; then he would trace the motives which had produced it. He said that the English invented nearly all folk dancing. When I asked him about the Scottish reel (for I consider myself a Scotsman rather than an Englishman), much to my chagrin he told me with gusto, *"Ach, der Englische ist viel, viel älter"* (The English one is much, much older).

Thomas also played the flute well. He took much pleasure in describing the music he had heard in Berlin. For him, Germany was not the greatest nation in the world—it was the only nation. In his opinion, the Fatherland had contributed more in every way to life and the arts than any other nation. His library consisted of *Deutsche Kunst, Deutscher Lebensraum, Deutsche Forschung*—in fact, everything portraying the greatness of Germany found a place on his bookshelves.

In civilian life he had been a school principal, and if he was a fair example of schoolmasters in Germany, it will take some years to eradicate his ideas from the minds of the children he taught. When on one occasion I began, "But when you declared war on Poland . . ." Thomas raised his eyebrows in a genuinely shocked expression. *"We* declared war on Poland! Why, it was Poland who declared war on us, and we simply had to protect our people in the east lands."

One afternoon a cheerful, plump man with a bald head arrived from Paris. He was a Berliner named Maurice Schmidt. He brought with him a morse practice set, and his duties were to teach me this art. This set was simply a battery arrangement with a tapping key which gave a signal such as can be heard over the wireless. The receiving was done by earphones. First, he gave me a series of dots, and after each one I would say "dot." Then followed dashes, when I would say "dash," after which "dash" and "dot" were combined. In a short time Schmidt announced that I could be taught morse. There are some people who cannot differentiate between dot and dash, and therefore will never be able to master wireless telegraphy.

Slowly I began to learn the morse alphabet, all the easy letters being taken first. Letters with only two tones in them, or one, such as *e, a, i, n, m,* came first. Afterwards came the more difficult ones having three tones, such as *o, k, s, b.* By the end of the first seven days I had managed the most difficult with four tones—*f, l, v,* etc. Schmidt was a good teacher and taught me various little phrases by which I could remember the letters; *l* was *"ich liebe dich"; q* was *"Wie scheisst die Kuh"*—rather vulgar, but good for memorizing.

◆ ◆ ◆

I was now growing accustomed to the life of *Dienststelle A .S.T.* There was a definite routine. The servants did not arrive before 9:30 A.M., which meant someone had to get up to prepare breakfast, which consisted usually of two boiled eggs, bread, butter, honey, and coffee. Eggs and coffee were bought in the black market. At 8:30 A.M. a bell rang outside the kitchen. This was the summons to breakfast. Down trooped the men, eight or ten of them. The number varied because occasionally some had duties in Rennes or Paris. Each had his place at the table according to rank.

First, they would greet each other by saying, *"Heil Hitler! Guten Morgen. Haben Sie gut geschlafen?"* Then they would line up behind their chairs. Von Grunen, the chief, would enter, intone "Heil Hitler," then solemnly shake hands with everyone. When this ceremony was performed the company gave him the Nazi salute. Then everyone wished everyone else *"Guten Appetit."* Von Grunen sat down; we all followed suit, and the meal began. It was an unwritten rule that one must not talk at meal times. Oh how I loathed those long breakfasts!

When the meal was finished, cigarettes were passed round and conversation began. Von Grunen detailed the duties of the day. Every morning someone went to the Wehrmacht Postamt to collect the mail. Letters came rarely, and these were always official. I was still a lost man, living with other lost men.

My own instructor told me when to begin my lessons. He was a strange but likeable little chap, this Maurice Schmidt—an excellent morse code instructor, being both an engineer and an operator. He could both give and take at a speed of 180 letters per minute, which is good time even for an expert. Under his tuition I was able to do 120 per minute. If the reader would like to discover what speed this is, let him take pencil and paper and write down the alphabet as many times as he can in one minute, then multiply this by three. This is about the average number of dots and dashes which must be heard and put on paper before one is considered a proficient wireless man.

Some time later Herbert Vosch, the sabotage expert of the unit, another strange type, told me that I was to begin learning sabotage. My training consisted in making homemade explosives by mixing simple chemicals, chemicals which could be bought in any chemist's shop. For some weeks I practiced every day with him, making thermites and dynamites from simple ingredients. For example, potassium chlorate or nitrate mixed with sugar makes both a dynamite and a burning substance capable of giving off some 3,000 degrees of heat; potassium chlorate with oil makes dynamite. Many more such formulae were taught me. All of these I had to memorize; nothing could be put down in writing.

Another point on which Vosch insisted was that I must on no account divulge any of these formulae to other persons in the *Dienststelle*. The number of people allowed to know such facts was limited, and each was sworn to secrecy.

An ordinary wrist watch was shown to me. Two wires were attached to it in such a way that when the hands turned they made contact with the wires. These wires were attached to a flashlight battery, from there to some burning mixture which contained a detonator and some gelignite. With this ingenious gadget one could make a timed explosion for any period up to twelve hours. If a longer period was required, a seven or fourteen-day alarm clock was used. The wires were arranged so that when the spring expanded it made contact with them, and the same result was obtained.

I was taught how to wreck a train, and how to place a contact on the rails so that when the wheels passed over it the charge exploded. The contacts were cleverly camouflaged. Anyone inspecting the rails would pass on, unsuspecting.

For sabotaging a ship, a piece of coal was drilled and the hole filled with dynamite. This was then placed in the bunkers. Naturally, when the coal was shoveled into the furnace the resulting explosion would wreck the boilers.

On Saturdays, the boys would go into Nantes for a night out. My rate of pay was fixed at 6,000 francs a month. This, of course, was simply pocket money, all other expenses being paid.

In 1942 there was as yet no shortage of food or drink in occupied Europe; everything could be had, though only in the black market. Butter was about 90 francs a kilo; eggs 24 francs a dozen; meat 40 francs a kilo; coffee about 800 francs a kilo.

Dienststelle A.S.T. nights were orgies. We drove into the town in three cars and started on a round of drinking. Usually we visited the Cafe de Paris, which had a good dance band although dancing was forbidden in France. The place was always full of German officers and men, and nearly all were accompanied by parties of girls. Popular tunes were played by the orchestra, but the place would really rock with the chorus of German marching songs. Somehow the German spirit comes through impressively (and not offensively) when the soldier sings these warlike refrains.

It was here that I heard for the first time that famous song, *Lili Marlene,* which the Germans took from the Serbs and which the British Tommy in turn took from the Germans in North Africa. Later, I was to hear it sung in Russian, Norwegian, Polish and Italian. It became my own favorite song, and I would sing it on any occasion at the drop of a hat.

How did the *Lili Marlene* craze start?

When the Germans marched into Belgrade they found that all the phonograph records in the radio station were broken. In the drawer of a desk only one record was discovered intact. It was a long-forgotten Serbian march, a folk song: this was Lili Marlene. It was played in between flashes of news. Soon people were tuning in their wireless sets to Serbia for the pleasure of hearing the song. Then the soldiers made a marching song of it—for the words express the hopes of every man who has left his girl behind and is fighting far away from her. In this respect every soldier is the same. He never forgets her, and here in Nantes the German conquerors would sit singing and dreaming with a faraway look in their eyes.

The refrain would swell:

> *Unsere beiden Schatten Sehn wie einer aus,*
> *Dass wir so lieb uns hatten,*
> *Das sieht man gleich daraus.*
> *Wann werden wir uns wiedersehen,*
> *Wenn wir bei der Laterne stehen*
> *Mit dir, Lili Marlene, mit dir, Lili Marlene.*

From the Café de Paris the *Dienststelle* boys would all proceed to a brothel. This was one reserved for officers of the Wehrmacht. One of the girls there told me that she was examined every morning by a doctor, and was only allowed to go out one evening in the week—*"Ce n'est pas beaucoup,"* she added. They had also stamped her control card, with typical German thoroughness, *"Reserviert nur für die Deutsche Wehrmacht"* (Reserved exclusively for the German Army).

The Germans regarded sex and women in animal terms. To them a woman was a physical necessity. It was healthy to have intercourse, therefore everyone, officers and men, visited the prostitutes.

Often I would see a colonel with his regimental officers wining and dining with the local prostitutes. This practice appeared in no way to affect discipline. One evening the colonel would be walking arm in arm through the street with some pretty tart. Next day she would be shopping, perhaps, with a corporal from the same regiment. Well, many men have drunk, at different times, from the same mug at an inn.

The French seemed to be apathetic, treating the Germans with frightened courtesy. It was the custom for the Germans, or those with German passes, to ignore the queues at theatres and cinemas, and to take a seat at once. The same applied to restaurants where people were waiting for tables. The "Master Race" came first, in all things.

I learned fast—and not only what my tutors taught me. I had a small house where I slept alone, so that I got into the habit of retiring early. When the others had gone to bed I would dress, tiptoe down to the garden, and climb over the wall. Walking at night always had a fascination for me. Besides, I discovered so many interesting things.

My personal relations with the Germans grew ever friendlier. They were always more than kind. In the dining room at the château they had started what they called their *"Heimecke"* (Home Corner)—a collection of views of their home towns. Von Grunen insisted that I, too, should have a photograph, and presented me with an excellent one of Berwick-on-Tweed. So there Berwick hung—indeed, it had a place of honor in the center: on its right Berlin, on its left Bremen. Other towns were grouped around it.

My work was progressing, and now I was taught a code. I practiced this for weeks until I could do it quickly and without thinking. The code was simple, and the following example will show how it worked:

a	b	c	d	e	f	g	h	i	j	k	l	m	n	o	p	q	r	s
1	2	3	4	5	6	7	8	9	10	11	12	13	14	15	16	17	18	19

t	u	v	w	x	y	z
20	21	22	23	24	25	26

The code word for the day was then chosen. The numbers of the letters of the message were added to the numbers derived from the letters of the code word. Of course, for deciphering, the reverse process took place.

At this time I was also taught how to use a transmitting set. Twice daily my practice was arranged with Paris and Berlin. At these lessons much latitude was allowed, and at the end of the transmission I would tap out all manner of things which provided many a laugh for the operators. I always ended up with *"he, he, ha ha* and *vy"* which means "many regards." Sometimes pretty rough, quite unprintable stuff was sent.

It was while I was being trained that I met a Frenchman of Italian descent—Pierre Coussins, who was undergoing a training similar to mine. This Pierre was a shifty-eyed fellow of medium height with a swarthy complexion, and he always wore hornrimmed glasses. We met sometimes for coffee in the town. Twice a week Pierre turned up for revolver training; he was an extraordinarily bad shot. Every morning I did half an hour's practice with an automatic, and soon the boys delighted in showing visitors my prowess. They would stand ten liqueur glasses in a row, then from fifteen yards I would blast them to pieces. Or to vary it, they would stick a franc piece in the bull's-eye, and I would knock it out again. I had never used a gun before, and I have not used one since.

Coming home from a binge one night I got mixed up in a nasty quarrel. Everyone was drunk. It was Maurice, the chief radio expert and a charming fellow when not in his cups, who picked the quarrel. He said I had insulted him. In true tradition, he suddenly clicked his heels together and demanded satisfaction, insisting that I do a *"fünfzehn-Meter Lauf"*—a 45-foot walk—with him. I laughed, because that meant fighting a duel. He called me a *"Feigling"*—coward. Whereupon I drew my automatic, and we both marched into the middle of the lawn. But von Grunen, hearing angry voices, came down, scolded us like naughty brats, and ordered us to our quarters.

Next morning Maurice came up to my room and apologized profusely, saying that he was so drunk he had not realized—or could not even now remember—what he had been doing. So we shook hands and became friends again.

◆　◆　◆

Herbert Vosch, from whom I had gratefully learned so much about explosives (outside of gelignite, of course!) was a man with whom I never came to be on good terms. But one day, in a burst of amiability, he tried to win my confidence. Before the outbreak of the war, he said, he had been sent by Germany to help the I.R.A. stir up trouble in London. He claimed, however, that he had worked entirely on his own; they did not even know him. He told me that he was the man who had made the well-known attempt to blow up Hammersmith Bridge.

My opinion is that many of the bomb outrages in 1939 were really the work of this man. If you ask me for conclusive proof, I don't have it. I can only report the facts.

The two simplest methods of sabotage can be carried out either with a watch attached to batteries, or with acid. An ordinary ink bottle is filled with sulphuric acid. The lid is pierced and a piece of cardboard is placed between the lid and the hole. It takes two hours for the acid to eat through the cardboard. This flows on to some specially prepared burning mixture which explodes the detonator and charge. Now Herbert Vosch was certainly in London during the time of the I.R.A. outrages, and in my opinion it would have been difficult for Irish Irregulars to have acquired the training essential for such hazardous work.

I sincerely believe that some of the unfortunate Irishmen who served long sentences for these offenses were not so guilty as people were led to believe at the time. Nor was this expert saboteur, Vosch, the only German agent who was in England during this period. Franz Schmidt, now also a member of my unit, A.S.T., was then working as a waiter at Frascati's, the well-known London restaurant. Was it an accident that a skilled saboteur and a radio man were in London at one and the same time?

Schmidt was a blond, blue-eyed man of twenty-nine. He spoke English with a cockney accent; his French was also good. His knowledge of the West End of London, its restaurants and clubs, was quite amazing. He loved to tell the story of a cockney in the underground, who said to him while reading the headlines in the paper: "Cor' blimey, one of these blinking days that bleeding Hitler is going to start a war."

Von Grunen, my chief for whom I had a real respect, was not a Nazi, and unless it was imperative he avoided using the mumbo-jumbo words "Heil Hitler!" He collected reproductions of good paintings, and his Raphael and Rubens prints were something to be seen. Rare volumes fascinated him, and von Grunen was never happier than when rummaging in some second-hand bookshop for a find. Old furniture, china, carpets— all held his interest. He would see something which caught his eye, and would expound on its date, its manufacture, etc. Rarely was he mistaken.

At night, after dinner, von Grunen would often invite me up to his room for a drink. Never, in my own considerable experience, have I seen a man drink so much. Every night my German chief consumed at least two bottles of wine, and then proceeded to cognac. It did not affect him in the least. If anything he became more lucid. He was a genuine lover of the British way of life, and often, when we were alone, he would tell me so. I think he was imagining that we were back in the days of Pitt and the "two-bottle men."

When I discussed the policy of Germany with him von Grunen would shake his head sadly and knowingly. "You and I, Fritz, we have a duty to do, so let us do it," he would say. "Personally, I think Hitler will ruin Germany. Of course I will stand by and see that whatever happens you will be looked after."

This was in 1942!

When he spoke of Hitler, von Grunen's view of the Führer was that of a small man who has lost all sense of proportion. True, by a few ruthless strokes he had won half a world. But could it last? "No, Fritz, I must be honest with you, I do not believe it will." Of course, in these arguments I did not support him, although I reckoned that I knew better than he that the British people would not fail to win the last battle.

An important visitor came to see me at Nantes. His name was Müller, a chief of the Counter-Espionage Bureau, then situated at Rennes. When he arrived I felt a twinge of apprehension. He was a brute of a man, five feet eleven inches tall and weighing about 210 pounds. He had a huge neck, a square Boche head, and was practically bald. His eyes were his worst feature—small, piggish, piercing, and cruel. Even his voice was ugly and rasping —he must have been one of the ugliest-looking and ugliest-sounding men in Europe. When he questioned me his eyes never left me. I sat there without any outward display of nervousness—this was an art I had learned through first-hand experience of police questioning.

First, he asked me if I knew a "Lord Lonsdale." I replied that I did not, and said the only man I had heard of by that name was a great and almost traditional figure of the English Turf, who presented the Lonsdale Boxing Belt.

"No," said the unattractive German heavyweight. "Not that one. This one was mixed up in a robbery in Mayfair."

I told him that I recalled the case in which a certain Lonsdale was mixed up in a jewel robbery with violence, and that he had been heavily punished for it. When my opinion was asked of him, I explained that I thought the gang a lot of weak sisters because they had all squealed on each other when they were caught, and also the robbery was a disgusting example of brutality. Müller looked surprised. "Would you not use brutality?" was his next poser.

"Well, yes, I would, but only if it was a case of self-preservation. Violence, like insurance, is reserved for emergencies."

Why these questions were put to me I never found out. When I repeated that this Lonsdale was no lord, the Gestapo man looked nonplused. When he departed he gave me 5,000 francs, and thanked me for the information.

He returned a few days later saying he had discovered that I knew a girl called Lydia. Did I also know her ex-husband, who by then had become a member of an embassy at Vichy? I replied guardedly that I knew of him. Did I know he was now married to an American? Yes, I did. What was my opinion? Was he liable to work for the Allies and turn traitor? When I answered that I did not know the man well enough to form an opinion, but that with an American wife anything might happen, Müller laughed, appeared satisfied, and gave me another 5,000 francs.

I was invited by him to work for his department in Rennes. I told von Grunen of the offer, but he would not hear of it. He said that he had more important work for me to do. Müller then made an application for me to go to Berlin; but thanks to my guardian angel, von Grunen, this was also refused.

My fate was, in any case, already decided in a different sense. The time was fast approaching when I would have to face it.

7

BIRTH OF A MISSION

A conference was to be held in Paris, and I went along with Thomas and von Grunen. Some of the chiefs of the German Secret Service were to be present. At this period the headquarters of the Service were in the Boulevard Raspail, but the conference took place at 8, rue de Luynes, which is near the rue du Bac.

We were the first to arrive, and went up to a well-furnished flat. Von Grunen told me it had belonged to a Jew. We sat in one of the rooms which served as an office. Drinks were brought in by a man of about twenty-eight. He was introduced as Albert Schole, and had, for a long time, been in South Africa, representing German firms. His English was good; later we became friendly.

Then the cloak-and-dagger chiefs began to arrive, first a Herr Brandy. I was amused at his choice of a name, but he was affable, and brought with him two bottles of his "namesake" as a present for me. He told me that I was to be sent to England, and that sabotage would be my mission. In addition there was a list of other matters in which the Germans were interested. The details would be divulged to me at some later date.

In walked a jolly-looking fat man. He was sweating, for it was a steaming June day. He was like something out of a musical comedy. He told funny stories and kept us all in fits of laughter. Cognac and champagne flowed freely. In between jokes Fat Boy would shoot me a searching question. He was shrewd, and asked if I had heard the Jersey people speaking of German espionage before the invasion, hinting that he himself had been there. With his round, chubby face, his stock of drummers' jokes, his common sense and a determination which this affable front did not quite conceal, I think he must have made a successful agent. His command of English was perfect. He was known as Colonel Gautier.

The means of getting me to England were discussed. I was asked if I had any objection to being dropped by parachute. I told them I hadn't. Orders were given to von Grunen that I was to be trained in parachute jumping. He was also asked what progress I was making in my general training. He gave me an excellent report.

Herr Brandy gave instructions that I was also to learn the use of invisible ink. They drank several toasts to my health. Then we all went out and had an excellent dinner at the Cafe de la Concorde. Afterwards we made a tour of the nightclubs. They were all chock-full of Germans; the conquerors were certainly enjoying the spoils of war. Frenchmen were treated with contempt, not so much by the Germans as by their own women. Loud war songs were sung. I noticed that many of the women joined in the chorus, and I myself had many invitations from Frenchwomen, in German. It was surprising how quickly they had learned the language of their overlords.

When von Grunen and I arrived back in Nantes, my training in parachute jumping began. At first I started with a ladder on the lawn. I would prop it up against a tree and for about a week I did twenty jumps daily. Then, every day, I began to jump from one rung higher until I was able to drop from sixteen rungs up without doing myself damage. A Luftwaffe instructor was sent to teach me the finer points of making a landing. This man, Wolfgang Blommer, was a good instructor; he taught me how to land and roll without hurting myself.

By this time I was very fit. Every day I was trained further in morse code, sabotage, and jumping.

Sometimes I found it hard to control my feelings, especially when we had finished our meals. The whole of the *Dienststelle* would then gather round the radio for the news. If it was a *"Sondermeldung"* (special news bulletin), there would be great excitement, and the martial song would be played—*"Wir fahren gegen Engelland"* (We are Marching Against England). Then the faces around the radio would light up. The voice of the announcer would tell of the huge losses inflicted upon Allied shipping. Fearful visions of my father and brother would float through my brain as I pictured them choking in the oily water near a sinking ship or sliding helplessly off some raft in the Atlantic after days of thirst, hunger, and lonely horror. Announcements of this sort, and news of the bombardment of London, filled everyone but old von Grunen with great glee. They would cheer, laugh, and yell *"Sieg Heil!"*

When my training was considered far enough advanced, I was sent, in the company of Wolfgang Blommer, to Paris, in order to make my first parachute jump. We stayed in a smart suite at the Hotel Majestic, and later drove out to Le Bourget, where I was introduced to a Colonel von Blecker, who produced an air crew consisting of a captain and two lieutenants, who were to fly me. The colonel had seen active service against Russia, and then was put in charge of an observer squadron working against England. The captain wore the Iron Cross.

When we arrived at the airport I was given coveralls and fitted out with a parachute. The plane we used was a Junkers bomber, and the parachute worked automatically. It was attached by a rope some thirty feet long to a bar in the craft. The trap doors opened and out I went, a dizzy dive into space. I heard the roar of the aircraft as it passed over me, and experienced a feeling that I was going to hit its tail. Otherwise I felt no special sensations. Then my parachute opened—and I was floating down in the sunshine, while far away the drone of the machine died away. The descent was made from 1,000 feet and I landed smoothly enough. Such shock as there was resembled jumping, say, from an eight-foot wall.

I did five jumps in the course of the next three days. On the fourth I had an accident. When I came out of the plane it was windy and I began to swing like a pendulum. As I neared the ground I was on the upward wing; my parachute landed before I did and I crashed to the ground with considerable force. My chin caught against my knee with a sound crack, and I broke several of my back teeth. A doctor was called in, and after some attention and an injection into my gums, I went back to the hotel and to bed. A French dentist did some pretty good repair to my teeth.

◆ ◆ ◆

One sunny morning in June, 1942, von Grunen invited me to take a walk in the château garden with him. We sat down on a bench and he took a bulky envelope out of his pocket.

"Here, Fritz, read this—it's a contract drawn up between you and myself, on behalf of the German government."

I read it. It stated that I, "known as Fritz Graumann," was to receive the sum of 100,000 Reichsmarks or, if I preferred it, the equivalent in foreign exchange, the rate of exchange to be ten marks to the pound. My mission was to be the sabotaging of the airplane factory making Mosquito bombers, to wit, that of De Havilland Ltd. The mission would be accomplished if I succeeded in blowing up the boiler house or destroying the electric plant. In addition, I was to report on troop movements. Especially interesting was the identification of the Corps signs displayed on American transport. If I could also send positions of flak artillery around London, such information would be interesting and well paid for.

During my absence from France my salary of 450 Reichsmarks per month would be continued. If, during my activities, I was jailed, I would be paid six hundred Reichsmarks per month during my imprisonment. If caught, I was not to divulge that I was employed by the German government nor mention any of the names of the German personnel with whom I had been trained. To help me see my mission through I was to be given £1,000 in English money. If any further expense was incurred, I would be reimbursed on my return. The penalty for divulging any of this information, or betraying the German Reich, was death.

I told von Grunen that I was satisfied with these terms. He then produced six copies of the contract, which he asked me to sign. Thomas and Schmidt were called in to act as witnesses. Von Grunen then handed the original and the copies to Thomas and told him to lock them in the safe. A contract had been truly made.

Toward the end of that month I again went to Paris and made two more parachute descents. Colonel von Blecker decided I should also do a night descent, in order to have more realistic training for the job in hand. For this purpose I was made to carry a full pack, weighing forty pounds, on my back. One cloudy summer evening, after dark, I took off from Paris, and they dropped me two miles from our château at St. Joseph.

This was my first night drop. The moon was up. Below me was the billowing eiderdown of the clouds. For a moment I thought I was over the sea. Then came inky darkness, the clouds were left behind—and then, *bang!*—I was on the ground. I had been dropped into a large meadow which was used by a radio location and flak unit. The soldiers had been warned to expect me. Some of my own unit were there, too, and after a few drinks in the artillery mess we drove home.

For my training in the use of invisible ink, a professor was especially ordered from Berlin. He was a bespectacled, grayhaired old man, tall, well-educated, and spoke good English. He produced from a briefcase what looked to me like an ordinary matchbox. He asked me if I had ever written in invisible ink.

I said, "No."

"Well, then, this match is secret ink. What you need is a good quality of white writing paper. You first of all place this on a sheet of glass or hard wood. Then you take a piece of cotton wool and proceed to work it around in circles on the paper, rubbing with a firm pressure, taking care not to miss any part of the paper and treat both sides the same. About twenty minutes should be employed on this treatment.

"Next, you take this match and you paint each letter of your message separately. The match need merely touch the paper—no pressure is needed whatsoever. The match will leave no trace on the paper, so you must take care not to forget what you are writing. It is advisable to write your message down on an ordinary sheet of paper first, after which you can copy it onto another sheet with the invisible ink (not forgetting, of course, to burn the original message you have written down, and destroy the ashes!). After each word you will make a dash—so."

He then gave me the following example:

LONDON — WAS — BOMBED — LAST — NIGHT — FIRES — WERE — LEFT — BURNING — AT — LONDON — DOCKS — FIVE — WAREHOUSES — WERE — DESTROYED — HEAVY — DESTRUCTION — IN — CENTER — OF — CITY — FRITZ.

"Now you will always write your messages holding your paper vertically," the professor resumed. "When you have finished, you will write an ordinary letter, as though to a friend, holding your paper horizontally. This you can then post through to an address in a neutral country."

I asked him about the degree of success in getting my messages through. He replied, "Ninety percent of messages sent in this manner reach their destination."

I asked him further questions about the development of this ink, but his response was guarded. All he would say was that the letter must go through three machine processes before it became visible, and with this reply I had to be content.

The professor stayed with us three or four days, then left for Berlin. Arrangements were made for me to write a practice letter to him every day through the *"Deutsche Feldpost,"* using the invisible ink. From time to time I received comments from him by radio transmission on the errors I was making, until eventually the old boy declared himself satisfied.

◆ ◆ ◆

Meanwhile, the everyday life of the *Dienststelle* unit went on. Every week some of us went on a foraging expedition to buy goods for the château, of course in the black market. For this purpose we were given ample supplies of money, for not only did we buy for ourselves, but also for our Paris unit at the Hôtel Lutétia. We visited all the outlying villages and talked to the farmers. They were only too willing to let us have their foodstuffs for the enormous prices we offered.

Sometimes, when the boys thought they would have difficulty in getting a farmer to part with his produce because they were Germans, they would masquerade as Frenchmen. Leo and Hans spoke perfect French, and looked like typical Frenchmen in their Basque berets. I often heard some unsuspecting peasant letting off a tirade against those unwelcome guests, the Germans, while Hans and Leo, agreeing with every word, made their purchases and departed. Once outside, they would treat the whole matter as a huge joke.

Eggs, hams, chickens, butter, and even whole sheep would be bought. The eggs would be parceled and sent to Paris or to relations in Germany, together with kilos of butter and ham. This black-marketing was done by all branches of the Wehrmacht, and was encouraged by the authorities.

Once, in the course of such an expedition, we met two young officers who were on leave from Russia. They had hundreds of thousands of francs, and were buying supplies for a whole battalion which was resting up in Germany. German soldiers going on leave were allowed to take as much home with them as they could carry. They could be seen at railway stations carrying suitcases loaded with loot, with perhaps even a sheep slung on their backs!

One day I bought a small live pig and turned him loose in the garden. I named him Bobby, and he soon became a favorite with everyone. He was a most intelligent animal, and I only needed to go into the garden and shout his name for him to come galloping toward me like some well-trained dog. When I stroked him, he lay down and stuck his trotters in the air. Sometimes I would set off for the river and he would follow me. When I called him, the French peasants, expecting to see a dog, would be amazed by the appearance of Bobby, panting and blowing, and would raise shouts of *"Regardez le cochon, comme il est drôle!"* amid bursts of laughter. While I was swimming, Bobby would lie patiently in the shallow mud taking his bath, then would walk home, docile, behind me.

In July, I went with Thomas from Nantes to Paris, and then on to Berlin. This was my first visit to the German capital. To my deep disappointment, I did not have much chance of sightseeing. Our train left the Gare du Nord at night and we had sleepers reserved through to Berlin. The blackout required all blinds to be drawn, and on arrival at the Potsdamer Station a car was waiting to meet us. We drove swiftly through Berlin to a house in the suburbs.

At this time I could make little assessment of the bomb damage, for the Germans took precautions not to let me see too much. We were met by a man called Professor Karl. He was an odd chap, aged about sixty-five, bent and scholarly in appearance. He tested me in sabotage, making me do everything I had learned, and showing me further ways of making dynamite and fuses. I made time explosives for his benefit with both fire and explosion, started fires with nothing but acid and a watch, prepared explosive coal for use in ships, and made many other small demonstrations. At the end of four days he declared himself satisfied, and I returned to Nantes.

In August, a Panzer colonel came to visit von Grunen (I think he was a personal friend). A Panzer colonel was a very important personage in the German Army. He arrived in a staff car—a big fellow, 6 feet 3 inches tall, broad, square-chinned, and blue-eyed. He had fought with his brigade at Kharkov. When describing this battle he said that it had been bitter, that losses had been heavy, but he expressed firm confidence in Germany's victory. Later I learned that he lost his life at Stalingrad.

What always surprised me about German discipline was that officers and men ate the same food together. At this dinner, the colonel's chauffeur sat on his right, and was often invited by his superior to have a drink or taste some delicacy. The *Gefreiter* appeared to worship his *Oberst*, and I felt sure would have followed him to hell if necessary.

During the meal, von Grunen asked the *Oberst* if he would like to see a homemade explosion, and if so, would he set a time for it. The *Oberst* looked at his watch and said that he would like one for nine o'clock; it was then seven. We all set our watches by his, and I went out to make preparations.

Now, it is a difficult job to time an explosion to within a minute. I took some care, and placed my explosive charge under a tree, as near dead set to my watch as was possible. At five minutes to nine we were sitting in von Grunen's study having drinks. Four minutes, three minutes to go—we were all examining our watches. Just as the *Oberst* said, "Well, it's nine o'clock now," there was a colossal explosion. I had used about ten pounds of dynamite. The tree was practically uprooted and some windows in the château were blown in.

Von Grunen never turned a hair. He smiled, took his cigar out of his mouth, and said, "Well, you see what it's like—easy." The colonel was dumbfounded, and kept repeating, *"Mensch, und genau auf die Sekunde"* (Man! And right on the button). Of course, the whole thing was an extraordinary stroke of good luck and my reputation was enhanced accordingly with certain members of the German General Staff when the *Oberst* told his story.

The Colonel offered interesting opinions on the political leaders of the Allies. He claimed to have been at Hitler's headquarters in Russia. Hitler, he said, regarded Churchill as a drunken old fool, who was so befuddled that he did not know what he was doing. "Why," Hitler had explained, "the man lives on brandy and whiskey and is an incorrigible cigar smoker. Look at him! His photographs depict the hardened drunkard. Is that a fit man to lead a nation? Consider the things he used to say about the Bol-sheviks—and listen to him now! It is only the fact that he is at the height of his ambition in leading England, and making the world secure for the upper classes, that keeps him alive at all." "Hitler," added the Colonel, "has, on the other hand, a great respect for Stalin, and regards him as the cleverest politician the world has ever known. You never hear Hitler talking of Stalin in the way he does of Churchill. Why?" (And here he banged his huge fist on the table.) "Because Hitler has a personal respect for Stalin which he will never have for Churchill."

This opinion represented, I think, many German officers' attitude at that time.

Von Grunen was very strict about my visits to Nantes. He told me a story, which had been well-publicized in the world press, of some German-Americans who had been sent on a sabotage mission to America. A vast plot had been hatched; much time and money had been spent. These men had gone through the same extensive training as I had, and several members of my *Dienststelle* knew them. A few nights before they left by submarine for America they were given a farewell party in Paris. Women were present; one of the mission talked. When they finally landed from the U-boat in the U.S.A., they had only been a few hours on shore before they were all arrested. They were tried, sentenced to death, and some were shot, von Grunen insisted.

◆ ◆ ◆

August in the Loire Valley was beautiful, with its sunny days, the grapes ripening on their vines, apples weighing the branches down, and a wealth of flowers. I remember a punt full of German soldiers passing down the river, all singing in harmony. Everywhere the men of the Wehrmacht swam, sang, exercised, flexed their muscles, and drilled and drilled and drilled.

Rumors of invasion were in the air. Von Grunen had told me that if the British landed I would be given a uniform. The *Dienststelle* might perhaps move. On August 18 we were told to stand by—something unusual was happening; what, I did not know. On August 19, the British descended on Dieppe. Obviously the Germans knew that an attack was to be expected somewhere. There was intense excitement; cars were filled with petrol and ammunition, but did not move. All day long planes flew over our garden. I wondered dully, "Will they make it? If so, I shall be doomed to die the death of a traitor at the hands of my own countrymen."

Our *Dienststelle* radio operators worked frantically all day. Robert Keller,

Thomas, Franz Schmidt, and another were continually rushing in with messages from Paris and Berlin. At nightfall came the news that the British had been repulsed with heavy losses, thousands killed, thousands taken prisoner.

The *Dienststelle* cheered wildly:

"*Heil Hitler! Heil Hitler! Heil und Sieg! Sieg! Sieg! Sieg!*"

And me! What a bloody war it was, and what a bloody mess I was in! I got drunk, then staggered to bed, and cursed and prayed and cried like a kid. Gerhardt in the next bed snored happily. The Boche once more had had his strength tested, and won.

The effect of this success upon the Germans was profound. They made a terrific propaganda drive. Newspapers screamed in sensational headlines, to the tune of mockery, ridicule, and contempt.

I went to see a newsreel; it was terribly realistic. At various points of the coast shots were shown of landing craft attempting to put British troops ashore. The men jumped down from the gangways, waist-deep in water. They were mown down by machine gunners who were waiting for them. A tank waddled slowly through the launching doors of a landing craft; it was blown to pieces and burned fiercely. Some infantrymen, clinging around the mouth of a small cliff cave, were blasted out. Everywhere slaughter reigned, with the Germans doing all the killing. Yes, I certainly believed that the Wehrmacht knew well beforehand all about that landing. Hundreds of bodies were strewn about the beach. The deepest penetration was skin-deep only. The Canadians had managed to take the casino, but were forced out with heavy losses.

The French people, during the whole battle, remained passive. Shortly afterwards, to reward them for this attitude, the Reich claimed that they had assisted the Wehrmacht, and ordered the release of all prisoners of war in that area. This, of course, was simply another Goebbels stunt to try to boost Franco-German collaboration, but it was not without effect on the morale of the local people. What was the sense in fighting these Germans? The faint stirrings of the Resistance were stilled again. The spirit of France was subjugated once more, judging by the conversations to which I listened at this time.

Von Grunen was a fair man in his verdicts. When the British or Russians scored a victory, he gave them credit for it. His opinion of the raid on St. Nazaire had been that it was an excellent piece of work, and succeeded in its mission of blowing up the sluice gates.

"This Dieppe business," he said, "seems to me to be the height of folly, and the British have made a bad and stupid mistake."

He then deplored the loss of life and the uselessness of war. He abhorred it all and declared with a sudden passion, such as he rarely exhibited:

"Never by force of arms can the question of world peace and security be obtained, for in the wake of bloodshed comes hate. One 'revenge' rises on the ruins of another. Nationalism is the curse of the world! Why is it not possible to have, or to breed, a *World* people? Instead of you, Fritz, being a Britisher, me a German, and these poor, robbed Frenchmen dying for their country, why can't we have a World Federation with equal rights for men, something like the system H. G. Wells advocates? Why can't we have the great, tolerant thinkers of the world from each nationality, to form such a Commonwealth of All Men?"

I am sure he meant it. I often speculated on his words, and sometimes wondered myself "Why not?" I don't know the answer. He certainly was a most unusual German.

◆ ◆ ◆

I was still forbidden to go out alone. This order annoyed me. One Sunday afternoon I jumped over the wall, went down to the river, and walked along its banks until I came to a roadhouse. Although dancing was prohibited, several proprietors disobeyed the order, and at this place the customers danced. I headed for the bar. It was thronged with fashionably dressed *jolie filles*, with and without escort. I was soon dancing with a girl; she was intrigued by my English accent. We sat at the bar. On a corner of the shelf among other bottles I noticed one of Johnny Walker. I asked for a drink from it; it was pre-war. Now prices for liquor ranged from 40 to 60 francs a tot, and liqueurs were about the same. I inquired about the price of the whiskey. We had been given at least half a tumblerful, and were charged only 15 francs.

I sat all afternoon with my charming companion, and we drank the bottle. Feeling hungry, I ordered dinner. By this time I felt like a schoolboy playing hooky. In the middle of it, in walked three of the *Dienststelle*. They had missed me and von Grunen had ordered them to take a car and search for me. I invited them to have a whiskey. Soon Leo and Gerhardt were having another and another. Thomas was not slow in following their example.

At last the party broke up. As it happened I was the only one still capable of holding the wheel, and I had to drive all four drunks home. We were singing the popular song *Belle Amie* at the top of our voices, and driving at almost 70 miles an hour. We went slap through the gates of the château, jammed on the brakes, and came to a screaming standstill. Outside the house stood von Grunen. He nearly had a stroke.

However, in the end he took the affair in remarkably good spirit. Unusually so, as it seemed, for he descended to his cellar and brought up two bottles of cognac! He insisted that we could not go to bed until these were finished. One by one each member left the table and was violently sick. Von Grunen and I kept on and on. A bottle of Chartreuse was brought up, but this was too much for my mutinous stomach. I walked out into the cool night air and retched violently. Von Grunen laughed. I think he was determined that evening that he would teach me a lesson. He certainly did. Von Grunen was a true German disciplinarian that night.

Shortly after the Dieppe raid came an order from Berlin stating that the whole of the kit I was to take to England must be British. I made a list of the following articles: shoes, landing boots, wireless set, detonators, revolver, ammunition, spade, money, identity card, coveralls, crash helmet, chocolate. When the list was completed von Grunen, accompanied by Wolfgang, my parachute instructor, motored to Dieppe.

After a week they returned, bringing with them all the articles needed. What they could not find at Dieppe they found at Paris. Four British wireless transmission sets were produced, and an American Colt automatic. The papers belonged to some dead soldier. One of the wallets they gave me contained the letters and diary of a Scots Canadian from Montreal. It told of his nights out in London, and clearly showed how fed up he was waiting for the fighting to begin. There were some moving letters from his wife and children, and the address of a girl friend in Hammersmith. An amusing printed card made us all laugh. It stated:

"I hereby give my permission for my husband Jock Mc—— to smoke, drink, and swear, and to go out with any woman he damn well pleases and have a good time."

This charter of liberty was signed by the soldier's wife.

I made a collection of these odds and ends, including a London hotel bill, packed them in a wallet, and had them all locked in the safe.

My mission was discussed at length, and the Luftwaffe sent photographs of the de Havilland works, which are situated at Hatfield, near London. These photographs were very good, and penciled over the different buildings was a description of the type of work carried on in each. The various machine shops, mounting hall, offices, testing rooms, and timber stores were all clearly marked. Then followed a larger photograph of the outlying district showing the approaches to Hatfield. There were views from various heights and angles. As I have said, it was suggested that I should try to blow up the boiler house and, if not, the electric powerhouse. As an alternative, I could set the timber stores on fire.

Next, my landing came up for discussion. Where did I think would be the best spot? They invited me to pick out three places. I chose Cambridge, Torquay or somewhere in the Midlands. I was told that just before the take-off I would be shown where I would actually land.

I got very jumpy waiting for the start. My liberty was still more sharply curtailed, and one day I complained bitterly to von Grunen about the delay. During my training, dates had been fixed several times for my departure, but for some reason they had always been postponed. I made the wildest suggestions to von Grunen to get things expedited, even volunteering for the Eastern front—though I knew that he would never consent to such folly. He told me that he was as anxious as I that I should be "on my way," but that unfortunately at this time the Germans had no planes of the type needed to take me to England. So I fumed and waited.

At dinner one night Coussins the Frenchman, who was being trained for sabotage work, turned up with two other students who were also working for the *Dienststelle*. One of them, a young, blond boy, looked rather ashamed of himself as he sat at table. I think at this time they were working on separationist propaganda. The Germans tried whenever they could to split French solidarity. Coussins was in charge of a small Nazi-controlled journal which advocated the separation of Celtic Brittany from France.

During this time the events of the war had taken a new, sensational course. The Allies had landed in North Africa, and this time they stayed ashore. The repercussions of this invasion were felt by the Vichy collaborationists. Admiral Darlan was on a tour of inspection at Algiers. Realizing that Germany might well lose the war, he went over to the Allies with several other Vichy officials.

This action was followed by a tremendous outburst from those unlucky enough still to be in France. Vichy declared the deserters to be traitors; newspapers under the control of Damand and Deat, leaders of the small French Nazi Party, urged the army to resist the British. German reaction was equally instantaneous. They decided to seize the non-occupied zone of France. This interlude imposed a further delay on my often-deferred journey to England.

◆ ◆ ◆

It was not until November 5, 1942, that von Grunen called me to his room and said that I was to be measured for a uniform. Rumor and speculation were rife among us, because neither Thomas nor von Grunen would give the reason for this action. On November 8, I received the uniform of a German noncom, which fitted me perfectly. The uniform was the usual field-green with gold trimmings around the collar. I was also given a large yellow armband with a swastika on it, and a belt with an automatic pistol holster.

This dressing-up took place in my room. When the servants had gone, Thomas gave me lessons in saluting. As I wore an armband belonging to Hitler's S.S. I had to give the full-arm

salute to all officers. After this was over, saluting with a rifle was practiced. This caused some amusement among the men. Von Grunen declared, however, that I looked better and smarter than the S.S. themselves.

While all this was in progress, one of our number, Hans, was in town with the car. It was suggested that I should try the effectiveness of my uniform on him. While the others stood behind a nearby hedge to watch the fun, I waited for the car to arrive. When it approached, I halted it. In it were Wolfgang and Hans. In a harsh voice I demanded, *"Ausweis bitte"* (your papers, please). Without a word, both of them produced their *Soldaten-Ausweis,* together with the papers "necessary to circulate."

I folded them, thanked them, and handed them back. I kept the paper with the permission to circulate. "Heil Hitler!" "Heil Hitler!" I replied, and they drove through the gates to the garage.

Von Grunen and the rest were doubled up with laughter. They dashed into the mess and sat waiting for the victims. I went upstairs and changed into my civvies. When I came down Hans was relating how a military police officer had stopped him and asked for his papers. I walked in and said to him in exactly the same tone of voice, *"Ausweis bitte."* With that, I handed him back his control paper. He was stunned, and it was not until I had dressed myself up again for his benefit that he believed the story.

During the next few days there was intense activity in the château. Everything belonging to the Germans was packed and labeled. My laboratory was dismantled; all wireless sets, documents, typewriters, books, and stores were put in boxes. We still had a considerable supply of British stores, food, coffee, and chocolate, which had been distributed to the various German units after the abortive landing attempt at Dieppe.

On the night of the 10th, the official news came through that it had been decided to seize the non-occupied zone of France. This, of course, was supposed to be secret. However, it was no surprise to us; we had been expecting it. All the boys changed into the battle dress of their various troops, for each of them belonged to some branch of the Wehrmacht.

Herbert Vosch was an *Oberleutnant,* and when he was dressed I noticed that he sported the Iron Cross, first-class, upon his breast. Walter Thomas had the rank of lieutenant; Gerhardt, my room mate, was a noncommissioned officer, as were Keller and Schmidt. Hans and Hannen, the two chauffeurs, had the rank of *Obergefreiter*.

On the morning of the 11th everyone, including myself, came down to breakfast in uniform. There were the usual "Heil Hitlers," and we sat down. It was the first time that I had seen von Grunen in uniform. He wore the green uniform of a cavalry major, and looked exceedingly smart in his highly polished boots and spurs. The only medal he wore was the Iron Cross. When the meal was finished, he put on a double-breasted leather trench coat and a swagger forage cap.

The effect was surprising—he looked like a real old war horse ready for any fight. Gone was the placid calm, the benevolent air. Instead, before me stood a typical German soldier in love with war and conquest. The arrogance of the Prussian was stamped upon his bearing. He thundered out orders and they were obeyed with much heel-clicking and saluting.

When our servants arrived they did not recognize us at first glance. The girls peered at me dubiously and fearfully, then "Ah! Mr. Fritz," they cried in relief, and started shooting questions at me: "What are you going to do?" and so on. I could answer none of them.

That night the *Dienststelle* unit moved. Von Grunen, Wolfgang, and myself were left behind; apparently permission had not come through for me to leave.

Then, at dawn, the telephone rang and the chiefs in Paris gave their O.K. for my departure. I was on my way—but not to England. I was off to help the Germans take over the rest of France.

8

ON HITLER'S PAYROLL

OUR CAR was packed with food and arms. We had two machine gun pistols, a string of hand grenades, and plenty of ammunition. Von Grunen sat in front, and Wolfgang drove. I sat in the back, with a pistol at the ready and orders to shoot if any disturbance occurred.

We drove to the outskirts of Nantes, bound for Limoges. The roads were thronged with military traffic, all moving south—great convoys of lorries, each bearing its divisional marking. In the midst of these rolled the huge-wheeled benzine tankers. For every forty or fifty lorries there would be flak artillery trucks, on guard against aircraft attack.

It was sultry weather. Motorcycle dispatch riders tore past, instantly to be lost in clouds of dust. Outside the country inns and cafes soldiers lolled, quenching their thirst with flagons of wine. They stood to attention and saluted von Grunen when they caught sight of his uniform. He gravely returned the compliment.

On we went, past rumbling panzers and grinding truckloads of troops. It seemed as though a battle must lie ahead, so dense was the traffic. When we passed through the demarcation line between the two zones a German guard was already stationed on both sides of the gates. These were lifted to allow us to pass through. Three of us raised our voices and gave the unit's war cry:

"Joli Albert! Terreur, Terreur!"

This cry had originated with Albert Schole, an unusually wild member of our Paris branch. He often went to nightclubs and drank a great deal too much. He was well known to the *filles de joie,* and when he was a little drunk the girls would cry, *"Ah, ce monsieur là, c'est une vraie terreur."* So the legend grew up round him.

That night we sped into Limoges. There were few troops there, and the H.Q. was in the town hall. Von Grunen spoke to the officer in charge, and we were given billets for the night in one of the best hotels. I was struck by the apathy of the French. The people looked frightened, and here and there groups were huddled in doorways. A curfew had been ordered for nine o'clock that evening.

Next morning I went for a walk with Wolfgang. People stared at us curiously. Soldiers passing me saluted smartly, and I in turn saluted the officers. It seemed to me like a game, unreal and strange. Some Jews, strained and scared, watched us despondently —poor devils, I felt terribly sorry for them. Soon they would be rounded up and made to wear the Yellow Star, herded into camps —deported, mutilated, murdered.

With Wolfgang I walked to a hotel opposite the railway station. It was here that we had a rendezvous with the others who had set out the previous night from Nantes. They had arrived safely. We saluted one another, then lunched in a restaurant. The place was full of chatter, which ceased as we crossed the threshold. We commandeered a table, and the eight of us sat down. An excellent meal was served. The food was much better here than in the occupied zone, especially for the French.

After lunch we went back to our hotel, where von Grunen, with a major from the Gestapo in Rennes, was to give us our orders for the day. We assembled in a room. The major, a tall, gray-haired, severe-looking man dressed in the uniform of the S.S., told us the plans for the evening. About ten other hefty Gestapo men surrounded him, and a more grim-faced mob it would be hard to imagine.

He told us that a list of people suspected of espionage or of being British sympathizers had been given to him by the German Secret Service. When it was dark, we were to split into two bands, sally forth, and arrest the suspects. The names and addresses were handed to von Grunen, who took half of them. The arrangement was that any suspects were to be brought back at once to the hotel for interrogation. For this purpose we took with us a small lorry and three cars. Our *Dienststelle* was to do half the work, the unit from Rennes the other. Von Grunen and our party left the room and went into conference. A map of Limoges was produced, and a plan worked out in detail.

Our orders were that should any resistance be encountered, we were to shoot on sight. We set off at dusk. The first address proved a miss. Our man had left the district some time before and had not been heard of since—or so the concierge told us. The next on the list was a Captain le Saffre. We hammered for a long time on the door of a large block of flats. At last a woman in a dressing gown opened it. She said that she knew of Captain le Saffre, but did not know where he was. Von Grunen ordered her apartment to be searched. Every drawer was turned out, and the cupboards emptied of their contents. On one bed sat her eighteen- year-old daughter, frightened to death. "Don't be afraid," I assured her, but she cried hysterically. I think she thought the soldiers were going to shoot or rape her. Her mother, hearing her cry, rushed forward and said:

"Captain le Saffre lives in the flat above."

We went upstairs, and von Grunen knocked on the door. No answer. He gave orders to break the door down. I helped, taking care to make as much noise as possible, telling myself that if the man were inside he could shin down a pipe into the courtyard and escape. When the door at last burst open all the lights were on. The bedroom door was locked. Again and again I banged at it; the door gave, but the room was empty. I noticed that the window was open. Had my ruse succeeded, I wondered? Had le Saffre escaped? I never found out. All his belongings, his papers, etc., were ransacked. He was a man who had the dangerous habit of keeping all his old correspondence.

I found a few letters to a well-known British personality, applying for a post as interpreter. These I gathered together, then went to the toilet and flushed them down. However, there were cases full of more letters, and I fear that many of them may have been incriminating. In addition, a revolver and a Verey Light pistol were found, also a large sack of sugar and a quantity of nitrate, which, mixed in certain proportions, makes a strong explosive. Von Grunen himself was by no means idle. He found a choice collection of wines and liqueurs. These as well as stores of food were parceled up.

We got back to the car and set out for the next big kill. We arrived in a poor quarter of the town, knocked on a door, and inquired for a M. Durant. The woman who answered said:

"Yes, sir, that was my husband, but he has been dead for seven months."

I could not help laughing—the German information must have been rotten indeed!

The next address was a private house. We knocked—again no answer. But from the garden in the rear a light showed from one of the bedroom windows. We shouted—no reply. Von Grunen and his eight trusty men, armed like walking arsenals, waited breathlessly, expecting at any moment a hand grenade or a volley of tommy-gun bullets to burst among us. The order to break the window and force an entrance was given.

When we had climbed into the room, two old maids aged well over fifty stood defiantly in a comer. They had on their night caps and gowns. Oh, were they indignant! They scolded us with all the virulence that only outraged old spinsters can muster. Never have I seen tough S.S. troops so nonplused!

We made hurried excuses and proceeded to search the house. We had first to dismantle the barricade which the old girls had placed before the door. As I went out, I solemnly winked at them. One of them looked surprised, then suddenly stuck out her tongue at me.

We went upstairs to a bedroom, and there found a man in bed with his wife. He answered to the name of Durant. His room was searched, but nothing incriminating found. He vehemently protested his innocence, but was placed under arrest and led away to one of the waiting lorries.

◆ ◆ ◆

Altogether, we had spent an unsuccessful night. Nearly all the names we had been given belonged to people who had gone away, died, or were not known. At the end of the raid, all we had to show for our night's effort was four or five miserable people who did nothing but protest their innocence, and upon whom nothing incriminating had been found. The only useful thing seized were the papers belonging to le Saffre and, of course, the loot which had been taken from his flat.

During the trip home von Grunen stopped the car and let three of the hostages go. One was a boy of seventeen whose mother had cried terribly when he was taken away. The two prisoners still held were men of about forty. All their personal possessions were seized and they were then locked in a bedroom. As a precautionary measure their trousers were taken away.

We then went to von Grunen's room where a division of the spoils was made. My share was a bottle of cognac and one of Benedictine. We celebrated our evening by drinking and singing. The following morning von Grunen released the two prisoners. Afterwards he said to me:

"Why should I send them to a concentration camp? They may be guilty, and yet they may be innocent. It revolts me to think of them pining away, as thousands of others are doing, behind barbed wire, for no useful purpose whatsoever."

Next day, we set off for Rodez. Night overtook us on the road. When at last we reached the town it was difficult to find rooms in any decent hotel because a panzer brigade was quartered there, and we had to be content with billets on the outskirts.

When our meal was finished, I went for a stroll. Suddenly two soldiers approached me, wearing the skull and crossbones on their lapels denoting that they were from the famous Death's-Head Panzer Division.

"Sir!" they began, as they saluted, "we are lost, and have had nothing to eat for two days. We have lost our troop and have no food coupons."

They had seen my yellow band, and had apparently taken me for one of the special police.

I told them to follow me to a neighboring café, and gave them food tickets. They did not speak a word of French, so I ordered a meal for them. During the meal we were swapping our various experiences, when one of them said to me:

"Excuse me, sir, from where do you come?"

"I am a Finn," I replied.

"What, you are a Finn?"

Thereupon they both solemnly shook my hand, and insisted that I drink a bottle of wine. They told me they were drivers of a petrol truck and it was parked higher up the road. This was a bit of luck, for we were short of petrol. Wolfgang had carelessly left our fuel orders behind at Nantes. Von Grunen was most annoyed—chits must be given for everything in the German Army. Up to that moment we had got along by borrowing, but this was not always easy.

I asked the two soldiers if they could let me have some petrol. Then I went outside, found our car, and drove with them to their lorry. They filled my tank and gave me several cans. I drove back to the hotel and informed von Grunen. He looked at the others and said:

"A fine state of affairs! An Englishman keeps the German Secret Service in petrol, while its own personnel cannot find a drop!"

November 16 was my birthday, and it was on that day that orders came for me to return to Paris. My trip to England was at last decided upon, and I was to discuss the final arrangements with the experts. That night I was given a birthday party by the *Dienststelle*. All our friends were invited, and after dinner von Grunen presented me with a gold cigarette lighter as a souvenir. In a speech I thanked him and the others, and assured these Germans that I would *never be ashamed of anything I did while working with them.*

Next morning Thomas, von Grunen and I left for Paris. The discussion which took place there with Maurice, my former morse code instructor, was technical and concerned the timing of transmission. Our plan was as follows:

It was arranged that I was to transmit only vital news. After my third day in Britain, I was to establish my first contact with the Germans, telling them only the spot where I had arrived, and whether or not all was well. They were to call first, and their calling signal was to remain constant. Mine was to change every day. The three recognition letters were to be taken from the first three coded in my message, and morning and afternoon times were set for transmission. If necessary, I was to let them know when I had something important to send, and they would go on

"Dauerempfang," which meant that they would sit by the receiver day and night until they heard from me. Then I returned to St. Joseph.

◆ ◆ ◆

It was now December, 1942. Great preparations were being made at the château for the Christmas celebration. We had bought a flock of geese, and these had been fattened up during the summer and were now ripe for the slaughter. Bobby the pig was truly the pig of pigs. His liberty had been curtailed in order to prevent him from trying to emulate a greyhound, and in his narrow confines he had become fat and contented. Wolf, the most recent arrival at the *Dienststelle,* was given the task of feeding him.

Wolf was a dapper, fastidious type of chap, always beautifully groomed and manicured. When he mixed the pig's slops he wore gloves and held the basin containing the swill well away from his nose, amid the jeers of his comrades.

He told me an incident which gave me quite an insight into the way the Germans behave among themselves. His brother was a first lieutenant in the Luftwaffe, a hard-drinking, reckless fellow but a good soldier. He had the reputation of being a crack shot with an automatic. In his mess, after a large number of bottles had been drunk, a dispute arose concerning the merits of William Tell. Wolf's brother declared that anyone could emulate the famous shot—that he himself from twelve paces could shoot an apple from a man's head.

To prove this, he ordered a soldier to place an apple on his head and stand the required distance away. The man demurred, and looked frightened. Whereupon Wolfs brother called him a coward and changed places with him, placing the apple on his own head. He ordered the unfortunate soldier to draw his own automatic and fire. That order was obeyed, and the bullet hit him squarely between the eyes.

From the Luftwaffe came large-scale maps of southern England, with photographic enlargements forming a mosaic of the country where I was to be dropped. I was told that the accuracy of the drop was within five miles, depending on wind and altitude. For some time I studied certain points on the photographs until I had a fairly good knowledge of the various landmarks and railway stations.

The scheme adopted was that I should be dropped within easy reach of London at about two o'clock in the morning. I would hide in the countryside until daybreak, taking good care to bury my parachute and destroy all traces of my landing. From there, I would catch a train to London, and from then on the Germans believed that I would be among friends in the underworld, some of whom I would try to recruit for my mission. To my old buddy, Freddie, I was to offer £5,000 if he would help me. Any other person who did the same was to be suitably rewarded. If any one of these people decided to return with me to Germany, then German nationality and protection were promised them.

The problem of my return to the Continent had been carefully considered. Von Grunen had told me that he had a scheme in mind, but that he could not divulge it. One suggestion was that a U-boat should pick me up at some point off the British coast, details to be arranged by radio. If this fell through, I was to try to get on a boat bound for Portugal, and a cover address in Lisbon was given me. The name was de Fonseca. If I got to this place and met him I was to use the password *"Joli Albert."* He would then put me in touch with German Secret Service agents, who would smuggle me or my friends through to the Reich.

I prepared my pack for the journey. It held a wireless receiver and transmitter, sabotage materials, chocolate, etc. A special oilskin moneybag was made to hold my cash, which was to be strapped to my back in case I fell into water and got it wet. Naturally, all details of my sabotage formulae, radio code, mission, and cover address had to be carried in my head. My wireless was fitted into a small English briefcase of brown leather, very innocent in appearance. Thousands of the same sort are carried in Britain every day. All these articles were enclosed in rubber- fiber packing. Even this packing was British, having been seized by the German Military Police when the R.A.F. dropped sabotage materials over France for the *maquis.* When my pack was ready it was placed in a specially prepared sack and sewn up.

My last day at Nantes was December 17, 1942. I helped the boys to kill the geese. I placed the birds one at a time on a wooden block, and chopped their heads off. The German Secret Service sat in rows and plucked them. Eighteen were killed, plucked, and strung up.

That afternoon I packed my bag and said goodby to all—I must confess, not without regret. Somehow I had come to know all these men so well by now. They had shown me genuine comradeship. When I thought of the uncertainty ahead, doubts as sailed me. Would I be treated as a traitor in England, or hanged as a spy? But it was too late for doubts now.

"Auf Wiedersehen," I shouted.

"Hals und Beinbruch, viel Glück" (Mud in your eye, and lots of luck), they shouted, and the car sped away from the first "home" I had known in ten years.

In Paris we stayed at Les Ambassadeurs. Next day I was driven to a small airfield with Thomas and von Grunen to meet the crew who were to fly me to England. The colonel in charge presented his men to me. The pilot was an *Oberleutnant*, who wore the Iron Cross. He was a small, thickset young man of about twenty-eight, with steady blue eyes. The navigator was a lieutenant, a blond youngster of nineteen, tall, and extremely shy. Next came the radio operator, another youngster of eighteen. I learned that this was to be their fiftieth operational flight over Britain. For this they would receive a special leave of seven days.

I was taken to the *Fallschirm-Zimmer* (parachute room), and my parachute was tested. It was, as is usual, automatic. It was a rule of the Luftwaffe that every man must roll his own parachute; this I had learned to do. I took the parachute out of its tin box and refolded it. The silk had been dyed dark brown for camouflage. My pack was left with one of the harness experts. He had been given instructions to sew it to the harness in such a way that it hung low on my back and my parachute rested on top of it.

Then I went to inspect the Junkers 11 which was to fly me. It was a twin-motored reconnaissance plane with four machine guns. Experiments were made as to my best way of leaving the aircraft, which had not been adapted for parachute jumping. In fact, the only way of getting out was for me to drop through the floor, which necessitated removing a machine gun and fixing a hinge door over the aperture. This meant that I had to fly the whole journey sprawled on my stomach, with a load of forty or fifty pounds on top of me.

At a given signal, I was to release a lever beside me, the door would fall out, and I would follow it head-first through that hole. The hole itself was small, and it was only by dint of much wriggling and squirming that I could get through it at all. However, it was the best they could do, so I had to run the risk of being stuck. A flying helmet and oxygen mask were then tried on me for size.

After this, we went to the colonel's office to study the landing place. It was decided to land me at Wisbech in Cambridgeshire. This spot was chosen because it is easy to fly in over the Wash, and also because here the density of population is slight. It further offered a favorable landing ground, being set in an agricultural district well served by road and rail. What was still more important, I knew the district fairly well.

◆ ◆ ◆

Von Grunen, Thomas, and I then left the colonel and his crew. We agreed to have a farewell dinner that night. Paccardi's Restaurant, on the Boulevard des Capucines, was chosen for the occasion. The Italian food was plentiful, and we managed to procure some excellent pâté de foie gras, with a good bottle of Chianti and plenty of champagne. Von Grunen paid me compliments on my work, and told me that whatever happened to remember that I always had friends and that I would be sincerely missed. He wished me every success and *"glückliche Reise."* He went on to say that he regretted having had to curtail my liberty while I was at Nantes, but hoped I would understand that it was for my own good. When I returned, however, I would be accorded complete freedom and helped to start a new life. Thomas also said he would miss me and made sentimental references to our lasting friendship. A *"Brüderschaft"* (a toast to camaraderie, which establishes the informal German *Du)* was drunk, and we went home.

Von Grunen had a single room at Les Ambassadeurs. Thomas and I had a double room, separated from it by interconnecting doors. On his arrival at the hotel, von Grunen was informed that two gentlemen were waiting for him in his room. We went upstairs and he asked Thomas to accompany him. I applied my ear to the crack in the door, and tried to catch the conversation. When I heard an American speaking I was greatly astonished, and even more intrigued.

Unfortunately, it was impossible to overhear much of the conversation, which seemed to be concerned with a mission to America that these men were planning. They were looking for a competent man to do the job. Von Grunen remarked that he had such a man, but he would not be available for four months. Sabotage discussions went on for some time. Then the American inquired whether the operator in question could speak English. The reply was, "Yes, he is a Britisher." So I gathered that he was alluding to me.

When the conference broke up I sneaked out to the lavatory. The two men emerged. Peeping from behind a crack in the door I was able to get only a back view of them.

Next day I went to the airport again. I had noticed on the way there that it had suffered little or no damage. This surprised me, because I had been allowed to listen to the British radio, and every fourteen days I received the British newspapers and heard of the bombing of these places.

The reason for this lack of damage to airfields was probably the painstaking system of camouflage. Large nets covered with leaves and foliage draped the hangars. Small planes were disguised with straw to look like haystacks. Petrol was buried deep in the ground, usually in some small forest at a distance from the hangars, and everything else was so scattered that a concentration of bombs would have little or no effect.

The afternoon before I was due to leave, a surprise was in store for me. Von Grunen took me by car to the Hotel George V. On the first floor we were shown into a room by a colonel in the uniform of the High Command. He wore a thick red stripe down his trousers.

At a long table a tall, impressive figure was seated. Von Grunen stood smartly to attention.

"Heil Hitler! This is the man who is going to England, Herr General," he announced.

Von Rundstedt—for it was he—stood up and stretched out a hand.

I "heiled" him and shook his hand. He asked me details of my mission and transport, and then wished me luck. He also signed a paper, authorizing my transit from France. Again we "heiled," and I was led from the room.

Thomas and I sat in the back of the car and sang some of the catchy American dance tunes we had learned over the radio. Von Grunen was amused at this and joined heartily in the chorus. One of the tunes was *I've got a Girl in Kalamazoo*. We did not know the words, so we roared in complete disharmony. Then, to please me, we all sang my favorite, *Lili Marlene*.

The colonel was waiting to greet us, and we went to his room to await the start. It was then six o'clock in the evening. Weather reports came through and were favorable—not too cloudy, and a slight wind. At twelve midnight, the moon would be rising. At two o'clock it would sink to the required level, not showing a gleam on the surface of the ground.

At ten o'clock we left the colonel's private room and went to his office. There I took off all my clothes and von Grunen and Thomas made a thorough search of them. Next, my money was strapped round me. I then put on an English lounge suit, the one which I had brought from Jersey and which had been bought originally in London. On top, I put on coveralls to cover everything. My knees were well-bandaged to help absorb the shock of the landing. Boots which came from supplies captured at Dieppe were fitted on me. A crash helmet was handed to me. In the plane I was to wear an aviator's helmet with fitted telephone and oxygen mask.

I was ready. I loaded my automatic and stuck it in my pocket. At the last moment, von Grunen produced a small brown tablet.

"Fritz, I hate to give you this—it is poison. You know if anything happens and you are caught, it is better to end it quickly than to be tortured."

I nodded, made a small hole in the turn-up of my trousers, and inserted the tablet. During that whole day and evening I had taken nothing to drink. Now the *Oberst* produced a bottle of cognac, and we drank to the success of the venture.

He telephoned for the crew, and they arrived. I only hoped at that moment that I looked as cool, calm and collected as they did. My heart was thumping. Yet somehow I felt the same thrill as I did in the old days when I had gone out to do some job in the night with Freddie—a mixture of fear and excitement. I kept saying to myself over and over again, "If you have enough guts you can do anything you want. In any case, if something happens, it's going to be over quickly."

A car was waiting outside. I was driven to Le Bourget airport. In the parachute room, an expert fitted my pack and chute; they felt terribly heavy. Outside, I could hear the revving of many airplane engines. My drop was timed to coincide with a bombing attack on Cambridge, and the other planes which were to accompany us were warming up. The noise increased until it was ear-splitting. A smell of petrol and exhaust fumes filled the air. We reached our plane, and I shook hands with the *Oberst*. Thomas came next.

"Fritz, I wish you all the best."

Last of all, von Grunen grasped my hand warmly.

"Fritz, *auf Wiedersehen*."

"*Joli Albert, Terreur, Terreur*," I answered.

I climbed into the machine, and lay on my belly. There was a practice attempt to see if the hinge door would work; it functioned perfectly. My oxygen was then plugged through, and my telephone tested.

"*Können Sie mich hören?*" the pilot yelled to me.

His voice resounded strangely in my ears.

"*Jawohl*," I answered.

"*Gut! Gemütliche Reise*," was the retort.

The engines rewed and roared, louder and louder. We bumped over the ground faster and faster—and then we were off into the night.

◆ ◆ ◆

Lying flat on my belly I could see nothing of what was happening in the nose of the plane where the pilot and the navigator sat. The radio operator was placed a little above me. About a foot from my face a machine gun gave him a full traverse of the tail. My head faced in that direction. Beneath me I could see through a crack in the badly fitting door the tiny receding lights of the airport.

We climbed and climbed. Below was inky darkness with occasional pinpoint flashes. I squirmed my back round, which was a difficult business, for my pack weighed me down, and six inches from the top of my head were various instruments. On my left side, squeezed against me, were more instruments; on my right side, also pressing into me, were the ammunition holsters. This plane had certainly not been built for comfort.

I was conscious of the rush of the wind and the roar of the engines as we mounted. The radio man switched on the oxygen. *"Alles in Ordnung,"* came the voice of the pilot in my ear. I replied, *"Jawohl, alles gut,"* though at the moment that was hardly true.

From time to time the pilot and navigator discussed our course and speed. The operator tapped out messages on his key, then began letting out strips of aluminum through a vent in the floor. I learned later that this was to avoid the risk of radio location.

"Over the Channel," said the voice in my ear.

Below, far below in the gleam of the moonlight, I could see water and white foam. The smell of the sea came up sharply through the crack. I began to feel cold. Owing to my unnatural position it was difficult for me to keep my circulation going. I rubbed my legs together to get rid of a slight cramp.

"Herr Leutnant," I asked, "will you tell me when we are over England?"

"Jawohl," came the answer.

I caught the flash of searchlights. There seemed to be hundreds of them sweeping their beams in every direction.

"Jetzt," shouted the pilot. "This is England."

Immediately all three of the crew gave their war cry: *"Buzz! Buzz! Buzz!"* It resembled the noise of Stukas going into a dive-bombing attack. From far below little colored balls came floating up. I watched them disinterestedly until I realized that we were being fired upon. Patches of cloud blurred the searchlights as we flew on.

Suddenly there was a tap on my head. The wireless operator was holding his fingers up—ten minutes to go. The plane screamed through the air—another tap on the head. This was the prearranged signal for me to take off my oxygen mask and replace it with my helmet. The operator then made signs for me to pick up something, I could not understand what. His signals grew more frantic, and he went through an elaborate pantomime of tying a knot.

At last I got it. We had forgotten to fasten the opening rope of my parachute to a bolt. These chutes were operated by means of a rope attached to their tops. It had to be fastened to something substantial in the plane so that the chute could be jerked open. In another few moments I would have pulled the lever and fallen to my death. I fastened the rope to a bolt jutting from the ammunition box, and waited.

Another tap on the head—and that was the signal to go. I wrenched the lever and the hinged door fell out. I waved to the radio operator, and saw him smile and wave back at me. I lowered my head, and suddenly heard a terrific crash of shots. I wriggled and wriggled. ... I was stuck in that accursed hole! I exerted all my strength, the strength of fear and desperation. In vain! Suddenly, I felt a hard kick on my bottom, and I was falling clear of the aircraft. The tail zoomed over me. . . . *Zack.* . . My parachute had opened. There was a crackle of machine guns; a night fighter had picked us up. For a moment, I could see nothing. I wondered if the British fighter would come hurtling into me.

The din of engines died away in the distance. My chute was swaying slightly. Emerging from the edge of a cloud, I saw a brilliant moon set amid bright stars. I looked at the time on my wrist watch—it was ten past two. Peacefully, quietly, floating gently, and absolutely without any sensation of falling, I was coming Home, out of the sky. Below me was England, my own country.

I looked down, and then fear gripped me again. The clouds far below seemed like waves, and in my confusion I thought that those German devils had dropped me over the sea. The Gestapo had betrayed me after all! I was sure of it, positive. This was the end. I fumbled in my pocket for my automatic—a cold, watery grave did not appeal to me. I fired a shot to see if the gun was working. Then, as I dropped closer to earth, I realized with relief that I was sinking into a cloud, and not into the sea.

Another glance at my watch—it was nineteen minutes past the hour. I had the feeling that I would never come down. Then I thought of that old saying, "What goes up must come down." I hoped it was true.

I stuck my automatic into my harness belt. I was through the clouds now, beneath the great blanket which covered the land. Darkness engulfed me, and I could see nothing. Suddenly, a roof top loomed up toward me a few yards from my feet. I sailed over it, straight into the middle of a plowed field. I was so surprised to see the house that I had made no preparations for landing. Next moment—*bang!* I was flat on my back, sprawled like a sack of coals, facing the sky. My chute was spread out behind me. I just lay as I had fallen, and felt the earth beneath me. This was England!

9

[This part of Eddie Chapman's story was censored by the War Office. The facts have been carefully reconstructed by George Voigt]

OUT OF THE NIGHT

WHEN CHAPMAN first offered his services to the Nazis back on the Isle of Jersey, he was prompted by a variety of reasons. He was indulging his zest for excitement and adventure. And he was seeking escape from the boredom of a tiny, sleepy island too confining for his appetites. But there was more in his mind than that. He never considered helping the Nazis against England. He had no intention of turning traitor to his country. Chapman has been a criminal most of his adult life, he has broken a multitude of laws, but he has never sunk to treason. On the contrary, he had a plan, a wild and grandiose plan, to dupe the Germans and emerge as a hero in his country. He had the kind of imagination to fancy such things: Eddie Chapman, crook, thief, fugitive; then—hero and patriot. Back on Jersey his plan couldn't have been worked out in any detail. There were too many unknown factors confronting him. But hazily he saw the many possibilities of helping his country through the connections he was seeking with the Nazis. And, being an eminently practical as well as an imaginative fellow, he was not one to overlook the corollary possibilities of gaining an amnesty in England for his services—if his plan succeeded.

On that frosty November day in France, on Chapman's birthday, when orders arrived for him to report to Paris for final preparations, he knew the time had come for an accounting of his intentions and a reappraisal of his plans. The months with the Germans had been fun, the kind of life that suited his tastes. In the years ahead, those months would remain pleasant memories. But the time had come for serious and dangerous business. He was going home, taking the big jump over to his own side—

the big double-cross that was the basis of his plan. At his birthday party that night, thanking his German friends for their presents and good wishes, the actor in him must have despaired for an audience to appreciate the true meaning of his final remarks, when he assured the group *that he would never be ashamed of anything he did while working for them.*

That night he began to accumulate information in a notebook. Everything he had seen or heard that might be useful to the British military he wrote down. He was confident he had completely won the trust of the Germans and there was no danger of his notebook being discovered or even suspected. A month later, when he dressed to leave for Le Bourget airport and the flight to England, he had the notebook, well filled with information, strapped next to his body under his money belt. But he had overlooked one thing: the thoroughness of the Germans—and that was almost a fatal oversight.

The Germans had no suspicions about Chapman. But as a matter of routine they had scheduled a final search of his clothing and equipment, a final safety check in case some item or mark that might reveal he had been on the continent had been overlooked previously. Luckily, in the course of the evening while idling away the last brief hours before his plane was due to take off from Le Bourget, von Grunen mentioned in passing that a final examination of his clothing would be made before he left.

In that moment Chapman came closer to panicking than at any time during his dangerous association with the von Grunen group. But his nerve held steady and his mind remained clear. He did the only thing there was to do. As casually as possible he rose from his seat, stretched, made some remark about the need to relieve himself, and sauntered from the room. The others laughed and made jokes, attributing his need for the toilet to nervousness over the approaching flight. Behind the locked door of the bathroom, Chapman jerked the notebook from behind his money belt, tore it into small pieces and flushed it down. A few minutes later, when he was taken into a private room and stripped naked for the inspection of his clothing, there was not a telltale item to be found.

Chapman's plan, on arriving in England, was simple. He would merely report to the nearest police station, ask to be taken to MI5, the British intelligence organization, tell his story, then offer his information and services. He thought MI5 would fall over him in welcome. But when he landed in England he scarcely had time to take the initiative in offering his services. And his welcome was not quite what he had expected.

As he broke through the clouds over the Cambridgeshire countryside, his parachute was spotted by a local farmer who, like all English farmers during the war, stood guard against parachutists. The sound of the airplane passing overhead had brought the farmer from his house. Scanning the dark sky, he had seen the parachute descending and already had turned in the alarm before Chapman landed. Local police were speeding to the spot as Chapman stumbled through the dark plowed field toward the farmer's house.

The farmer was there, waiting. Chapman spoke to him and asked directions. The simple farmer told him outright that he had notified the police and that they were on their way. Chapman waited. The police arrived a short while later, furious at finding an Englishman dropped by the Germans, obviously a traitor. They were in no mood to be reasonable, especially when Chapman calmly, almost haughtily, told them he would speak only to military intelligence, and steadfastly refused to answer any of their questions.

All the rest of the night the angry police questioned and threatened him. But Chapman, a seasoned professional at police questioning, stood by his demand to be taken to military intelligence before explaining anything. Once during the night one exasperated officer exploded into near violence, called Chapman a "traitorous son of a bitch" and threatened to shoot him there and then without bothering to take him in for hanging. But Chapman refused to be bullied or frightened.

In the morning the farmer's wife made breakfast, which Chapman ate sitting at the farmer's kitchen table as calm and collected as any house guest. Later, more tired than their prisoner from the night of uninterrupted interrogations, the police decided to take him in. As they left the farmer's house, Chapman used some of the crisp new pound notes from the Deutsche Bank to pay the farmer's wife for her food and hospitality. Like most people, with the exception of the police, the farmer and his wife thought Chapman utterly charming, a real gentleman.

◆ ◆ ◆

In London, military intelligence listened in amazement as Chapman told his story, from the beginning, leaving out nothing except the small fortune in Reichsmarks he still hoped somehow to collect from his German friends despite his double-cross. For three days intelligence officials kept him locked up, draining him of information about conditions in France and in German military units, much of it information that Chapman had written down in detail in the notebook he was forced to abandon at the last minute. They checked and rechecked his story for any inaccuracy or contradiction that might betray him. They examined his radio transmitter and other equipment, checked and studied the code he had been given to use.

At last, satisfied that he was telling the truth, they agreed to use his services, under strict limitations and controls. All messages sent by the Germans would be taken over by intelligence officers immediately on receipt. He must never send any messages unless composed and given him by Intelligence or unless they were thoroughly checked and approved by Intelligence.

With that matter settled, Chapman, nervy and brazen as ever, set forth his terms. While assuring the Intelligence officials that his actions were prompted by patriotism and a desire to serve his country, he also thought that he deserved something material in the way of compensation. His terms: that he be allowed to keep all money he had received or might in the future receive from the Germans; and that he be granted a full pardon for all his pre-war crimes. Intelligence officers were astounded at his brashness, but in the end they accepted his terms.

His transmitter was set up and he was given his first message to send: "Well. Am with friends. Good landing. Fritz." But he had transmission trouble on his very first try. He couldn't make contact and the message didn't go through. For a few alarming moments he imagined doubts creeping into the minds of his intelligence overseers. His own mind backtracked over the past few days, searching for an error he might have made to arouse the Germans' suspicions. Could they have suspected him and stationed another agent about to observe him making contact with MI5? His thoughts raced over the many possibilities for error that could have revealed his double-cross to the Germans.

But finally the Germans came through, sending their code signal to contact him. They were on the air, but they weren't receiving him. He sent his message again, blind into the unchanneled ether, hoping some other station on another frequency might pick it up. That worked. His message was received. The great game had begun. His plan was functioning.

◆ ◆ ◆

One of the greatest errors an intelligence organization can make is to underestimate the enemy intelligence. It would have been naive to presume that the Germans would make no effort to double-check the information relayed to them by Chapman.

Surely there were other German agents in England seeking the same information Chapman had been sent to get. Surely there were others available to spy on Chapman and report on his movements and associations. Chapman's usefulness to British Intelligence would last only so long as he retained the trust of the Germans. Every precaution had to be taken, therefore, to keep the Germans from learning of his duplicity.

There was little MI5 could do beyond what they would normally do to guard against a double-check by other agents of the information sent through Chapman. Security was already as tight as humanly possible. It was standard practice to employ various ruses to mislead agents into sending incorrect and conflicting reports that would confuse the enemy, making it difficult for them to determine which reports were true and which were false. Beyond this, British Intelligence could only hope that Chapman's information would be received with trust and confidence.

To guard against detection of Chapman's associations with British Intelligence, his contacts were kept at the barest minimum. Chapman was set adrift in London to fend for himself, find his own lodgings, make his own social contacts, occupy his time as he wished. Nothing was done to reveal that he was receiving any help or advice, or that he was under any control. His intelligence overseers were highly secret members of MI5 and their contacts with Chapman were maintained with the utmost discretion.

It was expected that he would make some contacts with some of his old underworld friends; the Germans expected him to do this too. It was part of the German plan that he would need some associates to help him with the sabotage of the de Havilland aircraft works. But he was warned to keep such contacts at a minimum, to keep his activities restricted—as becomes a traitor and a spy. He was to be neither too secretive nor too open in his movements, either of which might arouse suspicion.

Just how British Intelligence used Chapman's connection with the Germans, or with what effectiveness during this period, nobody outside of the War Office could know; and only a few inside would know. Chapman himself would be left in the dark about it. Of obvious value was the opportunity to misinform the Germans with the messages Chapman sent them. Misinformation in war can be much more disastrous than no information at all, and there are few properties more valuable to an intelligence organization than a clear and trusted channel through which to feed misinformation to the enemy. It may be assumed that British Intelligence received full value in this regard.

Also, the messages sent by the Germans would be of a certain value. By themselves these messages, blunt and succinct, wouldn't carry much information. But the kind of information the Germans demanded, pieced in with other intelligence, could reveal something of what was on their minds or in their plans, what was causing them doubt or fear. Whatever subtler uses British Intelligence could or did make of Chapman's connection with the Germans remains the War Office's secret.

◆　◆　◆

In all of this, Chapman played only the most subsidiary role. Occasionally his advice might be asked on matters he would have special knowledge of as a result of his long sojourn with the von Grunen *Dienststelle*. And he had to memorize and retain details of all the information sent over his transmitter in preparation for the day, if it ever came, when he would face a German grilling about his "mission." But he had little part in analyzing or deciding anything that passed through his transmitter or receiver. If the Germans asked for a report on bomb damage in London, or a listing of American divisions arriving in England, or a report on a new tank gun, British Intelligence provided the report for him to send back. In this respect, Chapman was little more than an attachment to his radio equipment, used by intelligence as they saw fit.

Chapman's main job was to stay alive and retain the connection; to live in such a manner as to avoid suspicion, to meet some friends but avoid most, to move about as though he was gathering information (for the benefit of any German agent checking up on him) but not to move about so much as to attract attention of police or acquaintances. For a man as well known throughout London as Eddie Chapman, this was not an easy task. But it was as important to Chapman as to British Intelligence. An error would deprive Intelligence of a valuable property, but it also might deprive Chapman of his life.

Within this restrictive and uneasy framework, Chapman settled down to enjoy life as much as possible. The thick stack of pound notes from the Deutsche Bank helped, but still it could not be the life he had known before the war.

While he lived this life, and tried to make the most of it, the War Office undertook the problem of what to do about the principal task Chapman had been charged with by the Germans: destruction of the De Havilland factory. Unless something was done about that without too much delay, Chapman's value would soon run out.

◆　◆　◆

It had been a long detour home from the island of Jersey. Only a cool and seasoned traveler could have made it without mishap. But it also had been the kind of detour that an adaptable fellow like Chapman could enjoy. There had been periods—during the months of carefree merrymaking with his Nazi friends—when Chapman almost forgot that it must all eventually come to an end, when he forgot about his plan—the plan that first led him to offer his services to the German occupation commandant on Jersey.

Now, home again, it was time to put the plan into effect.

10

OPERATION DOUBLE-CROSS

THE MORNING rush hour was on when I was turned loose at Liverpool Street Station. I was ravenous, and wondered how the hell I was going to get something to eat without a ration book.

Down the platform I saw the people coming and going at a door marked Buffet. I joined the crowd and went in through the swing doors. The man in front of me asked for sandwiches and tea. He didn't hand over any coupons, so I asked for the same, and in no time I was having my first taste of wartime Spam. It seemed pretty good to me, after the sawdust in the *Leberwurst* I was used to in Germany.

By now I felt much stronger and more confident, and was gradually becoming acclimatized to the unfamiliar scene. I went to a phone booth, put in my tuppence, and rang up a club in Soho which I used to frequent. I asked for the doorman who was an old friend of mine, and whom in the past I had tipped rather well, and they told me that he would be on duty at six that evening.

I thanked them, went into the tube, bought myself a ticket to Piccadilly, and spent the next three hours at a movie. When the program was over, I got up and went toward the door, but suddenly remembered that I had left my precious briefcase under the tip-up seat. I returned for it, and a great deal of groping ensued with the aid of the usher's flashlight. I could not help wondering what these peaceful people would have thought if they had known what that briefcase contained.

At six o'clock that evening, still carrying the briefcase, I rang up the club again. This time my doorman pal was on the job, and I arranged to meet him in half an hour's time at a neighboring club.

We met, and he asked me what the hell I'd been doing.

"Look, I'm in a spot of bother," I said. "I want to lie low for a few weeks. Can you find me a hideout?"

He promptly gave me an address in Finchley. I slipped him two more quid from the Deutsche Bank and made a few inquiries about friends of mine. Then I thanked him, and told him I would contact him later. We swallowed our drinks, and I took a taxi to the address he had given me. It was a quiet-looking house in a moldering Victorian street—beautifully inconspicuous.

The landlady answered the door and I mentioned the doorman's name. I found he had already telephoned her. Without asking any questions or making any fuss, she showed me up to the second floor in the back. I asked her what the price was, and gave her a month's rent in advance. Once again I felt very much at home when I saw the flyblown wallpaper, the large brass bed, the worn linoleum and the shilling-in-the-slot gasmeter. Anyway, this was all I needed for what I had come to do.

The next two days I spent wandering around London, inspecting the bomb damage and taking care to avoid my old familiar haunts. Dear old London! Still the same untidy, planless network of streets, with the same dilapidated taxis, horse-drawn vans and barrows, and traffic almost as dense as in peacetime. Everywhere the khaki uniforms of the troops of the free nations contrasted with the field-green I had come to know so well for nearly two years. It seemed to me that here was an immense piling-up of forces on a scale which would have seemed inconceivable on the other side of the Channel.

On the third day I unpacked my radio set, plugged it into the electric light socket, and laid out my aerial along one side of the room and my counterpoise along the other. I switched on and waited for it to warm up. This took about ten minutes, after which I tapped out my call sign and tuned in to my frequency.

No reply.

I dared not wait, so I flashed out a code message saying:

"Well. Am with friends. Good landing. Fritz."

Five coded X's were incorporated in this message. If I failed to include them it meant that I was sending it under duress. If they appeared, my message would be regarded as authentic.

The time came to check back. Tuning in, I could hear the German signal coming through in good strength. *G.W.T.* they called, then stopped. I started calling *V.U.T.*, and continued for some minutes. Then—disappointment! They could not hear me. After some further minutes of calling in vain, I tapped my message over the ether, blind. I knew that other stations in Nantes and the south of France were listening for me, and there was a possibility that they would pick up my message.

Next day, I again transmitted to the Germans, and this time had a reply saying my message had been received, and wishing me good luck.

At first the transmission did not work too well. Paris, the station with which I was in communication, could not hear me. My messages were being picked up by Nantes, so usually I sent them "blind." Later, I received confirmation from Paris that they had come across.

During this time I went out quite often, dining and visiting theatres and cinemas. For the first time in several years I saw a Christmas pantomime. I bought myself some clothes, the excellent quality of which surprised me, even though "utility" was then the order of the day. I also explored some of the bomb damage, and sent over a report on it.

◆ ◆ ◆

The ignorance of the German Intelligence astonished me. Up to the time of my arrival in England, they had no idea of the most elementary details of British life. I had been warned that perhaps it would be difficult for me to obtain food, for they believed this was drastically rationed in Britain. They did not know that anyone could get a meal in a restaurant without giving up coupons. London was portrayed to the German people as a mass of devastation, and even their own Secret Service believed this.

It was not difficult to understand why this was so. Under the twisted genius of Goebbels, German propaganda had so long deluded the "Master Race" that its sinister influence had penetrated even into the inner recesses of the Nazi war machine. It lied to everyone. Even its own Special Branch did not know the truth! Accurate reports must have flowed in from innumerable neutral sources, as well as from every foreign embassy and consulate. These were received by officials high in the hierarchy, who automatically filed them away in order to continue deluding the German public, and even their own bosses. They finished by deluding themselves.

A point had been reached at which even intelligent Germans had come to believe whatever Hitler wanted them to believe, and nothing else. If the British declared that they had bacon, meat and bread in abundance, it must clearly be lies—in fact, "propaganda." The Germans always firmly maintained that they were in a better position than their enemies. That is why Hitler was able to keep them fighting up to the twelfth hour, in the belief that the other side would crack first. Indeed, they are still wondering why that didn't happen!

Some light can be thrown on the bungling technique of the German Secret Service by their handling of my own case. When I unpacked my money I found that the *Dienststelle* had forgotten to take the bands of the Deutsche Bank from the packages; they had even left the *Dienststelle* number stamped on the bundle. Again, the new tubes which had been fitted to my transmitter were of German origin, and still bore their German markings.

One night at this time I was dining at Princes' Restaurant in the West End. I went to the toilet. As I emerged, I caught sight of a member of the underworld whom I had known in the old days. It was an awkward moment, for he accosted me and said: "Hello, aren't you Eddie Chapman?"

I gazed at him and replied, without batting an eyelid: *"Excusez- moi, Monsieur, mais je ne comprends pas l'anglais."*

He appeared bewildered, scratched his head and said:

"Good God! You and the devil must be brothers!"

Upstairs, sitting at a table nearby, he kept staring at me. Then, thinking that his memory must be playing him tricks, he started dosing himself with double Scotches.

Nevertheless, however furtive my life, it was a delight to be home again—to watch free men in a free country and to hear people discussing politics and praising or damning the government according to their personal opinions. The outlook of the ordinary man and woman seemed so much broader, and so far less one-sided, than in Germany. Instead of the eternal "Heil Hitler!" greeting, here it was a pleasant "Good-day." To feel the cheery confidence of the people was something I enjoyed after the fears and frustrations I had suffered among the Germans.

One night there was a bombing attack on London, and the next day I received orders from the Germans to report on it. I tapped out a message, mentioning that an unexploded bomb had fallen at Lord's Cricket Ground, St. John's Wood, and that traffic had to be diverted in that area. Another message came in one morning over the ether asking me to send a list of government offices, especially those which had moved because of the blitz.

The Wehrmacht had also requested me to make sketches of various subjects of interest—divisional signs, flak battery sites, airports, etc.—all in invisible ink. My radio by this time functioned beautifully, and a full communication (both "give" and "receive") took no longer than eight minutes. Naturally, transmission varied with the weather.

I had a good laugh one day. I went to see a spy film. The spy, the usual sinister-looking villain, carried his set around with him in a large black suitcase. When he wished to transmit he simply opened his box, took out a microphone, and started speaking openly over the air. In this case he was in direct contact with a German U-boat commander.

"Hullo," he would say, "this is Number Seven. Tonight, at nine, a convoy is leaving X-."

"Jawohl," would come the immediate answer.

With that, transmission closed down, with never any trouble in getting through again, and always the obliging commander ready to act on his instructions!

◆ ◆ ◆

I wondered if the man who had made this film understood the difficulties of wireless transmission, and the problems of frequencies, aerials, and weather conditions. Whether he realized how, at one period of the day, it is possible to receive a message and transmit with perfect clarity, while an hour later the ether may be disturbed, so that all that comes through the earphones is a crackling inferno? Sometimes conditions can be so bad that letters have to be repeated four or five times in succession to make them audible. And, of course, a real spy has to remember that the science of wireless interception and location has now practically reached perfection.

In every country at this time skilled men sat all day at receivers. Each had a small band on the short wave to watch. If an "irregular sender" was noticed, other stations were warned. The next time the "irregular sender" transmitted, sets from all over the country were tuned on to him, and the lines from one point of location to another drawn. This gave the approximate spot from which he was transmitting. Next, radio location vans were sent out. They did the same, always narrowing down the circle until finally the place of transmission was discovered.

I knew that in Rennes the Germans had such a location center. The men were relieved every two hours, and I believe they succeeded in catching several Allied agents.

An agent must do many things to avoid detection—change his quarters often, alter his frequencies, transmit at different times of the day, and use a different code call every day. Irregularity and, above all, brevity are the keys to success. Four to eight minutes for a full transmission is plenty. A finger should never touch the key more than is absolutely necessary. In this sinister world, as in that other underworld which I had known, "say next to nuffin' " is the way to remain in business.

It is not easy to fix up a modern radio set. Some require two aerials, good and highly placed; a counterpoise and earth are also essential. The work must be done as inconspicuously as possible. The ideal, of course, is to have two radios in the house, using the; aerials of these and laying the counterpoise around the room.

It can be seen from all this that the danger of spies broadcasting from hotels, so popular in films and magazines, is severely limited. The great temptation for an agent, once he has established contact, is to continue doing so despite the risk. This often leads to his undoing. A better idea would be to find out the call signs of a legitimate broadcasting station in the enemy country, and use its frequencies to transmit.

Another point, and an important one, is the use of ciphers. Yardley, who wrote *The American Black Chamber*, claimed to be able to crack nearly every cipher that had been invented. A cipher should be as foolproof as possible. My first one was much too simple, and I am certain that with a little study the experts could have solved it. Later, I was to be given another which I think could have been solved only after a long period. Thus, it can be realized that sending information is not just a matter of talking into a microphone and giving out the required information.

During the weeks that followed I sent many messages in answer to German inquiries. They were particularly anxious to know which American divisions were now in England, and what were their divisional signs. They also asked me for descriptions of the flak units in London, especially in the parks near Piccadilly.

After some time I was able to send a message saying that all preparations were completed for the really big job, and that with the aid of my old friend Freddie, who had accepted my offer, I would attempt to do it at six o'clock that evening.

Next morning I sent another message saying that the venture had been successful.

The Germans replied with congratulations.

In February I sent a message to Paris asking for suggestions on the method of my return. Von Grunen had promised me that I would be brought back by submarine, and that the details would be arranged by radio. I told them how urgent this was, because meanwhile Freddie had been arrested and the heat was on, so that it was imperative that I should leave England with the least possible delay.

The reply was astonishing. It ran:

"Impossible to send submarine. Suggest getting passenger steamer to Lisbon."

I had a good laugh at this. It wasn't so damned easy to do that sort of thing in wartime!

11

[The facts reported in the following chapter were censored by the War Office under the Official Secrets Act and have been carefully reconstructed by George Voigt]

THE BIG JOB

THE BATTLE of Britain had been fought and won long before Chapman parachuted into England. That small band of hard-pressed, hard-fighting Royal Air Force flyers who held back the Luftwaffe and stopped the German invasion threat—the few to whom so many owed so much—had grown to a formidable force capable of attacking as well as defending. The English skies were filled with ever-increasing numbers of Allied planes and the Germans were feeling the first sharp jabs of the R.A.F. and A.A.F. counterattack. And though they couldn't foresee the sledgehammer blows still to come, they were becoming desperately concerned over the rapidly changing balance of air power.

A prime source of the growing Allied offensive strength in England was the De Havilland factory at Hatfield, a few miles north of London, where Britain's famed Mosquito bombers were made. Above all else, the Germans were interested in Chapman's assignment to cripple the De Havilland works.

It was a tough assignment. The mission had to be accomplished, or appear to have been accomplished, to satisfy the Germans and retain their trust in Chapman. While Intelligence mulled over the problem, Chapman stalled the Germans with messages outlining the difficulties of the job. He could pull it off, he assured them, but it would take time. Finally, MI5 decided to attempt a gigantic hoax: a vital part of the De Havilland plant would be made to appear destroyed by an internal explosion. The plan involved one of the war's most demanding camouflage efforts.

Two power plants supplying the factory were selected for the fake explosion. Their destruction would bring production at the plant to a virtual standstill, and that would surely satisfy the Germans. Also, the power plants seemed the easiest buildings on which to work. They were away from the main, more heavily occupied buildings. There were fewer workers to notice the elaborate camouflage work and question what was going on. They were located at a point within the factory grounds that an accomplished saboteur and burglar like Chapman could conceivably reach and enter with a package of explosives.

Chapman was drawn into a direct and active role in this scheme. He had to be. When and if he was ever questioned by the Germans about the job, his answers would have to be detail- perfect. He would have to know exactly how he entered the yard, how he made his way to the power plants, how he set his explosives and how he got out again. Also, still acting on the presumption that Chapman might be shadowed by other German agents, he ought to be seen making trips to the De Havilland works and going through other preparatory motions: making his contacts with a fellow-conspirator, going on mysterious automobile rides into quarry areas, where explosives could be found. He had to thoroughly "case" the factory grounds and surrounding country, both to learn the details of the layout and to keep up the necessary appearances. The information about the layout that he could glean from the maps and charts of the De Havilland works provided by German Intelligence was no more than sketchy.

It was all a great gamble as well as a great hoax. The entire plan was subject to error at almost every step. To make a factory building appear blown up from the inside was an untried camouflage trick. The Germans might easily see through it. Some German agent observing the operation might smell out the hoax before the work was even completed. Chapman might be seen by a guard loitering about the plant and be picked up on suspicion. Or he might be spotted by a policeman who remembered him from pre-war days. There were many such policemen about England. But it was a gamble that had to be taken and British Intelligence carefully worked over every detail to narrow the odds as much as possible.

Before any work on the power plants could begin, a number of preliminary factors had to be considered and decided. What would be the force of the explosive charge that Chapman was supposed to set off in the plants? And what kind of charge would be used? It would have to be made of explosives Chapman could conceivably steal somewhere in England. Where would a saboteur most likely place an explosive charge if he had access to the plant? And what visible external damage would such an explosion cause to the power plant structures? These questions were considered long and carefully, with the most expert consultation available. Then, with the painstaking care of portrait restorers and using all their knowledge of the effects of explosives, they created the illusion of countless bulges and cracks and gaps, twisted steel beams and shattered transformers—solely by means of camouflage. When they finished they had a work of art.

It didn't look like much from the ground. To the thousands of workers who passed the plant every day it was just another camouflage job. But the Germans wouldn't be seeing it from the ground. To see it as the Germans would, a photo reconnaissance plane was sent over the factory grounds to take a series of pictures. They looked perfect. They were studied and restudied for telltale flaws. None were found.

From five thousand feet up, the power plants looked as if they had suffered a terrific explosion that most surely would have blasted them out of commission. If the Germans accepted the appearance as fact, Chapman's mission would be considered admirably and thoroughly accomplished. (Incidentally, it would also completely throw off German estimates of British aircraft production and strength.) All was now set for the final move in the gamble.

Chapman contacted von Grunen and told him that at last all details for the big job were arranged. He would make the attempt that night. That evening he and his accomplice left London and drove to Hatfield. They returned late in the night. The next morning he radioed von Grunen again. Mission was successful, he said. Von Grunen flashed back congratulations. The London papers that morning carried news reports of an explosion at a factory in southern England, cause unknown. To the British public—to everybody but Chapman and his British and German Intelligence associates—the news stories, as faked as the explosion itself, might have referred to any of hundreds of factories in southern England. Two days later, at the tail end of a bombing run over London, a German reconnaissance plane circled low over the De Havilland works.

Later, in Berlin, under questioning of top German intelligence men, Chapman was to see those pictures taken by the German reconnaissance plane. He would be amazed by their exact resemblance to those in possession of British Intelligence. And he would not know whether the thorough Germans had discovered anything overlooked by the British.

In the days that followed he had no way of knowing if the hoax had worked. He continued to receive messages as before. There was nothing in the German messages to reveal if the gamble had succeeded or not. He received the same kind of requests for the same kind of information as before. He continued to send the answers composed by British

Intelligence.

After the excitement and activity that had gone into the great elaborate hoax, life in London seemed duller than before. The waiting, without being sure, weighed on Chapman. And he had lots of aggravating work. For while awaiting some word or reaction from von Grunen, he had to spend most of his time studying and restudying every detail of the story he would tell the Germans when the time came. And when he had memorized every step of every action that supposedly went into the accomplishment of his mission, he studied and memorized them further. It was an awful strain.

MI5 was also anxious to know whether the hoax had succeeded or failed. Was Chapman still a "connection" or not? Did the Germans still believe in him, or was British Intelligence now wasting its time using him to feed misinformation to the Germans? They had no way of knowing. The only way to find out, it seemed, was to send Chapman back to the Continent. It was risky. But it was another gamble that had to be taken. And this time Chapman's life was at stake. If successful, he would be in an invaluable position to pick up fresh intelligence for the British. If he failed . . . British Intelligence would carry on without him. All agents are expendable in war.

Chapman wanted to go back. In the boredom that had become his life in London he was developing a great hankering to return to France. His reasons were simple, straightforward and Chapmanesque: he'd been hired to do a job; he'd done it, or a reasonable facsimile of it. Now he wanted the payoff. There were a hundred thousand Reichsmarks, or ten thousand English pounds, waiting to be picked up back there.

Chapman had no qualms about taking the money on a doublecross, if he could get away with it. He was never one to worry overly much about ethics. In the code he'd followed most of his life, it was getting caught that was a crime, not committing the crime itself. If he wasn't found out in the De Havilland hoax, the Germans had to pay him ten thousand pounds. If he was found out—well, when you go in for a criminal life, you have to be ready to pay the penalty. Chapman had never let the fear of getting caught stand between him and any sizable sum of money.

So Chapman made his requests to von Grunen for instructions to return, and fabricated the story of his accomplice's capture and the growing heat building under him in England. He demanded a submarine to chauffeur him back. The refusal of a submarine might have deterred a weaker man; it might have been interpreted as an indication of displeasure on the part of the Germans. Chapman wasn't deterred in the slightest. He knew full well that in Germany they still used the ax on common criminals. He had enough imagination to visualize what the Nazis would do to a double-crosser. But ten thousand pounds is ten thousand pounds in anybody's language, especially Chapman's. He set out to find a ship that would take him to Lisbon.

12

THE ROAD BACK

THE SHIP was a small sea-going tramp of about 1,000 tons. She had just been bunkered, and was filthy. Every part of her was choked with coal dust, and the gangways, hatches and berths had coatings several inches deep.

I knocked at the chief steward's cabin. A tall, tired, thin-faced man appeared. He looked as though he had a hangover or had recently been dead.

"I am the assistant steward," I began.

"Hell!" he yelled, exploding with unexpected violence. "Another bloody steward! Jesus! We've got two already! What's wrong? Has the Old Man gone batty?"

I ventured no answer.

"All right," said Corpse-Face, cooling down. "Start and lay up for breakfast."

"Lay up," I found afterwards, was the technical term for laying the table. Luckily, at that moment another steward arrived. I introduced myself and asked him if he would lay up as I wanted to put my kit in my berth.

I found that I was to sleep among the gunners, because the stewards' berths were occupied by the other two chaps. I made my way aft and down a gangway, and found myself among eight Navy gunners. In charge was an old cockney chief.

"Cor' blimey, mate, you bunking down 'ere?"

"Got a berth vacant?"

"Sure"—and with that he pulled some old cases and life jackets from the top of a berth. It was grimy, and water seeped into it through the plates of the ship. However, as I was not to be aboard for long, I dug myself down and made up my bed.

I produced a bottle of whiskey, and won the friendship of the Navy boys. Some of them had been torpedoed two or three times.

When I was settled, I went up to help with the breakfast. I explained to the chief steward that this was my first voyage, and asked if he would please show me the ropes, so the other two stewards served at table while I prepared the bacon and eggs. When everything had been eaten, we cleared the table and washed up. Our work was then apportioned to us. I was told to clean the cabins of the captain and the three wireless operators.

The ship's company consisted of about thirty men. These were the master and three mates; the chief engineer and three juniors; three Marconi radio operators; and a mixed bag of sailors, firemen, stewards and gunners. Practically all the crew were Liverpool Irish, and a tough mob they were.

That night we steamed out of the Mersey to join the rest of the convoy, which had formed up off the north of Scotland. The number of ships in convoy was about fifty, including an escort of four destroyers and three or four corvettes. The order of the ships was so arranged that those carrying the most dangerous cargoes had the middle positions. These were the tankers and ammunition carriers. Our ship was also in the center, although our cargo was mail, parcels for prisoners of war and pipes for buildings. We were in line with six other ships, and there were seven lines all told. The escorts steamed ahead, astern and on either side of the convoy. Our ship had an armament of ten-pounder and twelve-pounder guns, two anti-aircraft guns, and two machine guns.

I soon fell into the routine of my work. At six o'clock in the morning, I took tea to the captain and the "Marconis." At eight I served breakfast; from ten to twelve scrubbed out rooms; at one o'clock served lunch and afterwards washed up. After that, I was free.

On my first night out, I opened my kit bag, produced pajamas and began to undress. The gunners watched me in amazed silence. Then the chief said:

"Say, mate, you shouldn't do that."

I asked why not.

Said the chief gunner: "If Jerry sends a tin fish into this bloody can, you won't find it warm on a raft with those things on." Stubbornness is a human trait. I heeded not the words of wisdom, and soon was snoring in my night attire.

We steamed around the north of Ireland into the Atlantic. Nothing untoward happened until the third day out.

At three o'clock in the afternoon I was standing on deck, watching the waves, when I heard shots. Alarm flags were run up on all the ships. The roar of a plane sounded, and a Heinkel appeared. I saw it release a bomb about two hundred yards away. It was flying low, and the bomb missed a 5,000-ton cargo boat, which was carrying a load of 500-pound bombs and ammunition, by a matter of feet. The explosion rocked the ship, but she steamed steadily on her course as the plane roared into the clouds and was lost to sight. The whole incident took only a few seconds. The gunners had not had time to man their guns properly. The two men on watch had merely loaded and stood at the ready, waiting for a renewal of the attack.

Great excitement reigned on board. Frankie, a youngster of seventeen who shared my duties, whistled through his teeth: "We'll catch it tonight." When I went below after the alarm, the chief gunner made the same remark. I asked him why.

"Cor' blimey, mate, don't you know? That bleedin' Jerry plane will tic-tac to the blinkin' subs and give 'em our course. Mark my words! Don't go to bed in them pajamas tonight!"

Dinner passed quietly enough. I went aft and smoked a cigarette with the two gunners on watch, taking care to hide the glow—for in convoy it is a serious offense to show a light of any description. The talk was fairly primitive, as is that of most sailors—about women and drink, and the strange girls they'd met in distant parts. It reminded me of our home in Sunderland, and my father.

At last, tired out, I turned in. This time, I did not put on my pajamas but slept in my clothes. I was awakened by the sound of the alarm bell, and lay for a moment in a stupor, blinking at the light. The gunners shot out of their beds, had their life jackets on in a second, and dashed up the gangway with perfect discipline. As I still lay back, half asleep, the last man up cast a glance back at me:

"Come on, mate!" he bawled. "There's a bloody sub attack."

I flung myself out of bed, but could not find my boots. When I did find them, I put them on the wrong feet and had to change them back again. My life jacket seemed to have many more strings than when I had fitted it on before. I kept tying, untying and retying it—it was back to front!

A terrific explosion shook the ship. Dashing up the gangway, I found that I had forgotten my coat. I rushed back, put on my coat and ran up the gangway again. This time I had forgotten my papers and cigarette case; down I went again to retrieve them. At last I managed to get on deck.

I looked out to sea, and beheld a sight I will never forget. A tanker and two merchant ships were burning fiercely, and the whole convoy was lit by the flames. These ships were only a few hundred yards away. Then another deafening explosion rent the air, and our ship seemed to jump clear out of the water. Our sister ship was steaming to port of us about a hundred yards away. She rolled over, and disappeared under the waves.

The explosion had come from the munitions ship which that afternoon had so narrowly escaped being hit by a bomb. Now a torpedo had struck her fair in the belly and she had been blown into fragments.

I was standing by the cockney gunner. He merely said: "Poor bastards, they felt nothing."

No further attack took place. The hours dragged by, and dawn came at last. I made tea, and took it up to the captain and officers. Everyone was still pale and strained. The windows on the bridge had been shattered, and broken glass was strewn about the deck. About a quarter of a mile away I could see a large freighter sinking. She settled down slowly in the water. The boats were lowered, and her crew got away from her. Her bow vanished and then, after rising vertically from the sea, her stern sank out of sight beneath the surface. The convoy re-formed, and slowly we steamed on.

I went below to rest—to sleep was out of the question. I took out a piece of paper and scrawled some doggerel verses on the whole ghastly business. The cockney gunner was there. When I had finished my lines, I handed them to him. He looked around, called his crew together and read them aloud. When he came to the part praising the gunners his voice swelled with pride.

What a dreadful life these chaps led! They were the worst paid men on board. They belonged to the Navy and were used for the defense of the Mercantile Marine. They ran more risks than anyone else, worked harder and, in return, received far less money. It was a damnable scandal that nobody seemed to have bothered to expose.

We sailed on, and the time came when, with the two other ships which were also going to Lisbon, we parted company with the convoy. After another day's sailing we dropped anchor in the Tagus, but for two days the crew was unable to leave the ship, and it was only on March 14, 1943, that our passes came on board. I went ashore with the gunners. We made our way to a brothel bar—the English Cafe. It was a foul place.

◆ ◆ ◆

When the sailors were good and drunk, I slipped out, took a taxi and went to the address the Germans had given me. It was in the rua Sao Mameda, a street in the working-class quarter. I knocked at the door, and a little Portuguese girl answered it. I tried in English, French and German to make her understand that I wanted to speak to Mr. de Fonseca, but she could not understand what I wanted. Eventually her mother appeared, a woman of about forty, simply dressed, who gestured me to come in. Her flat was empty and carpetless. A kitchen table and two wicker chairs were the only furniture.

I wrote the name of de Fonseca on a piece of paper, and the woman managed to convey to me that, though he lived there, he was out. She gestured with her hands to imitate the use of a telephone—would I like to speak to him? *Yes! Oui! Ja!* Nodding, I made her understand. She motioned me to follow her daughter whom I accompanied to a café, where I telephoned the number she had given me. A voice replied, and, *"Je voudrais bien parler avec Monsieur de Fonseca,"* I began.

"Oui, monsieur, c'est moi," replied the voice.

I continued the conversation in French, for the people in the café were casting curious glances at me.

"I have only one thing to say to you, which is *Joli Albert!"*

A puzzled silence followed. Then:

"Comment, monsieur?"

"Joli Albert!" I said again.

"I do not understand," replied the voice.

"Good," I answered. "You soon will—get a taxi from wherever you are and come to meet me."

He agreed, and made an appointment for an hour later at his house.

I sat in the café with the little Portuguese girl, bought her a lemonade and drank an aperitif or two myself. When an hour had passed, I went to keep my rendezvous. De Fonseca arrived a few moments after me. He was accompanied by a short, fat man who turned out to be a German-Swiss. De Fonseca was a man of twenty-eight, slim and good-looking in the Latin way, with dark brown eyes. When he entered the room, I said to him:

"You are Mr. de Fonseca?"

He said he was.

Again I gave the code word, at which he nodded. Reassured by the German-Swiss, I told him briefly that I had just arrived from England and was anxious to return to Germany. What was the next step I must take to accomplish this, since it was dangerous for me to remain on board my ship?

"Es tut mir leid," replied the German. "I am afraid that my friend and I know nothing at all about it. We are simply businessmen here."

I was astounded by this turn of events and answered sharply:

"Well, if you know nothing, and have no idea what I am talking about, forget anything that I have said to you. Perhaps what you have already heard may be dangerous to you."

With that, I bade them goodby and left the flat.

I was in a jam, but I was resolved, by hook or by crook, to return to

Germany. With that thought uppermost in my mind I got into a taxi and ordered the driver to take me to the German embassy. It was closed. A notice outside stated that it would be open again at nine o'clock the next morning.

I went back to the English Cafe, drank some more with the sailors and spent the night at a cheap hotel. Next morning, I again presented myself at the embassy. A clerk answered the door.

"Heil Hitler!" I said. "I want to speak to someone in charge here. My business is secret and important."

He replied, politely enough, that none of the embassy staff had as yet come on duty, so I sat on a chair to await the arrival of an official who might help me.

After about an hour's wait, a well-dressed man came in, to whom I repeated my request, saying that I belonged to the German Secret Service. He sent me to an address in the rua Borges Caniera. When I arrived at an apartment house, a tough-looking German with a scar on his face was waiting on the doorstep for me. Apparently, someone had telephoned ahead of me from the embassy.

I gave this fellow some account of my mission in England, and repeated my request to get back to German territory as soon as possible. He asked me to wait for him in the hall and disappeared upstairs for a quarter of an hour. When he returned, he told me to go to the corner of the street, where a car was coming to pick me up. I went there, and soon a car drew up. Inside was a small, thickset German of middle age. He introduced himself.

"I am Dr. Braun, and you are Fritz?"

I nodded.

"You need not speak until we are back at my flat."

His flat was in an avenue behind the War Memorial. It was a luxurious-looking place, with comfortable armchairs, tapestries on the walls and low tea tables. He invited me to have a brandy and a cigar. I apologized for looking so unkempt—I had not shaved for a week, and wore a seaman's jersey and blue trousers. He smiled, and dismissed my excuses.

Next, he took a paper and pencil and wrote down the details of my work in England. When he had finished, he asked me if it were possible for me to remain on board for a few days more. I told him that it was, but pointed out that it was dangerous. He inquired if I had any money. I told him that I hadn't, and he gave me five hundred escudos. We drank each other's health and I departed, after having arranged to meet him the next evening. I then returned to the ship, and had some more drinks with the gunners.

Next evening I kept the appointment. This time I was introduced to two other men. One, a doctor, was a blond, good-looking and well-dressed man of about thirty, who spoke excellent English. The other, of about the same age, was a courier between Berlin and Lisbon.

Again I gave details of my visit to England, the attack on the convoy, and so forth. All this was written down once again. The purpose of these oral and written examinations was, of course, to check my statements for discrepancies. It is easy enough to be a bad liar, but very difficult to be a good one.

Next, Braun asked me if I thought it was possible to sabotage the ship. I said that it was.

"Good!" he replied. "For that you will be well rewarded. Meet me later this evening, and I will give you some explosive coal. The ship is carrying Welsh coal, and I will prepare it for you."

The reason for this distinction was that Newcastle and Welsh coal differ in grain. Should suspicion of sabotage have arisen, the coal would have been examined, and if a piece of Newcastle coal had been found in a Welsh bunker the plot would have been discovered.

I went out and ate a meal, and later met Braun and his companions once again. He handed me two lumps of coal about six inches square. I examined them; they were beautifully made. No one could have guessed that, far from being harmless pieces of coal, they were really infernal machines. A bag was given me. I placed the coal in it and hung it between my legs. Then I returned to my hotel and slept for a few hours. On waking, I dressed, again putting the bag between my legs, and returned to the ship.

The police at the dock entrance looked at my pass, and ran their hands over my clothing. They failed to notice anything suspicious. Arrived on board, I spoke a few words to the gunners, did one other important job, and went below to my bunk. Someone was sleeping in it. This annoyed me, and I awoke the intruder. He got down from the bunk and, without a word of warning, seized me by the lapels of my coat and butted me savagely in the face with his head.

I dropped to the deck, blood streaming from my eye and nose, then staggered up, blinded, and was butted again. Down I went a second time. Standing on the table was an empty whiskey bottle. As I dragged myself up I seized it, and hit my assailant violently over the head with it. This time he went down, and stayed there.

My face was now a terrible mess. I had a swollen eye which was rapidly discoloring, one of my teeth had been knocked out and my nose was bleeding. The sailors who had gathered around me advised me to see a doctor.

◆ ◆ ◆

I went ashore, my face still bleeding badly, found a telephone booth and rang up Dr. Braun. I explained to him that I had had an accident and must see him.

"Come straight along," he told me. When I arrived, he gasped at the sight of my battered face.

"Did you manage to plant the coal in the bunkers?" he asked.

"Yes, both pieces went in," I replied, "and I hope the bloody ship goes up with a bang, and blows that damned sailor to smithereens."

He produced water and bandages, and bathed my face. When it was bound up and I had drunk a glass of brandy, I felt a little better.

A few minutes later he was on the telephone. In response to his call the courier whom I had previously met arrived again. Briefly, Dr. Braun explained what had occurred.

"Now here is a photograph of Fritz," he said (I had previously given him one). "Go and get him a German Reich passport. Make it out in the name of Hans Christianssen, Norwegian-German; his profession—seaman. Tell everyone to hurry. I want that passport stamped and finished in an hour and a half. Fritz is flying to Madrid this afternoon. At the same time, arrange by wireless for one of our men to be at the airport to meet him. Tell our man Fritz will be bandaged, and will use the password '*Joli Albert.*'"

I ate a snack and rested for a while. Soon, the courier returned with my passport, stamped and in order. A car was waiting outside. I borrowed a suit of clothes and an overcoat, and off I went.

The weather was vile. A strong wind was blowing, and rain fell heavily. At the airport, we went into a private room belonging to the Luftwaffe. Dr. Braun stepped out to speak to the pilot. When he returned, he looked perturbed.

"The pilot refuses to take off," he announced. "The weather is too bad. I must wireless Berlin immediately and get an order for him to proceed."

Again he went out. He returned an hour later with an order for the pilot to take off without any further delay, despite the threatening storm. The pilot made him sign a note saying that he, Dr. Braun, took full responsibility for the flight, and I went aboard the plane.

Six other passengers made the flight with me, though several more refused, preferring to wait for a break in the weather. The journey was exceedingly uncomfortable. We bumped and lurched and battled with the wind for several hours. The rain slashed across the windows and drove through the plane itself, and two of the passengers were violently sick.

After three and a half hours' journey, we arrived in Madrid.

As I stepped down from the plane, a short, rosy-cheeked young man addressed me:

"Are you Fritz?"

"*Joli Albert!*" I replied.

"My name is Heinz Stromer. Have you any baggage?"

I shook my head.

"Good, come with me."

I followed him to the passport control. The official in charge looked at my bandages, then at Stromer, who winked. A stamp was affixed, authorizing my arrival.

A car took us to the Hotel Florida, where a suite had been reserved for me. Stromer accompanied me upstairs. He suggested that it would be better if I ordered a meal in my room because of my appearance, and we really had a first-class dinner. Suckling pig was the main item, and it was washed down with three bottles of Burgundy. I felt like a new man. My companion advised me to have a good night's rest, and departed, leaving me 1,000 pesetas.

That night I slept wonderfully, though next morning my eye was a vivid blue, with yellow and red streaks. I dressed and walked out into the streets, looking for a barber shop.

Madrid appeared to contain thousands of dirty, curious children, and I had the feeling that all of them were following me about that day. First they scampered in groups behind me, then the bolder spirits ran forward to stare at my damaged face. They pointed it out to their friends; passers-by stopped and gaped; soldiers regarded me with a sympathetic light in their eyes. I was relieved to find a barber, and sank down into the chair. He grinned at me when he discovered that I was a foreigner. I told him I was a Frenchman.

"*Ah! vous faites la boxe,*" he cried, and started mimicking a bruiser.

"Yes," I answered wearily. "Now, for the love of God, please cut my hair and give me a shave."

In the lounge of the hotel I met Stromer, and went with him on a short shopping expedition. I bought myself suits, shirts, and two good suitcases, also stocked myself up with coffee, tea, soap, chocolates and cigarettes, as well as many other articles which were unobtainable in occupied territory.

After lunch came another of my interminable series of interviews, this time with an official from the German embassy who questioned me again on my experiences. He was a fat, genial person who seemed quite easy to convince. When I told him of the food situation in England, however, he was incredulous. In fact, most of the Germans who questioned me doubted the truth of my reports whenever we came to this aspect of conditions in Britain. My fat friend was amazed to hear that the English people could eat in restaurants without food tickets.

Next day, Fatty from the embassy took me to the funeral of the late German ambassador. We had a fine view of the procession. Thousands of people lined the route, and troops of the Spanish air force, army and navy passed in battle array. As the flags of the regiments marched by, the people gave the Fascist salute. Dictator Franco, with several high German officials from the embassy, marched behind the coffin. The Italians also provided a good display of military uniforms. The Axis idea, of course, was to impress the world with the strength of Spanish-German relations. Nearly all well-to-do Spaniards seemed to me to be pro-German.

The press in Spain at this time, no doubt prompted by Berlin, had begun an outcry against the Allied bombing of Germany. Stromer translated some of the Spanish articles for me. They were plausible to anyone not versed in the ways of Nazi propaganda. Spain wanted the Allies to stop bombing German cities, claiming that these were nonmilitary objectives. Stromer also told me that the number of permits issued to British subjects to do business in Spain had been curtailed, and that those with existing permits were continually having trouble with the police.

I stayed in Madrid for six days. Then the courier from Lisbon arrived, and arrangements were made for me to travel with him to France. We left by train; a first-class sleeping compartment was reserved for us. The courier had ten sacks of mail with him, all of which bore the diplomatic seal. He was an interesting man, who spoke fluent English and Portuguese. He had worked at the embassy for six years and, except for the few days in Berlin in between each journey, had experienced nothing of the war. He, like myself, was taking a supply of food and other articles back with him.

It was thought that there might be some trouble in getting me across the frontier, so arrangements had been made for us to get off at an earlier station, where a car was to meet us and drive us through the inspection barriers into Hendaye. We left the train, but since it was an hour late the car had gone. The courier left me in charge of the luggage, and went to telephone Madrid in order to find out where the man lived who was to drive us.

There I sat, on the frontier of Fascist Spain and Nazi Europe, guarding the secret diplomatic mail of the Germans! After a wait of two hours our car arrived. The courier cursed the driver violently and promised to report him on arrival in Berlin. Without any difficulty, we drove across the bridge which separated the two frontier towns, and for the first time for three and a half months I again saw the familiar Wehrmacht uniform.

Next morning we caught the train for Paris. During the journey, I began to eat a banana. Some children playing in the corridor caught sight of me. Instantly their noses were pressed to the glass, and they were amazed to see a man eating so wondrous a delicacy. I opened the door and gave them a banana apiece. They departed, but as though by magic every kid on the train, and some grown-up girls as well, heard the news that bananas were being distributed. The corridor became thick with women and children, and long after all my fruit had been shared little faces were still pressed wistfully against the panes.

13

THE SUSPECT

THE TRAIN drew into Paris I spotted Wolfgang, a member of the Nantes *Dienststelle*, among the crowd on the platform. He stared at me without recognition. I did not realize myself how well I was disguised. Then suddenly he cried:

"Fritz! What *have* you done to your eyes?"

As I made my explanations we were joined by Albert Schole. A car drove us to a flat in the rue de Luynes, where I had previously taken part in a conference, and I was told that it was to be my home for the next few days.

No sooner had we settled in the car than Schole and Wolfgang started shooting questions at me. I stalled them by saying that I was hungry.

"Now look," I told them. "You go on to the *Dienststelle* and ask von Grunen to come to see me."

They told me that unfortunately von Grunen was now on the Eastern front. This was a blow, but they softened it by adding that if I wanted anything Colonel Gautier had given instructions that I was to let them know my needs, and these would be promptly acted upon.

"Fine!" I said. "The German government now owes me about 200,000 marks! Ask the colonel if I can have an immediate advance of 20,000 francs. Then I will invite you both to a really swell dinner."

While Wolfgang went off to arrange this, I had a bath and unpacked my clothes. He soon reappeared with the money, and I took them both to Maxim's. The dinner was stupendous—and so was the bill. During my absence, the price of food in Paris had soared by at least three hundred percent. I was informed that coffee was now 2,000 francs per kilo, butter 500 per kilo, meat 200 per kilo, and a pack of English cigarettes sold for 300 francs. Nor had Paris prices yet hit their final ceiling.

After dinner, we took a horse-taxi and went to the "Scheherazade," a

Russian cabaret in Montmartre. We chose a quiet table, and over a bottle of champagne Schole told me the inside story of von Grunen's departure for the Eastern front. Apparently he had quarreled with the chief of the *Dienststelle* in Paris on a question of policy. The chief had then used von Grunen's alcoholism as a pretext for sacking him from the Secret Service.

I pondered carefully over this development, because I regarded the old boy as a valuable friend. My contract had been signed personally with him, not with the German government. If I withheld certain information from the Paris bureau, and refused to work with anyone but von Grunen, he would most certainly be brought back.

I knew that Wolfgang and Schole also liked old von Grunen, and by their conversation I gathered that they were not satisfied with the setup in Paris. They grumbled endlessly about the rigidity of the present discipline and the many petty restrictions which were imposed upon them. Von Grunen had always shut his eyes to such lapses as staying out all night without a pass, and had often paid up restaurant bills through the official expense account. These good times were now over.

Schole told me that the Paris chief wanted me to work for him, and had promised to give me all I wanted, within reason. He had also asked Schole to try to get me to write a letter to Berlin saying that I did not consider von Grunen a capable leader, and suggesting that someone else should be appointed to handle my future work for the German government. This request I refused point-blank, and I further authorized Schole to tell the chief that I would work with no one except von Grunen.

Schole and Wolfgang agreed to help me, and in return I promised that, if von Grunen returned, I would send a request to Berlin for both of them to work with me. They made me promise to mention them in my reports and to stress that, while at Nantes before leaving for England, they had been particularly helpful to me. It was incredible how everyone in the Wehrmacht tried to curry favor with his superiors.

I then embarked upon probably the best evening out I had experienced since I joined the German Secret Service. After the Lido we went to Suzy Solidor's "Fashionable Club." It was one of the few places in Paris where the Germans seldom were seen. Suzy herself was clever and witty, and her lyrics and songs were admirable. When the cabaret closed at four in the morning, we went to bed—six bottles of champagne had helped me enjoy an extremely successful first night in Paris.

Next day I got up late, and soon afterwards Wolfgang appeared with a shorthand typist from the Hotel Lutetia. He had instructions to take down a detailed account of my landing and subsequent adventures in England. This is the story I told him:

I came down near Littleport, stayed the night in a ruined cottage, and early next morning made my way to the station and took a train to London. I got in touch with my old friend Freddie, who was in town, and I made a date to meet him.

At six o'clock next evening we met at Hyde Park Corner. "Hullo, bastard-face! How are you?"

"Where the hell have you been all this time?"

"Come along to the Star and I'll tell you."

Arrived at "Belgrave Mews," we ordered a couple of pints, and I sketched out to him what had happened in the intervening years. His face got longer and more surprised. I finished up by saying, "If you will work with me the Jerries will pay you £5,000 and we can both go back to Germany and have all the wine, women and song that we want."

"Christ," he said, "sounds all right! But how do we get there?" "Don't worry," I said. "Von Grunen will see to that."

We left the pub and went to Freddie's flat in Wimbledon, where I gave him all the details of my mission. Finally he agreed to come in with me.

The next two evenings I spent at his flat, plotting and planning. First we had to get the ingredients to make the explosives. I calculated that the job would require at least sixty pounds of high explosive. Now, in England it is not easy at any time to obtain materials for the manufacture of so much dynamite. In the past we had to rely on the powder magazines of quarries for our supplies; in wartime it was of course more difficult. However, Freddie knew of a quarry in the Sevenoaks district, where he hoped we might be able to find some "jelly."

A few nights later we went down to Sevenoaks and forced open the magazine of this quarry. There were several hundred sticks of gelignite and a couple of hundred detonators. Freddie had a car and seemed to experience no difficulty in getting fake petrol coupons. On our return to London we bought two suitcases and fixed up thirty pounds of gelignite in each, making use of a wrist watch and batteries for the time explosion. Freddie watched this with some anxiety when I explained the finesse required and told him that if one mistake was made the whole joint would be blown sky-high.

We then went down to Hatfield to "case" the factory. There is a large pub just adjacent to it. We went in and had a drink. There were several of the De Havilland employees there, and we could hear the roar of engines starting up in the background. We swallowed our drinks, walked right round the factory, and I compared it with the photographs I had been shown before I left. We noted where the powerhouses were. We also made mental notes of all obstacles to be encountered before we could climb in, and decided to come down later and have a rehearsal.

We returned to London, but came back that evening, climbed into the De Havilland factory grounds and, in stocking feet, crept up behind the sentries and made a note of their comings and goings. It was quite simple, we decided, to get into the powerhouses. After about a two-hour creep round the factory we felt that we knew every nook and cranny of it, and left once again for London.

When the day of the sabotage arrived, Freddie and I went down in his car at six o'clock in the evening. The suitcases were in the back. The time had been chosen as the most favorable because that was when the shifts were changed.

Disguised as employees in overalls, we climbed over the fence, taking care to avoid the guard. We separated.

I approached one powerhouse, scaled the surrounding wall and found myself facing six transformers. I left my suitcase underneath one (the fuse was already set), and returned the way I had come. Freddie meanwhile had done the same thing at the other powerhouse.

We then went back to the car, drove three miles from the factory, stopped the engine and waited for results.

At a few minutes to seven, we heard a tremendous explosion. We drove back to London without incident.

◆ ◆ ◆

What puzzled Wolfgang more than anything was that I had obtained meals in London without coupons. He could scarcely believe it. He then asked for details of the sabotage, and I had to draw a sketch for him of De Havilland's and the places which had been blown up, also a diagram showing how the explosives were fixed in the suitcases. After Freddie's arrest, I said, I got windy and closed the transmission. I buried my wireless set in the garden of the lodging house where I had been living.

When this had been taken down, I went on to give a full account of how I had managed to get on board a British freighter as a steward, and of my subsequent sabotage of the ship. I then related my adventures in Portugal and Spain, until the moment I had stepped off the train at Paris. When this report was finished it was a voluminous document of thirty or forty pages. It was read back to me, and I signed it.

Next day Wolfgang told me that we had to return home as some friends of mine were coming to pay me a "surprise visit." He would not tell me who they were. This "surprise" technique was a favorite with the German

Secret Service, and always left me with a funny feeling in my stomach.

At the flat, the surprise proved a pleasant one, for in walked Colonel von Blecker and two of the air crew who had flown me to England. The Colonel shook my hand and cried:

"Fritz! It's grand to see you back again. My! You must feel a regular hero now! A fine job of work you have done! Now tell me all about the flight. Did these chaps make you comfortable?"

We sat around a table and I told them my story. The young wireless operator told me how, just as I was going through the hinged door, a fighter had spotted them. He had looked down hurriedly and, noticing that I was stuck, had kicked my bottom hard.

"Then it wasn't so comfortable!" said the Colonel.

We all laughed. The navigator then told me that they'd had a few exciting minutes being chased until they had taken evasive action in a cloud.

The meeting was most friendly, and before the officers left I gave each of them a kilo of coffee, and sent another to the pilot of the plane. They invited me to visit their mess and dine with them. We saluted each other, and they departed. I heard soon afterwards that the whole crew had been shot down and killed over England: it was their sixtieth sortie.

My next visitor was an Army technician, who asked me many highly specialized questions about British armaments, none of which I was able to answer. Then, on April 2, 1943, Schole told me that I was going to meet von Grunen.

Next day Wolfgang and I left for Berlin. A first-class compartment was reserved for us, and Wolfgang had strict instructions that no one else was to be allowed to enter it. The train was crowded with officers and troops going on leave, or on duty, to Berlin. When the officers saw two civilians sitting alone in a compartment, some of them immediately opened the door.

Wolfgang politely but firmly told them that the compartment was reserved and asked them to leave. Glowering at us, they withdrew. Not so a grizzled old major. He refused point-blank, on the pretext that the Germans were living under National Socialist rule, and that "people's comradeship" should be practiced as well as preached.

Wolfgang called the train police and showed them his authority. They quickly bundled the "Socialist" major out of the compartment, despite his threats to report us and everyone concerned to Himmler himself.

His ejection did not meet with the approval of the officers in the corridor, who glared at us angrily through the windows. They could see no reason why two civilians should have a compartment to themselves, while officers of the mighty German Army were herded like cattle in a truck. They nearly had apoplexy when I produced a bottle of cognac, poured myself a drink and sipped it appreciatively. We lolled there with our feet up on the opposite seats, and watched the countryside go by.

When the train stopped at Metz some civilians boarded it, among them a woman carrying a child. She stood outside the door looking at me pathetically. I asked Wolfgang to let her come in and sit down, but he was adamant and said that if he disobeyed his orders he would be severely punished. So the poor woman stood during the whole journey. That ended the joke for me.

At the Potsdamer Station in Berlin a car met us, and we drove to the Hotel Petite Stephanie in the Kurfurstendamm. Awaiting us there was one of the chiefs of the Berlin *Dienststelle*. He put a few casual questions to me about England, and asked me to describe the explosive charge I had used, and how I had fixed it up in the suitcase. I told him that the batteries in the suitcase had been affixed on the right-hand side with drawing pins—and adhesive tape. He immediately pounced upon this.

"But in Paris and Spain you said the batteries were on the left-hand side."

His eyes glinted disagreeably. I felt hot.

"Oh, yes!" I replied. "That's true enough, but as you know I had two suitcases—one set of batteries was fixed on the right side, and one on the left."

Later in the evening I met a Captain Müller of the German Navy, a bronzed, blue-eyed, seafaring type and very amusing.

I was told that in the morning I was going to Oslo, Norway, to meet von Grunen. The old man had been recalled from the Eastern front. Müller produced a passport bearing the name of Fritz Graumann, domiciled in Berlin, bom in New York of German parentage; also a military pass with the description "Oberleutnant Fritz Graumann," and the *Dienststelle* number N.29803 endorsed upon it. The pass was signed by Infantry General von Blumentritt. My traveling papers were also handed to me.

Next morning at ten o'clock I said goodby to Wolfgang. He asked me not to forget to remind von Grunen that he too wanted to come to work with me in Norway.

◆ ◆ ◆

During my short stay in Berlin I was not able to see much, but the bombing did not appear to have had any great effect at this time (April, 1943). The Tempelhof airport had not yet been touched.

While passing through the barrier to the plane, which was a sixteen-seater Lufthansa machine, an official of the Military Control asked me if I had any money with me, for it was forbidden to take German currency out of Germany, or to bring in any money of the occupied countries. I replied "None," whereupon he asked me to produce my wallet—which contained about 10,000 francs. He looked at it, and at me. Hastily I took ten marks from my pocket and gave them to him. He folded my wallet and passed it back to me.

"Thank you, *mein Herr*," he said. "You have no money."

The plane was full of officers traveling to Copenhagen and Oslo. All ranks and forces were represented—Luftwaffe, Marine, Wehrmacht and one or two S.S. police officers. After an hour and a half s flight we came down at an airport in Copenhagen.

We got out and stretched our legs, but we could buy only ten kroner's worth of food, this being the total expenditure allowed on a trip through Denmark. It was the ambition of every German soldier to get hold of Danish currency, because he could then buy nearly everything he wanted there. For the Danes were far better off than any other peoples in the occupied territories. Butter, bacon, meat, eggs, milk, cream and many other good things were not rationed at all. Clothes and shoes were only lightly rationed, and were easily obtainable. So Denmark was regarded as the Promised Land by the Nazis.

I now ate a good meal of bacon, eggs and cheese, followed by several pastries with cream. Then we boarded the plane and took off for Oslo.

14

THE IRON CROSS

IN NINETY minutes we were over Norway. What a change of scene! Below lay ranges of rocky hills cut by deep fjords, carrying in their still waters the reflections of vast pine forests. Snow still clung to some of the hill crests, and it was cold in the plane. We glided up Oslo Fjord, passing over the U-boat pen and reservoirs which the Germans had-built.

Oslo airport is small, and must be one of the most difficult in the world to land on. We described a horseshoe curve as we banked over it. In front of the airport offices stood rows of Messerschmitt 9's, the German fighters. Antiaircraft guns were placed at regular intervals around the field.

At the barrier, I caught sight of a familiar figure—von Grunen! I ran over to him. He was overjoyed to see me.

"Thank God you are back, Fritz!" he exclaimed, as he shook my hand. He appeared genuinely moved. After he had cleared my papers, we walked to a waiting car, where he introduced me to a cheerful, chubby little man with a wide grin. His name was Johnny Holst and, as I learned later, he was one of the most dangerous men in the German Secret Service.

"It is most pleasing to meet you," he said in his quaint English. "Herr von Grunen has told me much around you."

We drove through Skoyen, a charming section of the Oslo Fjord. Most apartment houses lie on the outskirts of the town, away from the business center, and although built of wood they are varied in design, so that each bears the individual stamp of its owner. The gardens are large, but at that time of the year, except for the fir trees, there was not a patch of green anywhere.

Our car was driven by a combustion furnace at the rear, which burned wood blocks. These cars were in general use by the Germans in Norway. They ran smoothly, and could do a top speed of fifty miles an hour. They would also run on petrol. The electric Sporvein, or trolley, was an example of Norwegian ingenuity—a long, low vehicle, painted bright blue and white, and streamlined. These cars were really fast, and carried seventy passengers.

We drove by the Royal Palace, a simple but impressive building. There is a large open space in front of it which is not, as most palaces are, surrounded by high railings. Outside the building stood a guard of Quislings, dressed like the old Palace Guard in blue uniforms with tasseled forage caps.

Von Grunen's flat was just to the right of the palace and behind the park, in a building of modern bachelor flats. It was on the third floor, and consisted of a bedroom, kitchen and bathroom. We made ourselves at home, and von Grunen opened a bottle of aquavit. This was the first time I had sampled this potent national drink of the Norwegians. I found it ideal to keep the heat in and the cold out.

A peculiar smell of fish filled the building, and I remarked on it to Johnny Holst. He told me that I would soon get used to it, for the smell permeated all of Oslo. Apparently, the Norwegians lived entirely on boiled fish.

I gave von Grunen and Johnny Holst a short account of my adventures in England, and of what had happened in Paris. When von Grunen heard of the attempts there to place me under someone else, he became very angry. He said:

"Fritz, you and I are friends. Have I not always been fair in my dealings with you, and did we not arrange everything perfectly for your work in England?"

I nodded.

"Why," he went on, with rising indignation, "it was entirely the fault of that chief in Paris that I was not able to send a U-boat to pick you up. Also, he is to blame that something went wrong with your cover address in Lisbon. But do not worry about these things, for you are now going to receive the money I promised you. For that reason I am going to Berlin. In the next few days we must sit down together and make out a full report. Meanwhile, Fritz, you are to be given complete freedom here. You have already been made a German citizen, and you will be treated as an officer of the Wehrmacht. Furthermore, you will be in a better financial position than before, because you will have your Wehrmacht pay of 450 marks per month, plus your food and hotel bills. After that, you can draw your other money in any occupied country currency you choose."

Von Grunen continued, "For the next few months you will live here. Then we'll see what you want to do. There is no hurry. Perhaps you would like to start a business, or would you consider going back to England again?"

"No," I interposed, "I do *not* want to go back to Britain. After all, I have been lucky once but my luck may not last. I'd rather stay here and spend my money. Perhaps I may even find myself a wife. Who knows? I think it's time I settled down. Anyway, for the moment, I need a vacation."

It seemed that my refusal accorded with von Grunen's own wishes, for he looked pleased and said:

"Yes, take a long vacation. Johnny here will show you around. If you get into trouble over your English accent, here is my phone number. Tell whoever stops you to ring me. By the way, you should always carry your automatic with you—one never knows. Perhaps the British Secret Service may trace you up here, and we certainly do not want to lose you. Remember, too—beware of anyone trying to take a photograph of you, because we do not want you 'listed.' Finally, Fritz," he added, "I want you to promise me that if any overtures are made to you to work with other members of our Service, you will refuse."

The old man was speaking with great earnestness as he said these words. He laid his hand on my shoulder and resumed:

"After all, it was I who got you released from the Romainville camp, and taught you what you now know. From now on, do not regard me as your chief, but rather as your manager. Let me handle any business you have, and before this war is finished you will be a rich man. I am speaking to you now as I would to my own son—for you know that I have no relations—and I regard you as such."

I was sincerely touched. The old man was so pathetically eager to show his gratitude for getting him back into the limelight. Apart from that, I had always respected and liked him.

Von Grunen told me that Johnny Holst would take me to my hotel, which was at Slemdal on the Holmenkollen Bahn. The Fossheim Hotel was like most other hotels in Oslo that had been requisitioned by the Germans. It was a large, comfortable building, painted white and built of wood. At that time Oslo was crowded with the Wehrmacht, and was used as a place of rest and relaxation for troops on their way to the Eastern front.

◆ ◆ ◆

When I had unpacked, Johnny and I got back into the car and were driven into the town.

"I am going to take you to the only black market where we can really eat and drink good things," said Johnny. "There we can get a steak and cutlets, and drink as much red wine, cognac and liqueurs as we can hold. By the way, here is some money which von Grunen gave me for you," he added, handing over 1,000 kroner—about fifty pounds.

The restaurant was reserved for Norwegian Quislings and German soldiers; officers in uniform were barred. Originally it was called Humllin, but the Germans had renamed it Löwenbräu. A guard of the Security Police stood at the entrance to the staircase leading up to the restaurant. The place was crowded with hundreds of service men of all branches—Luftwaffe, Marine, Wehrmacht and, here and there, men of the Todt Labor Organization in their khaki uniforms with swastika armbands.

Our permits were asked for and closely inspected before we were allowed to move up with the throng of troops entering the restaurant, most of them with girls. On the third floor was a small room guarded by a sentry. To enter, one had to pass through swing doors bearing the sign: "Civilians Only." Johnny Holst gave his name to the guard, and we were allowed to go in. Inside there were about sixty civilians of both sexes, mostly Germans with Norwegian girls from the "National Sammling," the Quisling party. We were given a table in front of a glass partition through which we could look down into the main restaurant, where we saw a dance orchestra and cabaret for the entertainment of the German soldiers.

I took stock of my neighbors. They were mostly fat German businessmen, cramming food down their throats. There were a few newspaper reporters from the *Norwegische Zeitung*, the Nazi paper in Norway, and at a table in the corner, Holst told me, there were some artists from the opera. It was always easy to spot Germans in any restaurant in occupied Europe—they were all so poorly dressed, and most of them wore mass-produced suits made from wood or some other ersatz material.

The women looked equally dowdy. Those who were fortunate enough to be wearing original dresses from Paris also looked ill at ease and self-conscious. They spoiled any effect they might have made by wearing shabby shoes or unsuitable hats. As for their taste in colors—the most violent clashes never seemed to disturb their sensibilities, and the loudest were considered the most *chic*.

The German women who belonged to the various *Dienststellen* put on the most ridiculous airs to impress their less fortunate Norwegian sisters. They talked continually of "wonderful Germany" and the glamorous times they enjoyed in their small home towns, and boasted of the exquisite clothes they had been forced, by the exigencies of war, to leave behind.

The Norwegian women were, by comparison, smart and well turned out. They were tall, blond and blue-eyed, and used little make-up. The men were well-bred and good-looking. A sturdy six feet seemed to be about the average. They were dressed in well-cut suits.

As we ate and drank, I asked Johnny Holst why officers were forbidden to enter in uniform. He replied:

"It is because the soldiers need a place they can go and get drunk if necessary, take a woman with them and relax from discipline for a few hours. If officers were allowed in, the troops would be obliged continually to salute. Also, as a number of women come with officers, quarrels would follow."

I excused myself. Pushing my way through the swing doors, I stepped into another part of the restaurant. There, a piano and accordion were playing popular times which were sung with great gusto by the soldiers. A drunken sailor was standing on a table trying to dance a hornpipe, to the jeers of his compatriots. Women sat on men's knees. They seemed drunker than the men and came from the dregs of Norwegian life.

I fought my way back through the mob and returned. An acquaintance of Holst, who worked in the same office, was sitting at our table. We were introduced.

"Fritz Graumann, this is Peter Hiller."

The newcomer was about thirty, broad-shouldered, powerful, tough and shrewd-looking. An excellent cabaret show was in progress, and we watched it for some minutes. The cabaret artists had come from all over Europe to entertain the Germans.

Peter Hiller was an expert saboteur and morse code operator. Before the war he had been in South Africa. He had gone there as a seaman, and deserted his ship at Capetown. What his mission had been I do not know, but he was arrested by the authorities for illegal entry. He described his stay in jail as most comfortable; the authorities gave him good food and plenty of cigarettes. He was not under suspicion of espionage, and shortly before the outbreak of the war was deported to Germany.

Johnny Holst had taken his sea-going master's ticket. When war was declared, he was serving as chief mate on a 10,000-ton merchantman of the Hamburg-Amerika Line in a South American port. The captain received orders either to try to reach Germany or else to scuttle his ship. He decided to run the blockade, and they steamed past the Bahamas under Norwegian colors. They went north to Newfoundland, passing within sight of Ireland, then cut across the Arctic till they sighted the Norwegian coast. Two days out from Germany, they ran short of bunker coal. The wooden decks were tom up, doors pulled down, and everything that would bum was thrust into the furnaces.

Said Johnny, "It was a near thing whether or not we burned up that ship in her own boilers."

Several times they were sighted by British warships and planes. However, on showing the Norwegian flag, they were allowed to proceed. Finally, after a month's adventurous voyage, they put in at Bremen. Nearly all the crew were decorated, and Johnny himself received the Iron Cross, First Class. Later, he was given the job of sabotage instructor, and was now in charge of training agents who were going on missions to Allied countries.

When the restaurant bill was paid, Holst suggested that we go and meet a girl friend, who was working as secretary to the chief of our Bureau, Captain von Bonen. We drove to Drammensveien. Johnny introduced the lady as Mollie Serle. She was about twenty-five. Her flat was modem and more attractive than herself, and we sat around a comfortable log fire.

Another man, whom I later discovered was a Pole, was introduced. Before the fall of Poland he had been doing work similar to mine as a German agent. He looked rather striking, though he was the gigolo type and flashily dressed, with long hair and an extravagant display of jewelry.

Hiller, Holst and the Pole shared an apartment, and it soon became apparent that Holst and Hiller were rivals for the charms of the none too beautiful Mollie Serle. But if her physical allure was limited, she was extraordinarily gifted in languages. She spoke fluent French and English, but Norwegian was her specialty. When I became better acquainted with her, I noted that the Norwegians took her for one of them.

Before the Nazis invaded Norway, Fraulein Mollie Serle had been a stenographer. She had also been trained as a fifth columnist. At the time of the invasion she, and many like her, rendered valuable services to their country by numerous forms of sabotage. She had been rewarded with a good position and a smart flat. Invariably I found that when a German agent had done a successful job, he (or she) received some easy desk appointment as a reward.

We talked about the war. They were all still convinced that the Germans were going to win, although there had been some gloom about the Stalingrad reverse. But Goebbels had spread the story that nearly all troops of the encircled German Sixth Army had escaped, and this was blindly believed by all good Germans. They bragged that they would smash the Red armies once the Wehrmacht had been regrouped.

We were drinking cognac while these boasts were being swapped. When we had drunk more than was good for us, Holst and Hiller began to quarrel over the charms of Fraulein Serle. Angry words and insults were tossed back and forth between them. It was amusing to watch—or rather to listen to. Fraulein Serle observed all this with indifference.

Max the Pole then tried to intervene, but without much success. There was such a commotion that our hostess, fearing that the police would be called in, insisted that we quit the flat and that the combatants should settle their dispute outside. We picked up our coats. Holst, Hiller and Max rushed into the street, but I stayed on to thank my hostess. When I went downstairs I found everything in darkness and the street deserted. Also, the door had been shut firmly behind me.

Rather noisily I groped my way along the blacked-out pavements. I had not the faintest idea of how to get to my hotel. Worse, I had even forgotten the name of it! I walked on until I reached the Karl Johanns Gate. Ahead of me was the main street, and that, too, was deserted. I sat down on a bench. Strange, I thought, here am I, an Englishman, in the center of the Nazi-held Norwegian capital, and not even one damned German policeman to help me to find my whereabouts.

It was four o'clock in the morning. I reflected on the events of the last twenty-four hours with some satisfaction—breakfast in Berlin, lunch in Copenhagen and dinner in Oslo! But the next breakfast . . . ? Well, I thought, most wars are strange wars—and, putting my feet up on the bench, I slept as you can only sleep when you draw a complete blank.

When I awoke it was dawn, and the workers were hurrying to their jobs. Many curious glances were cast in my direction, but nobody bothered to ask any questions. The Norwegian is an expert at minding his own business.

I searched through my pockets and found von Grunen's telephone number. I explained to his valet that I had taken an early morning walk in the town and wanted to ring my hotel, but could not find the number in the directory. The reply came back, "Fossheim Hotel, Slemsdal." I took a Holmenkollen train to Slemsdal, and went up to my room.

One of the maids brought me a message that Herr Holst had rung me at least four times. She gave me his telephone number, and I got through to him. Johnny answered, and apologized profusely for last night's fracas. He had a black eye and a split lip, but he said Hiller and he were again friends. I made a lunch date with him.

The Ritz was a fashionable restaurant and, like every other place in Oslo, was thronged with German soldiers and officers. It was also the meeting ground of Norwegian Legionnaires of the "Viking Regiment," the Quisling troops used by Hitler on the Eastern front.

The food was bad. It consisted of *smorbrod*, which is a one- slice sandwich made with different sorts of salted fish. After that came the eternal *rollmops*, or pickled herring. Happily, to break the monotony, lobster was available too.

From my talk with Johnny Holst, I learned the true state of affairs in

Norway, which had always been the most difficult of the occupied countries to keep under control. As time went on I was able to gauge for myself the terrible hatred that most Norwegians held for Germany. In Norway you were either a Quisling or a Jossing (the latter being the name given to all pro-Allied elements). There was nothing in between. People of all classes and all walks of life openly defied the Germans. They dismissed with contempt every kind of social co-operation, or even civility. They distributed pamphlets, and organized protests and strikes. They committed sabotage, kidnaped, and even killed. Norway, as I can testify, never quit, and never looked like quitting.

◆　◆　◆

It was an uneasy feeling to be a German (or even a pseudo- German) in Norway in those days. Everywhere, a wall of hatred rose against you. The Norwegians are a truly brave and patriotic people, and I cannot speak too highly of the struggle they incessantly waged against their oppressors. Never did they lose hope. Never did they waver in their faith that they would eventually be free again.

When the Germans executed their leaders (to say nothing of many innocent hostages), or persecuted them by torture or concentration camp, the people bore their lot stoically. The horrors they endured served only to weld them more firmly together in their resistance to the conquerors. The Germans feared the Norse people, and respected them.

In the queues for cinemas and theatres, Germans stood patiently alongside Norwegians, taking their turn—a thing they seldom did in other occupied countries. In restaurants, a Norwegian would always obtain a table before a German did. In trains and on buses the Norwegians made the Germans feel how . much they despised them by giving them too much room. I have seen a German soldier get on an empty bus and sit on a bench capable of holding twenty people. In would come some Norwegians. They would all sit down on the opposite bench, and when that was full, they would stand up.

I had been told by von Grunen that Walter Thomas, who had worked with both of us in Paris, would soon be arriving, and on April 10 we went to the railway station to meet him. Thomas stepped out of a troop train, having traveled via Sweden. He was wearing the field-green of the Wehrmacht and sported a star on his shoulder, denoting the rank of *Oberleutnant*. He looked tired and dirty, and complained bitterly about the delays of his journey. He had been three days on the way. It had taken us as many hours in the air to cover the same distance.

Over lunch, he told von Grunen that Berlin again had required the whole of my experiences in England to be typed out and forwarded. The reason for this was, as I have already noted, that if they made me repeat my story often enough, I might contradict myself. The German Secret Service relied on the theory that a man can always remember the truth, but never a lie.

Thomas was not altogether pleased at coming to Norway. He had been attending an officers' course for the Eastern front, and was disappointed at having to give it up to work with me in Norway.

"Not because of you, Fritz," he assured me. "But you realize that I am an idealist. My life belongs to my country, and I think I could serve it better in battle against the Reds than by working in this Service. It is a shame, but orders are orders," he added morosely.

Thomas had a hero complex. He was stuffed full of Nazi ideas, and avidly read stories of the German war aces. He would identify himself with any highly decorated warrior, especially if he happened to know him.

"Look," he would exclaim, coming across a name in a German newspaper. "Captain Mucklin has been awarded the Iron Cross! And I was at school with that fellow! Now, perhaps if I had been there, I might have got one, too."

Sometimes, to tease or irritate him, I would reply:

"Yes, and by now you probably would be a nice stiff corpse out in cold, wild Russia."

He would retort sulkily:

"Better to die for one's ideals than sitting here doing nothing." April 20 was Hitler's birthday, and a great parade was staged in Oslo to impress the Norwegians with the might of the Wehrmacht. Thomas and I got a splendid view of the procession, which came up the Karl Johanns Gate, past the university, and on toward Drammensveien. A crowd, mainly composed of Germans, had gathered to watch it from behind the cordon of Security Police who lined the street.

First came the infantry, next a hundred rumbling tanks, then armed motorcyclists and, finally, a detachment of the Navy. The band played the marching song *"Wir fahren gegen Engelland"* (We are Marching Against England). They arrogantly goose stepped by, to the cheers of their compatriots.

Farther down the street, opposite the university, von Terboven, the hated Nazi Gauleiter, was taking the salute. It took an hour for the troops to pass, and they certainly made an impressive show. When several large mobile guns rolled by I noticed the thin-lipped faces of the few Norwegian spectators. They seemed to say, "You won't win after all!"

When the procession was over, I walked with Thomas, whose eyes were still glowing with pride, past the Grand Café. Next to it was a window used by the Nazis to display anti-Allied propaganda. Usually this took the form of a giant cartoon. That day it showed Churchill and Roosevelt as two monstrous airplanes dropping bombs on German churches and hospitals, while women in Britain were jitterbugging and drinking cocktails. I thought it did the German cause more harm than good.

The next few days were busy, for Thomas had to complete his report on me. It seemed to meet with his satisfaction. Nevertheless this recording process, as on previous occasions, left me with an oddly uncomfortable feeling.

When the report was finally completed, von Grunen took off by plane for the capital. After five days, he returned, and summoned me to his flat. He was in high spirits.

"Fritz," he said, beaming with pleasure, "they have decided to award you 150,000 marks—that is, 100,000 for the sabotage of the aircraft factory and 50,000 for blowing up the ship and the information you sent over."

I was elated by this news. However, I pretended to be disappointed.

"It is not enough," I complained. "They promised me 200,000 marks; 100,000 for the work at De Havilland's and another 100,000 for the ship sabotage and the reports."

"I am sorry, Fritz," replied von Grunen, "but unfortunately it was not I who promised you the money for the business in Portugal, but Dr. Braun. He had no right or authority to do so. However, do not forget that 150,000 marks is a lot of money, and in the future you will have opportunities of earning much more. Why, if you play your cards right, there is no reason why you should not end by earning a million marks."

With bad grace, I accepted the money.

It was now formally arranged that von Grunen should be my banker. I was to draw on him for whatever amounts I needed, and the money was to be payable in any country I happened to be living in. I signed a note saying that this was satisfactory to me, and Walter Thomas witnessed it.

Then came an extraordinary incident. Von Grunen stood up, rather solemnly, behind his desk.

"Now, Fritz," he said, "this is a presentation which I have decided to make to you myself. It was sent to our *Dienststelle* to be awarded to the member who had shown the most outstanding zeal and success during the year, and after consultation with the chiefs here, you are the choice!"

He then handed me a small case. I opened it—inside was the Iron Cross!

I was astounded—and almost burst out laughing, not at him or at the circumstances, but at myself. Not bad, I told myself—*Oberleutnant* Fritz Graumann, with 150,000 Reichsmarks and the Iron Cross!

I thought, if I stay with this mob long enough, I might end up as a *Reichsmarschall.* . . .

15

INDOMITABLE NORWAY

T HOUGH I WAS still officially "on vacation," Thomas told me that it had been decided to keep my morse code training up to scratch. So I was taken along to the school, which was in Drammensveien at Skillebekk—in the same flat where I had met Mollie Serle on my first night in Oslo. This lady had now moved to Skoyen. The captain in charge tested me, and after a few minutes of typing out letters and taking them down on paper, he told me that I was all right though a little rusty. Under him were three other instructors, who were teaching morse to some Norwegians and Icelanders. These Quislings would be used on intelligence work and therefore their presence was strictly secret.

The flat had been divided into practice rooms, and each pupil was allotted a specific time at which to present himself for instruction. On arrival, he was hustled into his room and the door locked, the idea being that no two agents should recognize one another or even see one another. The same precautions were observed when leaving the room. First the instructor went out to make sure that all was clear, after which the pupil was free to go.

Some of the Germans apparently were still doubtful about me. One day, they sent around a psychoanalyst to look me over in von Grunen's flat. He was a hawklike creature with gray hair, aged about fifty. He gave his name as Herr Koenig, and spoke with an American accent. He pretended that he wanted to know the whereabouts of the radio set I had left behind in England, so I drew a map of where I had buried it. He watched every movement I made. This questioning was accompanied by liberal doses of cognac. Sometimes he would speak to me in German.

"How far were you from the station when you landed?" "About a hundred and twenty miles," I answered.

"Ah!" he said in German, "but I thought you said only two?" "Yes, two from Littleport, but a hundred and twenty from London," I answered.

Herr Koenig questioned me for about two hours on one point. He wanted to know if I had any friends in London who would help an agent of his. I gave him the address of a club which was owned by one of my friends. I also provided him with the telephone number.

Later, we went off to dinner. Toward the end of the meal he suddenly looked me squarely in the eyes and said:

"You know, what you lack is integrity. You are not sincere." "Of course I'm not sincere," I replied. "Do you expect me to be?"

"Well," he confessed (he had become very benign), "you beat me." He shook his head sadly and added, "I beat myself sometimes."

"*Prosit!*" I toasted him.

On another evening in the Löwenbräu I became the target of a "spy-suspect" scene. I was sitting alone at a table when in came a woman of about forty-five who, in good German, asked me if the chair at my table was free. I told her "yes," and she sat down. We started talking. She was a Norwegian known as "Frue Anne." She noticed my accent and exclaimed:

"But you are not a German?"

"Yes, I am a German," I replied, "but I was born in America." She then began to criticize German policy. It so happened that I knew she was an *agent provocateur* who had rendered the Germans many services by supplying information leading to the betrayal of Norwegian patriots. I listened and made no comment. We soon switched over to English, which she also spoke without accent. I bade her good night, declining a dinner invitation to her house.

Next evening I was again in the Löwenbräu, dining with Captain Etling, when in walked "Frue Anne," accompanied by an officer from Etling's unit.

They sat down at a nearby table. She pointed me out to her friend. He looked, and nodded. Then he made a respectful sign to Etling to come over and talk to them. Etling went over, chatted with them for some minutes and came back to me.

He said: "She has reported you to my bureau, on suspicion of being a British spy!"

We both roared with laughter, much to "Frue Anne's" discomfiture. She was furious.

But that was not quite the end of it. A few days later I saw her once more alone in the same restaurant. Apparently her defeat still rankled. She sat glaring at me, downing aquavits and getting steadily drunker. Finally she got up, lurched to my table, and said in a loud voice, in German:

"I still think you are a British spy."

I did not reply. All the Germans around grew quiet. I got up from my seat, went to the door and called in the Military Police who were on duty outside. I produced my Wehrmacht pass, explained I was in the German Secret Service, and reported that I had been insulted.

The cops came in, arrested the woman and led her off. Several Germans who had witnessed the scene came to my table and expressed their indignation at such an accusation being leveled against me.

Next day, I phoned von Grunen and explained what had happened.

"You have done right," he commented. "Leave it to me. I will see that she does not interfere with you again."

What happened to "Frue Anne" after that I do not know. Henceforth I kept clear of her.

◆ ◆ ◆

Meantime, sabotage continued unchecked—sometimes with terrible, but also occasionally with amusing, consequences.

One early morning, I went down to my boat with a girl friend for a sail. It was a beautiful warm day; not a cloud broke the blue skies, and hardly a ripple stirred the water. I made my boat ready for departure.

At that moment, a staff car with three German generals and a Japanese admiral drew up at the pier. They were followed by several high-ranking German Navy officers. The parade of uniforms was impressive. The green with red stripes of the Wehrmacht contrasted vividly with the dark blue and gold of the bemedaled and bespectacled admiral from Nippon. Newspapermen pressed forward to take photographs. The formalities were prolonged. The party then moved off in dignified procession to board the motor yacht which was to take them on their tour of inspection of the fjord.

I glanced at the boat. Curious, I thought, she seems to be lying very deep in the water. I watched. Suddenly shouts of rage disturbed the quiet of the morning.

"Sentry! ... Sentry!" bellowed one of the generals. A guard had always been kept at the pier to prevent sabotage. At the double, up rushed the startled soldier on duty. His body frozen in a salute—so much gold braid and so many brass hats were more than his nerves could stand—he remained there, taut with terror. Although I was thirty yards away I could see his knees trembling.

Violent voices were raised on all sides, questions were shot at him, angry fingers were jabbed in the direction of the boat. Standing slightly apart, impassive and imperturbable, the Pride of Japan looked on.

I followed the gist of the row. During the night someone had sabotaged the boat by boring two-inch holes through her bottom while no doubt the guard had peacefully slumbered at his post.

Elaborate apologies and explanations were offered through an interpreter to the Japanese admiral, who seemed the only one to see anything funny in the incident. He grinned appreciatively.

The big hotels in Oslo did not escape the attention of the saboteurs. They could not sink them like a ship, but they could at least send them up in flames, and this they sometimes did. One afternoon, as I was having tea in my bedroom at the Forbunds Hotel, where I had moved, the cry of Fire! resounded through the passages.

Now, in this hotel the Luftwaffe had a reserved suite where films were developed for the Information and News Section of their Intelligence. Panic-stricken German officers rushed past me as I looked out of my bedroom door. A fire had mysteriously started at about five o'clock, and already the staircase was full of smoke and the top floor was blazing. To make matters worse, the soldiers had opened all the windows to let out the smoke. This merely fanned the flames.

My companion and I watched the scene. It seemed certain that the fire was going to spread still further, so I packed my suitcases and went downstairs.

Everyone was shouting orders, and no one was obeying them. Fire-bells were clanging, and telephone bells ringing, while outside, throngs of grinning Norwegians had begun to gather. The fire brigade, after a long delay, arrived amid cheers and laughter. Slowly and deliberately, the firemen mounted their ladders and fixed their hoses. They were plainly in no hurry. Inside, the Germans fumed at the delay.

They would have been better off if the fire brigade had not arrived at all. Water was squirted everywhere—into the rooms, on the roads, on the roofs, anywhere but on the fire. After an interlude which would have delighted a Marx Brothers audience, the Gestapo arrived, and under its vigilant direction the blaze was finally put out.

The damage was considerable. Scores of unmenaced rooms were ruined by water (the menaced ones had largely succumbed to the flames). My own bedroom on the first floor was so flooded that it was uninhabitable. Water had seeped through ceilings and walls, and something like Niagara Falls had come in through the windows. The chief damage, of course, had been to the prestige of the conquerors. The Oslo onlookers returned home that night feeling gratified.

There were other, grimmer incidents.

One of them occurred the day after my birthday, November 16, 1943.1

had forgotten this occasion, but not so von Grunen. He rang me up and invited me to his flat. When I arrived, he bade me shut my eyes while I entered the room. On opening them, I saw on the table a collection of gifts from the various people I had worked with. A Van Gogh print was from von Grunen himself; books from Fritz Stube, an ivory ashtray from Johnny Holst, two bottles of cognac from Captain Malinin, while others had bought me a radio. Finally, a birthday cake had been baked. I was very moved by the kindness of these people, who had done so much to make me feel one of themselves.

Little speeches were now made by the guests, who complimented me on my work. Later, we all sang songs. When it came to my turn, slightly high and homesick I gave them "Annie Laurie." Everyone joined in, and seldom has that sentimental song been sung in such a United Nations of accents. It got me down, I must confess.

◆ ◆ ◆

Through it all flitted visions of home, *my* home—even if it had meant only hardship and bitterness; even if I had never known the freedom of walking on those "bonny braes"; even if half of the fairest part of the land was covered with slums far worse than any I had seen in Europe. Even if I had become an outcast, a criminal; even if the Army had written on my record "Discharged, services not required," and refused them even in the dark days of 1940 because I was a man with a past. Here, in German-occupied Norway, I was respected, among friends and comrades. The bitterness welled up within me, but was swamped once again by sentimentality.

My birthday party continued late into the morning. Next day, as I was walking toward the National Theatre, I noticed excited crowds in the streets. German Security Police and plainclothes Gestapo men were mingling with them.

A boy of about seventeen rushed past me, pursued by a handful of panting S.S. men. The boy dodged in and out of the trees, and the people laughed to see how he eluded his hunters. Stung by the mockery, one of the Germans drew a revolver and threatened to shoot the boy unless he gave himself up. He then surrendered, amid cheers and jeers from the Norwegians.

Farther down Karl Johanns Gate, in the square formed by the university, were a thousand people guarded by soldiers. From time to time a Norwegian would be dragged out of the crowd to join them.

As I came up, an old man who might have been a lawyer was picked up. He did not understand the command given to him—whereupon the Gestapo officer hit him in the face with a knuckle duster. He fell, and the blood broke from his face as he lay on the ground. He got up shakily, and was shoved roughly toward the other prisoners.   '

Suddenly, I felt a violent hand upon my shoulder. A harsh voice said:

"You seem rather too interested in all this. You had better go and join the rest!"

The Gestapo man who had addressed me shoved me violently into the crowd. I turned on him instantly, and told him briefly what I thought most Norwegians would have wished me to have said:

"You stupid oaf, you block-headed blankety idiot—not enough brains to be a pig!"

In German, I poured forth all the abusive wealth of a language designed for swearing. An officer came over. I pulled out my pass and told him what had happened. The Gestapo man became abjectly apologetic. The officer turned on his man. He cursed him with even greater fluency because he was covering up his own inefficiency.

"Make sure, you stupid swine, that next time it is a *verdammter* Norwegian that you are arresting," he shouted.

I asked the officer what the uproar was all about. He said that for months the Germans had been having trouble with the university, which played a prominent part in the Resistance movement. Several of its teachers and professors had been deported to concentration camps in Germany. The principal, Dr. Seik, was also under arrest, and had been replaced by a collaborationist. The students had been ordered by him to wind up their union. He had, furthermore, made it plain that admission to the university would in future depend on the measure of friendship the applicant displayed toward the occupying power. The students and their teachers had protested. These were the consequences.

In the midst of this mass intimidation, another student was playing hide-and-seek around Ibsen's monument, opposite the National Theatre. I looked up at the statue of old Ibsen. Although his face is perennially lined with care and sorrow, on this day it seemed to me to bear something resembling a smile of sympathy. On this day, I swear, he actually winked. "This is the beginning," he seemed to be saying, as he watched the youth of his own land being led into captivity.

All day long the arrests went on. The Gestapo seized anyone and everyone they pleased. In all, sixteen hundred students were rounded up. Many of them were placed in concentration camps in Norway. Hundreds of them were herded off to Germany.

Sweden, a neutral state, made strong protests against this inhumanity.

Bowing to public opinion is not a weakness of the Germans, but this particular protest had some result, for many students were released before Christmas.

♦ ♦ ♦

Though German cruelties in Norway never approached the degree or the scale of their atrocities in Poland and Russia, they placed the land under real terror. In return, they reaped sabotage and murder from the Norwegian side, provoking more reprisals.

Not all the killings were political. Both Norwegians and Germans took advantage of this atmosphere of violence to settle private scores.

One day, I remember, a German soldier was found murdered in the streets of Oslo. An investigation was started, and von Grunen was asked to take charge of it. It was established that on the evening on which the murder took place the soldier had visited "Le Sphinx," the brothel used by the troops. Von Grunen asked me if I would care to visit it with him, because he wanted to speak to the girl who was the last person to see the soldier alive.

We went there that same evening. The soldiers were queueing up to go in. There were accommodations for two hundred men, who sat at crowded tables, drinking beer. They took turns in going with the women, the military police controlling the waiting queue. Twenty women were employed.

As fast as a girl came downstairs, she was taken up again by a soldier, who had already paid his money. These whores were the typical products of any third-class French brothel—old, tired and worn-out.

It was a disgusting scene. The men were stamping their feet with impatience. Jeers and mock cheers would come from the soldiers as they recognized some friend mounting the stairs.

We found the girl who had been with the murdered soldier. Von Grunen looked at the control book, which showed the number of times she had climbed those stairs with a man in one week, not counting Sunday or a holiday. She had in fact gone to bed 180 times. These whores only worked on a four months' contract.

After that they were sent home with thirty or forty thousand Reichsmarks.

The girl remembered that the murdered man had told her of a quarrel with some of his friends over her, for on her evenings out she had gone with him. She knew the names of these friends, and gave them reluctantly to von Grunen. He sent the military police to arrest them.

When they were confronted with the evidence, three of them confessed that they had shot their comrade in cold blood because of this quarrel over a whore's love.

They were court-martialed and sent to the penal battalion serving on the Eastern front. From this assignment few or none ever returned alive.

16

BERLIN BLACKOUT

TOWARD THE end of 1943 came an order from Berlin asking von Grunen, Thomas and myself to fly there at once to attend an important conference on sabotage. We left by plane via Copenhagen that afternoon, and reached Tempelhof airport before dark. A few bombs had fallen there, but not enough to hold up traffic.

Thomas and I stayed at the Hotel Metropol in Friedrichstrasse. It appeared that, despite von Grunen's trust in me, it was still considered necessary to keep an eye on me. Here I was introduced to a German named Fritz Walders, who had just returned from the Eastern front, and who had previously been deported from America. He was a timid fellow, and seemed to regret having returned from Uncle Sam's safe haven.

I found it interesting to be in Berlin, but rather inconvenient. Everything was rationed. If you ate in a restaurant you had to produce food coupons, which were demanded for potatoes, bread, fats, meat and even sweets. There were two meatless days a week; otherwise, one received about fifty grams a day. There was just enough food on a coupon card to satisfy one's hunger. At our first meal I asked the waiter what was on the menu.

"We have a specialty, sir," he answered. "Salted fish."

We groaned.

That night I went with Thomas and the "new man," Walders, to the Winter Garden and saw an excellent variety program. Next day, von Grunen groomed me for the conference. We decided to drink nothing at lunch in order to keep our brains clear for this discussion, for von Grunen declared that the officers who would be present carried great weight in the Nazi war machine.

I presented myself as well-dressed as possible. Mentally, I turned over all the questions which were likely to be put to me. I was, to say the least, a little on edge.

A car took us to a flat off the Kurfürstendamm. We were shown into a room in which there was a long table. Three men sat there. One was a colonel of the Luftwaffe—he sat at the head; the other two were civilians. A half-empty bottle of cognac stood at the colonel's elbow, and some glasses stood beside their owners, all of whom looked half-drunk.

The Colonel who presided wore the Iron Cross. He was tall, gaunt and gray-haired, and about sixty years of age. He spoke English with a slight accent, which was further blurred by drink.

"Have a drink, Fritz," he said, patting me on the shoulder. "So you are the young man who has been doing such good work for us? Well, I hope you do not think that we are unappreciative."

I took my place beside a small man who looked like a well- known English actor. We all raised our glasses, toasted each other, and drank. The colonel then opened the ball by saying, rather thickly:

"Now, what we would like to know first is your opinion of sabotage possibilities in England. What special points and objects do you think are worth striking at in order to do most damage to the British war machine?"

I felt a strong desire to laugh at this silly old burbler, trying to look at me seriously through a drunken haze.

"Well, why not blow up the House of Parliament, or bump off Winston Churchill," I suggested.

"*Nein! Nein!* We are not interested in political assassinations," said the colonel hurriedly. "What we are after are factories or airports."

Such were the ideas of these politically childish people.

I sketched over for them my experiences at De Havilland's.

"Yes, that was good work. But do you not think that if some highly specialized machine were to be destroyed, one of those which would have to be replaced from America, it would be better?" asked a clerk-like figure sitting opposite.

I agreed that it would, but pointed out the difficulty of penetrating into a factory at night, at a period when most of the staff was working overtime or on around-the-clock shifts.

A complicated discussion followed in German on the output of different American machines in use in Britain. By this time the brandy was finished. Another bottle was opened. Finally when that bottle was polished off the meeting was over. We said *"Auf Wiedersehen,"* and von Grunen and I departed.

Outside, he was furious.

"My God, Fritz!" he exploded. "And with men like that in our Service, we expect to win the war! They were all drunk! Why we were called to this meeting is utterly beyond me."

It certainly baffled me too, for all the questions could have been answered from Norway by letter.

That same afternoon, I walked over with Thomas to see the Olympic Sports Palace. It was not possible to go inside, for the vast building had been taken over by the Wehrmacht as a store depot and training ground. On the surrounding walls, heavy flak batteries could be seen, which promised a warm welcome to any raiders. The building and the monuments outside looked dilapidated: the pavements were cracked and the concrete badly chipped. It reminded me of the Nazi regime, once so proud and haughty. Now it was falling apart, and soon would be in ruins.

◆ ◆ ◆

Thomas was pressing von Grunen for his leave, which was in any case long overdue. This had become a bone of contention between them. It was agreed that Thomas should stay on leave in Berlin for three days, but that did not satisfy him, and he grumbled continually to me about it.

Next day, a car came to our hotel to take me to the airport. I said goodby to Thomas, and was driven to meet von Grunen. Our plane did not appear, and we sat in the restaurant at Tempelhof waiting for it. While we were talking, in walked our acquaintance of the previous day, the one who resembled an English actor. He had coffee with us. I noticed a book under his arm and inquired what it was. He handed it to me—it was *The British Secret Service*, written by a Frenchman. Then he began to explain to me the workings of that body. He finished up by saying to von Grunen:

"If I had my way, I would make Fritz here the chief of our Service."

We all laughed at the idea.

Before the war, this man had sold airplanes to the Norwegian government, and he had the dispassionate kind of mind which is most useful in Secret Service, since it is immune to illusions. Many of the Norwegians whom he had known, he said, had gone to fight for the Allies. One—an admiral, he believed—had been awarded the Victoria Cross for some act of bravery, an achievement which somehow appeared to please him.

He was now flying to Poland. His plane arrived and we said *"Auf Wiedersehen."* He promised that when time permitted he would come to see me in Norway.

Our plane had broken down, so back we went to the Hotel Petite Stephanie, where von Grunen phoned Thomas at his house. Thomas was angry at having to look after me again, and made a grumbling remark to that effect. Von Grunen flared up.

"I am giving you an order!" he roared. "Come instantly to this hotel!"

We sat in the lounge waiting for Thomas to put in an appearance—he lived only about half an hour's journey away. After two hours, during which von Grunen continually fumed and threatened to have him cashiered, Thomas had still not arrived. I was looking out of the lounge window when at last he came in sight. His eyes were fixed straight ahead of him, and his face was white with suppressed anger. He was so upset that he walked straight past the hotel without noticing it. A quarter of an hour later he presented himself.

He marched briskly up to von Grunen, gave him the full Nazi military salute, although we were in civilian clothes, and clicked his heels.

"I await your orders, *Herr Rittmeister*," he announced.

"Take Fritz around Berlin, and see that he has a good time. Take him back to the airport at 11:30," was the laconic order.

Outside, as we walked up the street, Thomas gave vent to his anger. Was it true that the plane had not left? Did I think the *Rittmeister* was plotting against him to stop him from taking his leave? This leave of his still worried him; in fact, it was on his brain. Even in Norway it had been his *idée fixe*. Thomas was one of those people who always believe they are being victimized. Nothing I could say would have changed his mind. We walked morosely around the city.

Although there was nothing to buy in the shops, by order of the government the display windows were still full of good things. Notices informed the public, however, that they were not for sale. But there appeared to be no dearth of entertainment, and every theatre was full of badly dressed, badly fed people apparently trying to forget their troubles.

That evening, we went to a circus. It was packed, and we would not have got in if we had not received seats from our bureau. We saw a good animal act, composed of tightrope-walking tigers. Clowns and jugglers, trapeze artists and blaring music made up the rest of a first-class show. I wondered idly how they managed to feed the tigers.

Next day, von Grunen and I left for Oslo. Soon I was again sailing my boat up the bright waters of the fjords.

There was big news from the war fronts, but none of it was good news for the Germans. Norwegians had hardly stopped cheering Britain's North African victories before the great story broke in July of the first Allied landing in Europe. True, it was at the southern end of Sicily, but that did not dampen the optimism that swept through Oslo.

Then came the real bombshell—Mussolini himself had fallen in a counterrevolution. On street corners, in buses, in cafes, the great event was discussed. I went to book a table at the Löwenbräu the day after the news was announced. The headwaiter asked me what I thought of it. Everywhere the Germans were besieged by Norwegians who took this opportunity of rubbing in the bad news by asking the most deadly questions in the most innocent way, and intimating the dire consequences of the event.

Von Grunen was pessimistic. Up to that time no suggestions had been made about the work I was to do. The latest events seemed to galvanize the bureau in Berlin into action. I was asked if I would consider undertaking another mission. At first I pretended it was out of the question. Later, I inquired what the mission was.

"Sabotage," was the reply.

"How much are you going to pay me?" I asked.

"The same as last time," replied von Grunen.

"That is not enough. I want at least 500,000 marks or £50,000," I told him impudently.

"They will never pay that much," he protested. "Why, it is a fortune."

I told him I was not interested in anything less. He got angry, stormed at me and tried to force my signature to a contract which had been sent from Berlin. I was adamant, and refused to sign.

For a week I steadfastly resisted the cajolings of von Grunen, Holst and Thomas, who had now returned from Berlin. In desperation, von Grunen blocked my drawing account. I did not see him for a week. I wrote a strong letter to him, however, expressing my indignation. I told him I would see him in hell before I was forced to sign a contract that did not suit me. At the end I said that if it was O.K. with him, I was prepared to go back to the concentration camp. This was a bluff, and he probably realized it. But next day he gave in.

Then he wrote a detailed letter to Berlin. A week later a radio message came through. Its contents were disclosed to me by the head of the German Secret Service in Norway—Captain von Bonen. Von Grunen and I were invited to his flat opposite Frognor Park. It was a well-furnished apartment on the first floor, in which everything was in meticulous order, giving an impression of parade-ground efficiency.

A portrait of von Bonen hung on the wall behind the dining table. It was an extraordinarily good likeness of him, with his piercing blue eyes, bald head and weak chin. Here, in his blue uniform with the four gold rings on his sleeve and the eternal Iron Cross on his breast, was an exact replica of the man who now sat exchanging politenesses with me. It had been painted by a sailor in a ship which von Bonen had commanded. He complained about the chin, which apparently hurt his vanity because it had not been rendered in the usual powerful Boche style.

"Look," he kept repeating, "it should have been heavier, much heavier."

As he did not speak English, we talked in German, at which I had become quite proficient.

"We are prepared to pay you 500,000 marks if you will successfully carry out a mission for us," said von Bonen. "I will explain the undertaking to you briefly. The British, as you may know, have practically stopped us from using our submarines—by means of an invention which enables them to locate their distance and position. This is done from considerable ranges. It is now impossible for our underwater craft to operate without great risk of being sunk—they can even be located when they are lying with their engines dead on the bottom of the ocean.

"If we can discover this device, or devices—for it may be a series—we can take steps to counteract them, just as the British did with our magnetic mines. At the present moment, I cannot give you any exact information regarding these inventions. Indeed, there seems to be little or none available. In due course, however, all the pertinent facts will be placed at your disposal. If you agree, will you sign this contract?"

He drew the contract out of his pocket—it was a replica of the first, except for the sum of money. I signed. We discussed several methods of my obtaining the secret, and von Bonen told me that I would be taking a trip to Bergen, where the submarine defense school would give me instructions in what was known of various devices.

About this time Thomas, who had not ceased to complain of his bad luck in being sent to Oslo, was at the request of von Bonen transferred back to Germany. Later, I had a letter from him. He was quite happy. Instead of being sent to the Eastern front, he was assigned to teaching sailors the sword dance—folk dancing, as I have said, was his hobby. The whole idea struck me as hilarious. He had told me that he would never be content until, gun in hand, he had defeated the savage Russians or the decadent British. . . .

17

THE DECLINE OF THE THIRD REICH

To INCREASE the usefulness of my work, the Germans decided to teach me photography. I owe them this much—they taught me another trade, to which I reckoned I might turn if all else failed when peace (with unemployment for the likes of me) descended again.

An excellent photographer named Rotkagel was in charge of that particular section of our unit. He was a funny little chap, with shrewd tired eyes. Before the war, he had been manager of one of the Leica factories. His hobby was color photography.

One night at Kapelveien, Rotkagel showed us pictures he had taken in Norway. He had obtained the most exquisite effects of red sunset falling upon the snow. He pointed out the tonal differences in the color of the same view taken at different hours of the day, and maintained that these were the true natural colors, which it was impossible to recognize with the naked eye.

His work in Norway consisted in photographing any sabotage committed against the Reich, any German soldier found dead in the streets (and I was told, there were plenty), and any suspected spies under arrest.

Rotkagel taught me rapidly the rudiments of camera work, how to hold and focus the instrument, and how to read the light meter. Then he gave me some film and a list of subjects to photograph.

After I had become fairly proficient, Rotkagel taught me how to photograph documents, charts, maps, etc. The results obtained in this type of work were interesting. For practice, I would photograph leaves and flowers, the minutest details of which would appear in the subsequent enlargements.

I was also taught portrait photography, which became a fascinating pastime. In the park near the Palace I often took pictures of the kids playing there. The young Norwegians are good-looking children, with chubby cheeks, blond hair and blue eyes. One day I saw a group of them sitting on a bench. I focused my camera and shouted *"Boo!"* The startled little faces spun round. That photograph was the best I ever took.

◆　◆　◆

The war was now imposing terrible ravages on Germany. Besides the mounting casualties in Russia, the Allied air campaign was daily increasing in power and ferocity.

The horrors of the bombing attacks were brought home to me by several friends who had lost their homes. Johnny Holst was the first. He had the misfortune to go on leave in July, 1943, to visit his wife, who was then living in Hamburg. The day after his arrival came the first thousand-bomber raid. It seems that the warning sirens did not sound until the bombers were well over the target, and the destruction was frightful.

Hearing the drone of planes, Johnny had stepped outside his house. He saw the bombs come whistling down, and huge buildings split in two. Fires seemed to break out simultaneously all over the town. Entire streets, said Johnny, seemed to curl up like tissue paper. The use of phosphorous bombs added to the horror. Many people were burned to death by this chemical, for the stuff burned as long as it was in contact with the air. Screaming with pain, victims would dive into the water; when they came out, the pitiless burning began again.

Several other of my personal friends, such as Captain Etling and Fritz Stube, also lost their homes. Since they lived in widely separated parts of Germany, I gained a fair idea of the magnitude of the Allied attack.

Many intelligent and humane men have since tried to assess the effect of this savage destruction upon the character of the Germany of today. I can only report its deadly effect upon German morale at the time. Despite all the ingenuity of Goebbels, there slowly descended upon the German people a sense of impending doom. The neutrals were the first to grasp this significant fact. Everywhere, from the exultant enemy camp to the German home front itself, Hitler's stock was falling.

No detailed mention had yet been made of my future work. I had insisted to von Grunen and other officials that I had no desire to return to England because the risk was too great. I had made enough money; now I only wished to lead a life of pleasure for a while. However, my suggestion of an indefinite well-paid holiday by no means accorded with their other ideas for me, for they wanted more work out of me as soon as possible. Their plan, therefore, was to see to it that I squandered all I had earned as rapidly as possible. They reckoned that when my loot was exhausted I would again be ready to undertake any dirty work required by my paymasters.

Johnny Holst or one of the others would invite me to the Löwenbräu. There would invariably be four or five friends present. Cocktails, champagne, liqueurs and cigars would be consumed—and I was the one who always footed the bill. Anything I wanted and could buy, I bought. I don't pretend that it wasn't fun! I drank and drank, but at the same time I tried to keep my brain clear, for the shadow of death was always looking over my shoulder.

A friend of Johnny Holst called Captain Hausemann, the commandant of an artillery regiment, arrived in Oslo en route for the Eastern front. When I met him at the "Deutsches Haus" restaurant it appeared that this smartly turned out German officer was thoroughly depressed by the idea of leaving for Russia, as well he might have been, for nearly everyone I knew had lost friends or relatives there. He was due to leave the next day, and so, of course, there had to be a farewell party. Captain Hausemann's thirst proved to be gargantuan.

During dinner he drank enormous quantities of every kind of liquor, but it was only afterwards that he settled down to really two-fisted drinking. As he sank bottle after bottle, the gallant captain grew more and more melancholy and recited tearfully the names of his pals who had been bumped off. "Albert, Fritz, Heinrich, Georg—all dead, killed by those bloody Russkies. Now it's my turn." At that point he looked anything but a hero. I never saw a man who tried so hard to drown his sorrows.

Eventually I took him back to my hotel, but found that the captain was by no means through. Once more he started drinking. He sang, recited, wept, and told me his entire life story. By now his tunic was open, his shirt half out, and his eyes bloodshot. At three in the morning he regarded me drunkenly.

"Fritz!" he cried. "You are the only bastard who understands me! And the only one who is capable of drinking with me." With that, he fell flat on his face and remained in that position. I went to bed and fell asleep.

Next morning the telephone awakened me. It was Johnny Holst, terribly agitated. Had I seen Captain Hausemann?

"Yes, he is still sleeping here," I answered, looking down at the inert form on the carpet.

"*Gott im Himmel!*" shouted Johnny. "He has to be on the train in an hour's time!"

I yawned sleepily. "O.K. Come around and collect the body." Johnny arrived in a staff car. He tried to bring the captain around, but it was hopeless. Water was thrown on his face, massage was tried, and even blows, but he was too drunk to stir. Finally, we made him look as respectable as possible and dragged him to the waiting car. The chauffeur sprang smartly to attention and saluted, and we explained that our companion had suffered a fainting spell.

When we arrived at the station, Hausemann's company was lined up, awaiting its commander. He sat propped up between Johnny and me. The lieutenant called the men to attention; we drove past them and acknowledged the salute. I called the lieutenant over and explained that the captain was indisposed. He then ordered the men to board the train while we carried the "body" and deposited it in the corner of a reserved compartment.

As the train pulled out, I waved goodby to the still motionless figure of the captain. Long afterwards I learned that the man with the most monumental hangover I have ever seen in my life behaved with extraordinary courage and distinction at the front.

◆　◆　◆

Just before Christmas, I made the projected trip to Bergen. Johnny Holst, von Grunen and another officer, a German-Finn called Johann, accompanied me. During the trip I had an interesting conversation with Johann. He had been a newspaper reporter before the war. As the train rumbled on we swapped experiences, while Holst and von Grunen slept off the effects of their last bottle. Johann had been doing work similar to mine but against the Russians. His stamina was astounding. He was well built, six feet tall, and had a reckless do-or-die air about him. We became firm friends.

Once this remarkable fellow had been dropped by parachute behind the Russian lines, dressed as a high-ranking Russian officer, with pro-German Russians acting as his escort. He had successfully accomplished his task, which was to photograph convoys, strongholds and munition dumps, and to indicate by signals strategic points to be bombed by the Luftwaffe. He and his group of four men had traveled hundreds of miles on skis, living entirely off the land, fishing, hunting and stealing. They were surrounded one day by Russian soldiers. They fought, and Johann was wounded in his face. He still had the scar. Two of his companions were killed; he and the other two escaped.

After days of blizzards, alternating with intense cold during which the temperature sometimes dropped to twenty below zero, they made their way back to their own lines with a complete record of what they had set out to find. This man's exploits had gained him the nickname of "Johann the Devil" among the troops. He was treated with great respect by all at our *Dienststelle*, for he held a distinguished rank not only in the Wehrmacht but also in the Finnish army.

On my arrival at Bergen I went with von Grunen and Johnny Holst to visit the U-boat defense chiefs, who had their headquarters in Mordness Gate. I was introduced to two captains and a lieutenant. First, we told them what my mission was to be, and asked them to co-operate by giving any information which would aid me while in England to locate and recognize the various antisubmarine devices.

The interview took place in an office. We sat around a large desk. Maps with colored flags covered the walls. The senior captain, a bald, ugly fellow with a huge wart on his face, answered as many questions as he could in German. Von Grunen translated whatever technical terms I did not understand.

I gathered that, so far as the Germans knew, the British used several radio-location devices in their planes, warships and merchantmen. If I saw on the deck of a destroyer, for example, an aerial made up of short rods, I would know that it was an antisubmarine locator. It was pointed out that the measurements of these rods would be most useful, for they would reveal the frequency which was being used to locate enemy submarines. These aerials could be rigged on any part of a ship, and the rods might either be vertical or horizontal. Usually they were placed behind a casing of wire netting. The senior captain emphasized that if it were possible to obtain a diagram or photograph of the radio equipment which operated this locator, that would be the ideal solution.

Another German theory was that the British had an electronic device which worked on the same principle as the automatic gadget which opens the door of a garage when a car approaches, or causes a burglar alarm to go off. When a U-boat came in contact with such electronic rays, the distance was registered on a screen, and its position located. Some of the U-boat commanders had reported that, when trapped, they had heard explosions from a detonator. It was assumed that this detonator worked in conjunction with a measuring device which, on explosion, gave the distance and depth by sound.

A "heat-measurer" was also considered a likely instrument. Apparently it is possible to measure the heat of the exhaust of a U-boat, when she is cruising on the surface, from many a mile away. The solution to the riddle the German Navy sought might lie in any one of these directions.

Another report had been received that an instrument known as the "Hedgehog" had been sighted. This was an object shaped like a giant hedgehog, which was towed between two ships by a cable, and was in fact an aerial, or series of locating feelers. Further information came from a skipper who claimed that he had seen a reddish glow on the underbody of a Sunderland flying boat which was trying to spot him. The glow might have come from some instrument used in radio location. Even the use of television was not beyond the realms of possibility.

These conjectures, some of them reasonable but most of them wild, showed that the U-boat commanders were badly scared, for without warning they had certainly been accurately located, bombed and, in many cases, sunk. At sea, too, it appeared that Hitler's Reich was on the way down.

As the discussion continued interminably, I became certain of one thing: the Germans had no positive plan for combating the menace to their U-boats. They could not supply me with the names of any of the firms making the British devices they feared so much, or even give me worthwhile descriptions of the instruments used other than what they had offered on the aerial and the "Hedgehog." Since they had to admit that they could help us no further, it was suggested that the Luftwaffe headquarters in Berlin might be able to produce some clues. It seemed that Germany, and not Norway, was the proper base for our activities. A few days later I took a plane for Berlin.

18

AVENUE OF THE DEAD

A FTER A brief stop at Copenhagen, we soon found ourselves over a town. At low-level approach I did not recognize it. Rubble, bomb holes and craters were everywhere. I asked Stube, who was sitting next to me, the name of the town.

"I think it must be Hamburg," he replied.

Opposite sat an old Wehrmacht colonel.

"Can you tell me what this town is?" I shouted above the drone of the engines.

"*Das sind die Ruinen von Pompeii*," he replied, sadly shaking his head.

We arrived at Berlin—and what a Berlin! Immense devastation was the result of the terrible hammering inflicted by thousands of Allied bombers day and night. The last attack had been made only seven days before by a thousand Flying Fortresses.

We taxied onto the remains of the airport. As we came to a standstill the air-raid siren sounded again. Officials leaped up, shouting, "Quick! The air-raid shelters, everyone!"

We all jumped out of the plane and, without waiting for our luggage, dashed for a deep underground shelter nearby.

Dignity was thrown to the winds. Generals, colonels and other important personages vied with lesser ranks in a hundred-yard sprint to get there first. I stepped on someone's toes, and pushed another chap head-first down some steps—but we obtained quite good seats! The rest of our party had to stand, for we had beaten them to it. The raid lasted for about an hour, and we listened even longer to the bang and rattle of the flak and the heavy explosions far away. Then the "All Clear" sounded.

We piled into a car and were driven to a temporary office in the Luftwaffe building. During this brief journey, I noticed the change which had taken place at the Tempelhof airport since my visit in July. Hangars were burned out, offices wrecked beyond repair. The main booking office and restaurant were completely gutted—a mass of broken masonry and twisted iron girders. The immense Luftwaffe offices themselves were a shambles. The runways were a series of craters, littered with the charred hulks of aircraft. A smell of escaping gas filled the air. The people in this depressing area bore the stamp of resignation and misery.

We drove through Berlin. The capital of the Reich offered an unforgettable spectacle. In every street branching off Friedrichstrasse, rubble was piled twelve to fifteen feet high, running the entire length. The once proud Unter den Linden—even it had become one long Avenue of the Dead.

It was difficult to find any object which had escaped the cyclone of the bombs—though what keenly aroused my professional interest was the number of safes which had crashed through the floors as the wooden boards had given way, and had come securely to rest on the ground level. Sometimes four or five of these would be piled up among the blackened debris. I surveyed them regretfully. They had defied the blockbusters, but Freddie and I, merely lock-busters, could have done a wonderful job on them!

At the hotel we met von Grunen with a Luftwaffe captain. As a result of the alert, no hot meal could be served and we had to put up with a cold salad, to which we added the content of one tin of preserved meat, our traveling ration in Berlin.

As I entered the hotel, I spotted a poster on the wall. It was the figure of a masked man in a cloak, wearing a dark hat. A huge question mark was displayed beside him. The aged doorman was standing beside me, and I asked him what it meant. With a whimsical smile, he replied: "That is the last Berliner, looking to see if his house is still standing."

I laughed. Von Grunen then explained that this was Goebbels' latest propaganda stunt to stop people from talking indiscreetly. The figure represented the enemy spy who was supposed to be everywhere. In my bedroom, above the bed, was a large notice advising guests not to unpack their luggage because of the possibility of air raids. All windows had been boarded up by thick layers of compressed paper.

I went down to von Grunen's bedroom to cheer myself up. For Berlin was even getting me down! Von Grunen was entertaining a young man of about twenty-eight, wearing the Iron Cross and Observer's Badge on his uniform. It appeared that he was the officer in charge of getting me to England. He told me he had several times flown over London in a reconnaissance plane during the blitz, taking photographs. "It burned well," he said, but added wryly, "though Berlin burns better!" He had been shot down over France by a British Spitfire, and had been temporarily grounded.

◆ ◆ ◆

Von Grunen told me, with some diffidence, that instead of the plans already discussed, another mission had been decided on for me. German Intelligence had come to the conclusion that certain Air Force stations in England were assigned to the bombing of specific targets in Germany. For example, planes stationed in Cambridge bombed Hamburg, while those at Bedford bombed Berlin. The same applied, so they said, to American planes.

The Germans wanted to know the exact schedules of each station. They proposed to supply me with a simple wireless set and, once in England, I was to instruct some accomplices in its use. For instance, one was to proceed to Warboys. When he saw the American planes assembling there he was to transmit a three-figure code. That would enable the German defenses to know where the air raid was to be expected. They could then concentrate their fighters and flak, and clean up the Allied raiders when they came over.

The wireless set was produced. It was a small transmission set. It was equipped with a keyboard, with the numbers one to ten engraved on it in small brass morse figures. An aerial and an earth were the only attachments necessary; it worked off the A.C. mains. A wireless operator who was present showed me the mechanism. When the set was rigged up, all one had to do was run a brass pencil over the slightly protruding morse figures. The code was elementary. Three figures had to be touched (say, 123 or 456—any three consecutive figures). A powerful listening station on the Continent would then pick up the signals.

We fixed up the set there and then, and I went to my room and picked up signals on a receiver. They came through with bell-like clarity. The underlying idea of the set was brilliant, for it enabled an operator to work without any experience of morse and send messages rapidly.

Afterwards, we dined and then sat in the lounge until bedtime. A peculiar tension could be felt throughout the hotel; everyone appeared grim and anxious. I went to bed and dreamed of fires, and once I thought I heard a fire alarm. I awoke. The air-raid siren was screaming! It was a few minutes before midnight. Damn it! I turned over and tried to sleep, preferring to risk the bombs rather than face the discomfort of leaving my bed. But a damnable noise beat upon my ears from the corridor.

I slipped on my dressing gown and looked out. A mob of hotel servants in steel helmets was parading up and down the corridor, banging on doors, ringing bells, beating tin cans with sticks. Everyone was shouting at the top of his voice: *"Alert! Alert!"*

I put on some clothes over my pajamas. Von Grunen and Stube came to my room, and we carried all our luggage down the stairs. Women, soldiers and officers were all doing the same. In the hall I bumped into a group of Japanese. They were officials from the Japanese embassy, carrying boxes of secret and confidential papers down into the air raid shelter.

An air raid warden directed us to our bunker. We passed through the courtyard, went down twenty steps and found ourselves in a fairly comfortable cellar. Wooden posts helped to reinforce the concrete ceiling above our heads.

Soon voices were stilled, and faces became white and strained as the bombing mounted in intensity. An uncanny factor was the radio, which was now switched on, with a voice plotting the positions of the planes. We listened to the grim news.

"Now they are re-forming, and flying in the direction of northwest Berlin."

"Another squadron," said the voice a minute later, "is coming in from the west."

Then ... "The enemy aircraft are now almost overhead .."

So it went on until shortly before dawn.

People looked at each other without speaking as the directions indicated that the heavy planes must be near, and death close at hand. Each person seemed to derive some confidence or courage from his neighbor . .. some hope, some comfort. Each would strive to behave bravely; most of them did. But sighs of relief would rise when the planes droned over without releasing their deadly cargo upon the cellar. At last the "All Clear" sounded. We carted all our luggage upstairs, and I went back to sleep.

◆　◆　◆

Food was now even more strictly rationed in Berlin, as I found out next morning at breakfast. Although I had a double issue of coupons, it was not enough to satisfy my appetite. A cup of ersatz coffee, very bitter, and served with skimmed milk and one lump of sugar; two rolls and a slice of black bread with a tiny pat of butter—such was the morning meal. Fats, potatoes and meat were scarce. Clothing was unobtainable, except for those who had been bombed out. Cigarettes were rationed at three per day—I got eight. There was no black market. The death penalty was sufficient to keep even the most reckless individuals under control. Wines and spirits were nonexistent in restaurants. A near-beer—which should have been called far-beer—was the only beverage to be had.

A major of the Luftwaffe arrived by car, and I drove with him to Luftwaffe headquarters in Leipzigerstrasse. The Hotel Kaiserhof had been completely destroyed—all that remained of it was a mass of debris. How long would the Reich Chancellery itself remain standing?

Luftwaffe headquarters was housed in a huge building with hundreds of offices. It was built of reinforced concrete. Heavily armed guards barred the entrance to all but pass-holders. On the fifth floor, we went into an office and I was introduced to two majors and a captain, all technical experts.

I was left in a room with the captain, a small, smiling man of about forty, who was to begin my instruction. He said, in good English, "I will talk to you in your own language. Before the war, I was often in England. Now, we believe that the answer to the anti-submarine device is also the answer to our losing so many planes over Britain. It's all done by radio location. The British have installed in their home-based fighters a device which enables them to locate our night fighters and bombers with the greatest of ease.

"Their fighters are not allowed to leave Britain," he continued, "but we managed to shoot one of them down. It crashed in France. The instruments were badly damaged, for they had been fitted with a detonator so that in the event of a crash they would explode. That was what happened in this case. However, we were able to reconstruct them to some extent, and I will explain them to you."

He rang a bell, a secretary appeared and was told to bring in the reconstructed instruments. They were indeed badly damaged. The captain explained that a small screen in front of one of the components registered the enemy plane. There were two sets of lines by which to steer—one horizontal, and the other vertical.

When the target was sighted in the center of the screen, where the two lines crossed, the attacker was in position to fire. It was in one of these components, the modulator, that the Luftwaffe was particularly interested. In this instance, however, it had been destroyed.

"That is what we want," said the captain. "If you can get us one of those, you will be very well rewarded." He then produced photographs of Spitfires and other machines fitted with these devices.

From my questions, I gathered that the Germans did not know the name of the firm which was manufacturing these devices. Cossors, of Hammersmith, were suggested as possible makers. The captain proposed that I should try to find out where the home-based fighters were stationed in Britain, and, either by theft or bribery, obtain the required components. He let me take a list of the aerial numbers which would help me to recognize the instruments when I saw them.

The interview was finished for the day, and I went back to my hotel. There I sat in the lounge, reading the Berlin newspapers. They were full of secret weapon hints and threats of the fearful vengeance which was to be inflicted on England.

Promptly at midnight the air raid siren wailed again, and I endured a repetition of the night before. These raids had now become routine with the Allied air forces. Nearly every night, shortly before or after twelve, the sirens would chase the weary Berliners to their bunkers.

◆   ◆   ◆

At Luftwaffe H.Q. next day I was introduced to another expert, Herr Weiss. He was dressed in civilian clothes, and looked like an untidy student. He began by explaining that they were going to give me still another mission in case I found it impossible to fulfill any of those so far proposed.

"As you probably know," he said, "both sides are experimenting with remote-controlled aircraft. There are two methods, one by fuel control, the other by radio."

He produced photographs of different planes made by Frenchmen and Italians, and showed how propellers had been dispensed with and exhaust was the driving power. He went on:

"Now, we believe that the British may be manufacturing these planes. If by chance you come across them, we would like the following details: length, height, and what color of flame comes from the exhaust. This will tell us what type of fuel is being burned, also whether they are radio-controlled or not. Further, we would like to know how much in pounds per square inch is the pressure from the exhaust. Where they are being manufactured, and by whom? How they are being distributed, and in what numbers? When do the Allies intend to use them? Do they think that we possess any and intend to use them? If so, what precautionary measures have they taken? Is our threat of a secret weapon being taken seriously in England?"

As he enumerated his list of questions, I made a note of them for reference. The interview lasted about four hours.

That night I sat in the lounge with von Grunen and Stube, who told us the latest joke which was making the rounds of Berlin. "A man went to buy some bread. At the shop he found a long queue waiting. Impatiently, he walked on to get some razor blades—another long queue. He tried to buy meat, clothes, papers, cigarettes and skimmed milk; everywhere he found long queues. Furious, he dashed home, loaded his revolver, determined to assassinate Hitler. When he got outside the Reich Chancellery, he found another long queue of people waiting to do the same." Von Grunen laughed heartily at this, and turned to Stube, who was a corporal.

"Do you know, Fritz, G.H.Q. have decided to shoot all corporals."

"Why?" asked that worthy innocently.

"Because they do not want it to happen again."

The following day I again met the expert at G.H.Q. This time he gave me a lecture on the working of rockets, asking me again to find out if the British had them, or were developing them.

I asked how large these rocket planes could be.

"Any size," he replied, "although the fuel tanks will be much larger than the explosive carried." His estimate was from fifteen to twenty tons.

After we had finished our technical discussion, we talked of wars. "Yes, war is good, and thank God, it is eternal," said the German. "It kills the softness and the rottenness in a nation. Any people which has gone through the fire of battle comes out better, stronger and with higher ideals. War is so vital a part of human nature that it can never be eliminated. If it could be, competition would die out and the world would stagnate.

"It is a question of evolution and natural selection," he went on. "Plants, birds and beasts fight—the best survive. So it is with war—the weak perish, the strong and virile come into their own. Look at Germany, attacked from all sides, for many years misunderstood. She will be victorious. England has gone soft, and is now a decadent race. As for America," he turned down his hands in contempt, "it is only a land of jitterbugging and hooey, where graft is rife, where the criminal is honored and the honest man scorned."

These ideas were the stock-in-trade of most leading Germans with whom I talked about the causes of war. Though they brought Germany to ruin, they certainly helped to keep the Old Guard going up to the last hour.

That night, we went to the Winter Garden and saw a good variety show. It started at six o'clock and finished at nine. All places of entertainment and all cafes had to be closed by nine-thirty. An exception was one all-night cabaret, reserved for the relaxation of troops on leave from the fronts.

Berlin, in 1944, had become a Tower of Babel, with its foreign workers and Satellite and Quisling troops. In the subway one heard every language spoken except, maybe, English. French, Italian, Russian, Danish and

Finnish were common. Most of those who spoke these tongues were workmen sent to do forced labor in Germany. They looked unhappy and underfed.

Every one of these ordinary people, Germans and foreigners alike, was tired out. Men and women would lean back with their eyes closed, a pathetic resignation upon their faces. They were near the end, and for all that most of them cared it might as well come at any time.

19

PARIS REVISITED

MY TIME in Berlin was up, and all the instructions for my various jobs in England had been given me. I knew positively now that the Germans intended to use some new weapons. I was pretty sure that a propellerless aircraft was one of them, and that a radio-controlled rocket was another.

Next day—in the company of von Grunen, Stube, the parachute captain who was arranging to drop me over England, and two other Luftwaffe officers—we took the train from Potsdamer Station for Paris.

The train was crammed with soldiers, sailors and flyers. The corridors were impassable, for men huddled on the floor between the legs of others who were standing up. The smell of this sweating humanity was unbearable. Up in front about twenty French workmen, going home on vacation, filled a compartment, squatting on top of each other and even perching in the luggage racks. I thought of Goebbels' propaganda, which still spoke of the wonderful conditions prevailing in the Reich; of the posters showing happy Frenchmen traveling in the luxury of first-class carriages or attended by waiters in dining cars while they ordered their favorite wines.

Sleeping berths had been reserved for our party, and we sat drinking a final tot on our beds before turning in. The parachute captain entertained us with stories of his flights as an observer over London, and described with relish the fires and the devastation he had seen. As soon as his duties in connection with my trip to England were finished, he was due for leave and was going to be married. I promised to send him a wireless message of congratulation.

The discussion turned upon the trains that were not running on time, and bets were made as to how late our own train would be. In 1944, Allied bombings of railway centers were having a dislocating effect on German transport. On our Berlin-Paris route, seven-hour delays were common. This was quite a change from 1941, when German railwaymen were boasting of their records for punctuality.

When we reached Aachen next morning, our train was already hours late and we did not arrive in Paris until 10:30 that evening. We were dirty and our nerves were frayed. To top everything, no car was waiting to meet us. Von Grunen stormed his way into the command post in the Gare de l'Est, and after many fruitless calls succeeded in getting a car to pick up our luggage. This was also late in arriving, and for some minutes he paced up and down muttering to himself. The captain and I were laughing at some pointless joke about the gaiety of Paris when von Grunen exploded in a burst of fine old Prussian wrath.

"Why the hell are you fools laughing at me?" he screamed. "Do you think it is funny being stranded here like this? For you two the whole trip seems to be a huge joke! For two pins I would call the thing off. This is war—*bloody* war! We are here on serious business. If we succeed, our efforts may have a considerable effect on the course of the war for Germany. *Herr Kapitän!* I am surprised, and ashamed of you, and I will most certainly report you for conduct unbecoming to an officer."

At last the car arrived. The chauffeur was soundly cursed by everyone for not arriving more quickly, and we drove to the Ambassador Hotel in the Boulevard Haussmann, where Stube and I were to share a room. Von Grunen went on farther, still in a temper. The rest of us had some drinks, and felt better.

Next morning, I took a walk up the Champs-Elysées. Spring was in the air. The lovely women of Paris strolled past. The sophisticated fashions, the challenging attitude of French women of those days seemed to me to reflect that deeper spirit which burned even during the capital's darkest hours. And Paris! I sat fascinated by so much beauty. Not even the drab green uniforms of the Bodies who strutted about could impair its grace and grandeur.

◆ ◆ ◆

During the course of the next week I was introduced to an officer who wore the Iron Cross and the uniform of the H.Q. staff of the Luftwaffe. He was a smart young man of about twenty-four, and we met at the Hotel Scribe, where the staff of the Luftwaffe was then quartered. He was a liaison officer in touch with the various squadrons flying over England, and the date of my departure depended upon him. He gravely informed me that it was not going to be so easy this time, since British night fighters were bringing down an alarmingly high percentage of German aircraft. He said I must wait for a few days, as he wished to make certain of a successful landing for me.

The Luftwaffe officer then asked me if I minded being parachuted into Scotland, but I insisted on being dropped near London.

Every day, von Grunen went around to the Luftwaffe H.Q. in the rue Miromesnil to find out the date of my departure. One morning he came into my room. He was excited, and said:

"Fritz, you are off tonight, conditions permitting. We are going to an airport just outside Paris. Get everything ready, have a final check-up on your codes, go through your missions with Stube, and see that you have forgotten nothing."

We left Paris by car that afternoon with all my luggage, my parachute and the briefcase containing my two wireless sets, and my money. The airport, which was near Le Bourget, was cleverly camouflaged. After passing through the usual identity checks by the guards, we were led into a small office where I was introduced to the two camp commandants. Both wore the Iron Cross.

The older man looked like an artist, with his long hair and delicate manners. He was old beyond his years, with prematurely gray hair, and I could plainly see that he was feeling the strain of too much air fighting. Despite his shy gentle manner, he was credited with fifty victories over Allied planes. He held the rank of major.

His second-in-command, a captain, was credited with thirty victories. The captain was a tough little man, with a devil-may-care air. He told me that he had not missed one operational flight for six months. That very week he had been shot down over the Channel, losing his plane but saving his life by baling out. Next day, he was flying again.

All my kit was examined, my parachute tested, and my pack (which weighed about fifty pounds) adjusted. Then we went into the mess, where I met a number of Luftwaffe officers. We sat down to a decent meal, and when it was over the commandant asked me whether I would like to hear some music. I said yes, and three of the young lieutenants who had dined with us disappeared and returned with an accordion, a guitar and a saxophone.

To my surprise, they began to play modern American swing. A flaxen-haired officer started singing in broken English "Yankee Doodle Came to London." All joined in the chorus. Then came several of the old favorites, "Suwanee River," "Take Me Back to Dear Old Blighty," and other Anglo-American songs. The accent may have seemed strange, but the harmony was fair enough. I asked them where they had learned these songs, since it was forbidden for anyone to listen in to the Allied radio.

"We are the Luftwaffe," answered the artist-major. "We are not naughty children to be told what we may or may not do. My men like dance music. We are lonely out here, and I have given them permission to listen to foreign broadcasts."

The man fascinated me. He produced some masterly sketches of fighting scenes he had drawn. They must have been inspired by some of the personal tragedies in which he had played a part. One showed a comrade waving to him from his plane through a mass of flames as he crashed to his doom. "Return from Britain" was a striking study of pilots gathered around a stove, some of them wounded, but all depicted with that fanatical glow in their eyes which the German loves to call "Duty and Faith."

Meanwhile the weather reports continued to come in, and at last I was told to get into my coveralls. I went with von Grunen and Stube into an adjoining room, where I stripped and allowed them to search through my belongings. When I dressed and got ready for the take-off, a last good-luck toast was drunk to the success of my venture. Just then a subaltern entered, saluted smartly and handed the commandant a message.

"I am very sorry, Fritz," he said, "but you are not going tonight. Plans have been changed. Instead of flying over England, we are attacking shipping off Portsmouth. It's a pity, because I myself was to be your pilot, and I would have enjoyed the experience. But orders are orders. Let us hope we will manage it at some future date. Now I must be off. *Auf Wiedersehen.*"

I took his hand and looked into his tired eyes. He was a Boche, but a brave one. I stripped off my kit, took the money bag off my back and handed it to von Grunen. We were all disappointed, but there was nothing to be done. In silence, we returned to Paris.

◆ ◆ ◆

The following Sunday morning I was walking through the Place Pigalle with Stube. Painters were exhibiting their work, and children were playing on the swings, to the accompaniment of hurdy-gurdies and accordions. People were gathered in small groups singing the latest dance tunes. I loved this quarter of Paris. The cocottes, with their gigolos, swaggered from bar to bar.

Suddenly I felt a nudge in the back. I turned and saw Amalou, the Arab boy, with whom I had been friendly in the hostage camp at Romainville two years before. It was an awkward moment, for Stube stood at my side.

"Ne dis rien," I muttered to Amalou, knowing well that Stube did not understand French. I stepped away from the crowd and, under the watchful eyes of my companion, quickly told Amalou not to say anything but to give me his address. He reacted swiftly, shaking my hand and pressing his card into it.

"What did that fellow want?" Stube inquired.

"Oh, I met him at some club or other and bought some tea from him. He is good at getting things in the black market."

My explanation was accepted. When I arrived home, I looked at Amalou's card which bore the address of a café in the Latin Quarter.

I made it my business next day to go down to see him alone. The café had an attractive cocktail bar. Amalou's wife, a good-looking blonde, was soon being entertained by tales of our experiences in Romainville. Amalou had left the camp after me, and he was able to give me news of Anthony Faramus, the young man who had been arrested with me in Jersey. From time to time Amalou had sent him food parcels. Naturally, he was curious to know what I was doing in Paris. I did not enlighten him.

"Well," he said, "whatever game you are playing now, if you are ever in need of help or want to hide somewhere, you can count on me."

I shook his hand warmly, for I felt that he was a staunch friend. I left Amalou, promising to return at the earliest possible opportunity.

Next morning, von Grunen called me to his flat. He said:

"Fritz, I want you to come with me to the Hôtel Lutétia. A friend of ours would like to meet you. He is a clever young man, and most influential. He is going to talk to you, and will ask you to leave some money and a camera in England for one of our agents."

I met the young man, a Herr Krauser, in a small park along the Boulevard Raspail. He was of slight build, effeminate, quite obviously a homosexual.

"I have heard so much about you," he murmured. "What fantastic luck you have had!"

While he talked, he never took his eyes off me. Von Grunen had told me something of this man's reputation. He had caught more British agents than any other member of the counterespionage *Dienststelle*. He would frequent all the "queer" cabarets, sitting at cocktail bars, looking like a gin-sipping little pansy. Actually, he was watching everything and nothing escaped him. He worked on the theory that British agents, if they had known Paris before the war, would always revisit their old haunts. As the British used quite a number of agents familiar with prewar Paris, he was extraordinarily successful.

Von Grunen excused himself, and Krauser and I went to lunch at "Le

Frog," a small dirty restaurant, its walls cluttered with old iron pots. The place was crammed with French people.

"Please, we will talk only French here," said Krauser.

At a nod from him, the proprietor rushed forward and provided us with a table, although people were lined up outside. From the meaningful looks that passed between Krauser and the owner, I gathered that this man, too, was working for the Germans.

During the excellent (black market) meal, Krauser fired seemingly innocent questions at me. I inwardly writhed under them, for I sensed that here was one man who was absolutely convinced that I was a fraud. He thought that with his singular intuition he had unearthed a guilty secret. Outwardly I laughed, raised my glass, slowly and deliberately puffed at my cigarette, and put on as casual an act as possible.

At the end of the meal, Krauser suddenly said: "Do you know Dennis W——?" and mentioned the name of a well-known man-about-town in London.

"Yes, I know him," I replied.

"Is he working for British Intelligence?"

"How the hell should I know?" I answered. "I have never yet had the pleasure of meeting any gentleman from that illustrious branch. What is more, I am not particularly keen to meet any."

He laughed sardonically.

"Sorry, old man. I thought that perhaps on your travels you might have run across him and learned what he was up to."

I left him, and in a thoughtful mood walked homeward. Some time later I went to a dinner party given by von Grunen for Krauser and a woman working at our *Dienststelle*, a Frau von Lipper. She was a charming, cultured lady in her early forties, still extremely attractive, and was greeted by von Grunen with great civility. Her husband was a wing commander in the Luftwaffe. She knew of my visit to England and asked me numerous questions. Krauser listened intently as I replied to them. It was rather like a cat watching a mouse. I was not sure who was the cat, or if there were two of them. However, the evening was a social success.

Every day von Grunen, the parachute captain and I went up to the Luftwaffe H.Q. to find out the date of my departure, but always got the same answer: "Not today." Apparently, the Germans were nervous about sending planes over Britain, owing to their huge losses. The newspapers at this time were full of news about the possibility of an Allied landing in France. Von Grunen came to me after a conference, and told me that, when I got to England, discovering the place and date of the Allied landing was to take priority over all my other tasks.

◆ ◆ ◆

Early in May, 1944, I was told that I was to fly out from Brussels. We set off for that city. During the journey I saw ample evidence of the force of Allied bombings. Burned-out trains, coaches and wreckage littered the track. We arrived at Brussels at night, and after meeting a member of our Brussels branch, who was arranging to introduce me to the crew who were to fly me out, we went to bed.

I got up bright and early in the morning to see the sights. The economic situation here seemed much better than in Paris. Clothes, food and cigarettes were more plentiful, though only in the black market. We stayed in Brussels for three days.

Alas! After a few days it became obvious that it was quite impossible to fly me out from Belgium, so we decided to return to Paris.

It now appeared that we would be staying in Paris for an indefinite period and von Grunen, who did not care for hotel life, decided to take a private house. Through his connections, we were installed in an exquisite flat in the rue Miromesnil, which had once belonged to Marshal Petain's doctor. It contained a fine collection of Chinese lacquer paintings and china. My enemy, Krauser, who came up one night for dinner, was knowledgeable about China. He had spent his youth there and spoke Chinese. He reckoned that the stuff must be worth £20,000, and remarked that if the Germans were forced to evacuate Paris, he would take this collection away with him as a souvenir.

Though this sinister pervert always treated me with the greatest courtesy, I felt that his underlying hostility never abated. He was determined to follow up his hunch that I was really a British spy.

You had to be damned careful with the Germans at that time, even in small matters. There was always the possibility that the mere fact that I was an Englishman was enough to arouse or confirm sudden suspicion, and that arrest and even execution might follow. Fear was rampant. I was often afraid myself.

I remember walking with von Grunen one day near the Folies Bergeres when he suddenly stopped dead. Two pretty Jewish children, about six or seven years old, were playing in the street. Sewn on to their clothing was the yellow star of Judah.

"Oh, my God!" muttered von Grunen. "The swine! The brutes! Even children are branded! Don't they realize that kids, whatever their color, skin or creed, are God's creatures?"

Tears stood in the old boy's eyes; he was profoundly moved.

"Here, Fritz," he said, "go and give them these 2,000 francs, and tell them to buy something." I did so, and the two youngsters ran off happily. I wanted to say a kind word to him, but I checked myself. I could not permit myself to make such a gesture. We walked on in silence.

While we were in Paris, von Grunen often bought toys and clothing for a German-Jewish child he had adopted at home, and he was never in a happier mood than when going on such a shopping expedition. He would read excerpts from her letters to me. They were addressed to *"Lieber Onkel Stephan,"* and he, a lonely old man, was overjoyed with the child's words.

Nearly every afternoon on those cloudless days in May I would bask in the sun, or bathe in the Seine or go to some of the nearby beaches. Listening to the chatter of the Parisians was always interesting. They speculated continually and quite freely on where the Allies would land. Bombing was particularly heavy in the region of Normandy, and some hostile feeling had been worked up against the Allies, because, unavoidably, there had been casualties among French civilians.

Once, I witnessed an air raid on Paris by the R.A.F. It was an unforgettable sight. When the sirens wailed, I was in the Ambassador Hotel and went up on the roof. The planes were clearly visible in the searchlights, and sky markers were drifting down like wreaths of electric lights. Flak was thundering and bursting above the city. Bombs were falling to the right of the Sacre Coeur, which was soon bathed in a red glow. From where I stood, it looked as though half of Paris was burning. From all sides came the clack and bang of falling shrapnel. A plane was hit, leaving a blazing trail as it crashed, smoke billowing in its wake.

An aviator came floating down, twisting and turning his legs in an effort to control his chute. The glare of the searchlights showed every particle of his clothing, as though made of the purest white. The airman sank amid the flak fire until his body banged helplessly against a chimney, and was lost to view.

20

THE SECOND FRONT

I was sitting with a couple of Germans in von Grunen's flat when I heard the news of the opening of the Second Front. Von Grunen himself came in and told us that the Allies had landed.

"Another Dieppe?" I asked.

"No, the real thing," said von Grunen.

We tuned in at once to London and heard the announcement. At the end of it the national anthem was played. Von Grunen gave the sign and we all stood up, raised our hands and gave the Hitler salute.

"Well, they've really started now, and we are fully prepared. We will show these *Scheiss* British and Americans what war is," said von Grunen.

I took a walk alone through the streets, and made a round of the Paris bars in order to judge what effect the announcement had made upon the population. The news was received with a superficial calm; indeed, the Parisians seemed quite indifferent to it. Food, as usual, remained the chief topic: would the Allies bring food with them, for Paris was getting desperately hungry. Many people had such faith in a quick Allied victory that they went out and purchased the whole of their ration supplies for a month.

A few hours after the invasion began, posters printed in large red type were displayed on the walls proclaiming that anyone assisting the Allies would be treated as a *franc-tireur* and shot. On the whole, cinemas, theatres and restaurants continued as usual. Three days after the landing, the commandant of Paris decided that, since the Parisians had remained so well-behaved (he had expected sabotage and rioting), curfew would begin an hour later.

The German cause received a boost a little later in June when it was announced that Hitler had finally used his much-vaunted secret weapon. To me it was no secret, for while eating in the Luftwaffe restaurant I had run into several of their experts who had given me my orders in Berlin. They were surprised to find me still in Paris. These men had told me weeks before that "Hitler's Toy" was ready to be used at any moment.

The German propaganda machine worked full blast on these weapons, describing the colossal damage and claiming that everything within two hundred yards of an explosion had been wiped out. London was in flames, according to Goebbels, and traffic was totally disrupted. I was impressed and worried. I wondered if it could be true.

Even von Grunen said to me:

"Fritz, this is such a fearsome weapon that I am afraid the British will begin to use gas in retaliation. Why, the blast effect is so terrific that it even penetrates into the deepest shelters."

"Let us hear what the British have to say about it," I suggested.

We went back to the flat in the company of the sardonic Krauser, and the wireless was switched on. First came the usual war news, followed by a brief announcement that the Germans had at last launched their much boosted secret weapon against southern England. A few casualties and some damage were reported, nothing more. Von Grunen and Krauser were furious at the casual reference. They sprang from their chairs in anger at what they termed the hypocrisy of the British.

"They simply cannot write it off like that," snapped von Grunen. "Wait and see! There will be a public outcry in England against it! The truth must out, and it is terrible for the British. We will soon bring them to their knees."

These words expressed the opinion of most leading Germans. They wanted to believe, and did believe, the most terrible and gruesome stories of the devastation caused by the V-l. When the next British newscast came through, everyone clustered around the set. Again they were in for a disappointment, for the same noncommittal communique was issued.

It was one of the best pieces of propaganda of the B.B.C., this deprecation of the "doodlebug." The German likes to hear his victim's cries of anguish, and hates to have his spectacular efforts ignored. Besides, the German propagandists had as good as told their own people that they could win the war with this weapon. When they eventually realized the truth that the V-weapons had come too late, their reaction alone would spell the end.

It was actually not long before the High Command itself wrote off the effectiveness of V-l, though it probably continued to place some hopes on the pending V-2. Meantime, it was preparing to yield some of its conquests.

◆ ◆ ◆

It was in July, after the Allied beachheads had been established in Normandy, that von Grunen called me into his office. He said: "The chief here considers that you understand the psychology of the British, and he wants us to start recruiting suitable agents to remain behind in Paris to work for us should the Allies capture the city. They will be used only for general intelligence work, and you can train them in radio and codes. He suggests we approach some of the hotels, for if the American and British armies ever do get to Paris they will obviously take over the same big hotels which we have occupied."

At the Ambassador Hotel was a friendly old porter who spoke perfect English. He had lived for many years in Jersey and in London. I thought it might be a good idea to approach him. On the pretext, therefore, that I wanted him to buy me some cognac and liqueurs, I got the old boy to come to the rue Miromesnil. There I put my proposition to him, something like this:

"As you know, every nation has an intelligence service, which employs people to collect information of different kinds. The rewards for this work are high, and the dangers are not great. Now, supposing the Germans were to evacuate Paris, they might conceivably leave behind a group of agents, some for sabotage, others for intelligence work. You, as a porter at the Ambassador Hotel, could be of great service to us if the Allied troops decided to occupy this hotel. Your work would consist in compiling a list of the officers and, if possible, of the divisions from which they came. If any of them continually phoned a certain number, this would be valuable, for it might lead to the discovery of their headquarters. You would be thoroughly trained in this work, and would receive twelve thousand francs per month. Now this is a rough outline of the proposition. Think it over carefully. If you are not interested, you are free to go. But in that case, you had better forget about this interview, and, above all, tell nobody about it."

The old man looked increasingly worried as I spoke. When I had finished he began, in hesitating tones:

"Monsieur, I am an old man, and am past the age for fighting. I do not want to die an unnatural death. At the end of my life I do not want to be considered a traitor to my own country. Please, monsieur, you have been very kind to me, let me go. Do not tell me any more in case you involve me."

I called von Grunen and a young lieutenant from our bureau into the room and explained what had happened. Von Grunen gave the old man a drink, and spent another half-hour trying to convince him that he was wrong in throwing away so golden an opportunity. The old boy was respectful, but adamant. We had to let him go.

We next tried to contact two girls whom we had met several times at the Luftwaffe restaurant. For a week I carried on a mild flirtation with one of them, and von Grunen and I took them around to various cabarets.

Both were young and attractive blondes. Hélène, the older one, had been employed in the German Work Bureau in Paris, and had had a violent love affair with a young Luftwaffe officer, which had lasted until he was shot down and killed. She was tall and athletic. Her friend was half Italian and half French, with unusual coloring, for she was blonde and blue-eyed. She had been a dancer and later a secretary to a German businessman. Both these girls were now unemployed, and appeared to be enjoying life among the demi-monde.

Hélène had already asked me if it were possible to find her some work. I now invited her to come to my flat. I put the German proposition to her, and she jumped at it. I arranged to pay her eight thousand francs a month, with a promise of ten thousand when she had finished her training.

Von Grunen himself had given me instructions as to her work. In the event of the Allies enlarging their bridgeheads, she was to be left in a town directly in the path of their advance. She was to be given a camouflaged wireless transmitter. She would endeavor to get employment with the Allies, contact Allied officers, identify their units and discover their troop movements. She also was to make a list of provisional signs of transport. This information was then to be wirelessed to us wherever we might be.

All this was agreeable to the fair Hélène. Her only preoccupation appeared to be how much she could make out of it. She asked me whether—should she be able to contact any F.F.I. personnel in Paris and betray them—she would be suitably rewarded. Another girl friend of hers, she said, was working for the Gestapo in tracking down the Maquis. By pretending to be anti-German, this girl had penetrated different underground movements and then sold her information to the Germans for a high price. I told Hélène that we were not interested in the Maquis, but only in her abilities as a military spy.

She signed a contract, and I witnessed it. From then on she came twice a day, morning and afternoon, and I gave her morse code training. She learned extraordinarily quickly. In three days she had mastered the alphabet, and in six days she had a speed of twenty words a minute—an accomplishment that usually takes from six weeks to two months.

Another person whom von Grunen roped in was a German bookseller from Nantes. This man was married to a French woman. During the bombing of Nantes by the Allies he had lost not only his foot but his business; and his wife, who was pregnant at the time, had been severely wounded. He felt especially bitter toward the Allies. He agreed to work for the German Secret Service, and as he had lived in France for many years and knew the type of people the Germans could rely on, he was assigned to do the recruiting.

♦ ♦ ♦

It seemed odd to me that at this early stage the Germans should be preparing for the occupation of Paris by the Allies. The landing was barely fourteen days old and had been thoroughly played down in the French press. Meanwhile, huge convoys of German troops and tanks were passing through Paris. Photographs of Allied prisoners were crowding the pages of the newspapers, and one batch had been marched through the capital on their way to internment camp. Clever propaganda announced the huge losses sustained by the British and Americans at sea, in the air and on land. The note was one of such sustained confidence that it seemed impossible that the invaders could carry on. Soon they would surely be pushed back into the sea.

Whatever Goebbels said, however, or whatever Hitler thought, the German High Command must have realized how impossible it was to hold Eisenhower's forces; hence its frantic haste in recruiting agents to stay behind. Von Grunen himself volunteered for such a job, though I imagine that this offer was made under the influence of too much brandy. He proposed taking over an antique shop and passing himself off as a Frenchman. He would be the commanding officer of the other spies, and if I stayed in Paris, I would be his assistant.

Alerts became more frequent as the battle on the coast developed; every day and night now the sirens sounded. It was like Berlin! Bombs could be heard dropping on the various military targets on the outskirts of the city, and flak filled the sky. One day, a magnificent formation of some hundred Flying Fortresses came sailing across Paris. They flew at about six thousand feet, and how they weathered the storm of flak I do not know, for it seemed to burst right among them. On they went, however, in stately contempt. Several were hit; two made arcs in the sky and plummeted to destruction. Several airmen came floating down to earth. But the air-borne armada proceeded on its way.

While all this was in progress the crowds beneath gaped and gasped at the audacity of the Americans. In the Boulevard des Italiens, where I was standing, the police were trying to force the unwilling crowds to take cover in the Metro and other air raid shelters. It was a punishable offense for any German soldier to walk in the street during an alarm. As soon as the sirens wailed they could be seen running to the nearest bunkers, while the French urchins grinned and jeered.

Paris, like Berlin, was full of every type of soldier at this time: Cossacks with their long swords and fur hats, Poles, Czechs—and I even saw some Japanese officers. Strangely enough, this did not surprise me nearly so much as when I encountered a group of Frenchmen in the uniform of the Boche, swaggering along the streets and followed by the curses of their countrymen.

Staying at the Ambassador Hotel were many Spaniards from the Blue Division, which had been fighting on the Eastern front. I was told that they were good soldiers, and brave in battle. The one snag was that as soon as they were rigged out with the excellent German army kit, they went out and sold it. One regiment had been fitted out three times before it actually reached the front line. The Spaniards must have found a good market, for they always had plenty of money and spent most of their time getting drunk.

Since it seemed that I would be staying in Paris for some time, I decided to buy myself some clothes. The Germans had organized a black market for themselves, which one could use only on producing a military pass. Once this was done, everything could be had on demand—tea at 5,000 francs a kilo; coffee at 3,000 francs; soap at 120 francs a bar, and so on. I went there and bought some cloth at 2,500 francs a yard. It was good English pre-war material.

All the stalls in this black market were owned by Italians or Frenchmen, who received permission from the Germans to carry on their illegal trading. Around the stalls were grouped officers and soldiers of all ranks, buying everything they could lay their hands on and putting their purchases into their little black briefcases. How much plunder was taken out of France and the occupied territories in those small bags we will never know.

A girl called Lilli whom I knew, and who worked at the Lido cabaret, heard that I needed a tailor, and took me to one in Romainville. I had a shaky feeling as I passed the gates of the grim fort where I had been interned. Where was Anthony Faramus? And what had happened to the other prisoners?

When Lilli introduced me to the tailor she said I was a Norwegian, for he was a Jew who was not wearing a star, but was keeping his real identity hidden from the Germans. As soon as I spoke to him, his eyes lit up with surprise and joy, for he recognized my English accent. He inquired if I knew England, and I told him I had lived there for two years.

"You know a place called Golders Green?" he asked.

I nodded. He then produced some photographs of his family. They were obviously Jewish, and I warned him not to show the photograph to any stranger.

"I may be a German for all you know," I told him. He laughed.

"Sir, you are a friend, I am sure," he said. He urged me to have a drink, and was so pleased with me that he would have kissed me if I had let him. I left him, but not before I had given him a warm handshake.

◆   ◆   ◆

I now paid another visit to Arab Amalou's café. It was called, appropriately, "Le Refuge." After closing time I was having supper with him and his wife when there was a knock on the door. Four customers, all friends, appeared for a final drink. One of them began a conversation with me, and appeared puzzled when he heard my English accent. He sat with his fingers to his face, surreptitiously giving me the V-sign. I did not respond, and he then started a political discussion.

He was a young, fiery-eyed type, and claimed that his mother was English; but his own English was atrocious. He had been in the Maquis, fighting in Haute Savoie. He claimed that owing to lack of support in arms and money, they had been forced to surrender to the Germans. For this he blamed the British.

"We fought to our last bullet, and many of my comrades were killed," he said. "I was put in a camp for two weeks, and then the Germans offered us our freedom if we would work for them. We accepted—why fight for Allies who do not support you? I am now driving a lorry for them, and I am content. Even if the British or Americans do take Paris, what kind of a life is it going to be for us Frenchmen? We will be expected to treat them as the great liberators, and cheer them as heroes. They will have the best of everything, like the Germans, only perhaps they will not be so polite."

I spoke a few words with his two companions. One was from Alsace-Lorraine, and the other from Dijon. They seemed all to be of the same mind, not caring whether the Allies liberated them or not. They were determined youngsters, and in the dim light of the café, as they sipped their cognac, I felt sorry for them, for they were men who had lost an ideal.

Two days after my visit to Amalou, I ran into Herr Krauser. He greeted me with his usual smooth cordiality and invited me to dine with von Grunen and himself. Whether or not it was an accident that he chose the Latin Quarter for his display of hospitality, or because he had been informed that I had visited Amalou, I will never know. Naturally, I took precautions to hide the fact that I had been there. Krauser took us to another Arab club, within a stone's throw of Amalou's.

Here, a dancing girl wriggled her belly, and the guests put coins down the neck of her costume and tucked notes in the elastic of her tights. Over our drinks, Krauser began talking of other places he knew in the Latin Quarter. After mentioning one or two *boites* he added, "I know of another quite amusing place called 'Le Refuge.' We must go there some time, it is a lot of fun."

This was Amalou's place, of course, and after my conversation with him, I did not wish to be confronted with him while in the company of my two German colleagues. I replied as nonchalantly as possible that I did not object to going anywhere for another drink, but this type of club was not really my idea of fun. Besides, I had an appointment at the Lido with a girl friend. I pressed them both to come along and share a bottle of champagne with me. Luckily, von Grunen agreed. It may have been my imagination, but I thought I saw a knowing smile on Krauser's lips.

On Frau von Lipper's birthday, it was von Grunen's turn to give a dinner party for her at the "Scheherazade." It was clear to me, from the way he courted this lady, that he was in love with her. I brought her some flowers, and he presented her with a magnificent watch. The meal cost about 14,000 francs, but von Grunen did not care. It was probably my money, anyway!

I say this because I never kept check on how much I had in my own account—I simply asked von Grunen for money, and it was given to me. For some time I had suspected him of feathering his own nest. He had only his *Rittmeister's* pay, yet his wallet was always stuffed with 1,000-franc notes. However, I was in no position to complain. Nor did I care; for he was my bulwark against any too inquisitive member of the Gestapo. I knew full well that, even in my absence, he would fight in my behalf against anyone who cast aspersions on my sincerity in working for the Germans, and that was enough for me.

Von Grunen was sentimental over small things. His own birthday was on June 28. Without mentioning this fact, he took me to a cabaret. He had ordered a birthday cake, and produced it as a surprise when we were halfway through a bottle of champagne. When I asked what was the occasion for this festivity, he replied:

"Why, Fritz, have you forgotten it is my birthday?"

He was obviously hurt that I had not remembered. I apologized. Next day, I went out and bought him a small ivory statuette as a present. He had it engraved as a remembrance of our stay in Paris.

On July 27, von Grunen telephoned me in a state of great excitement. "Fritz," he said, "you are definitely going at last. We start tomorrow for

Holland. You are going to fly with another squadron. Start checking up on your codes. Also, run briefly through your instructions, so that you are certain you understand your mission."

Von Grunen then told me to meet him at the Hôtel Lutétia, which was Secret Service Headquarters. Now a special pass was needed to get inside the building, and I had not been issued such a pass. Before I could tell this to von Grunen, he had rung off. I walked down to the hotel.

Outside the main entrance stood an armed guard who demanded to see everyone's papers. I was looking in through the door when suddenly I caught sight of Hannen, one of the men I had known in Nantes. I called him by name as I dashed up the steps past the guard, seized his hand and started a rapid conversation with him. The guard, thinking I was one of the staff, did not challenge me for my papers. After a brief conversation, Hannen left me and I made my way into the bar. I had sat there leisurely drinking for about a quarter of an hour when von Grunen entered.

"Good Lord!" he cried. "How on earth did you get in here without papers?"

When I told him, he went into another room and reappeared with two other officers. Both of them laughed heartily and told me that although they had been coming here for two years, never once had they been allowed to pass inside without producing their identity cards.

These officers knew of my mission, and we were discussing details of it when in walked the venomous Krauser. He shook hands all round, took a seat and listened, wearing his disturbing half-smile, to our plans. Von Grunen then asked him if he wanted me to proceed with the idea of leaving a camera and £.1,000 near London for another agent to pick up. Krauser replied that he did. Then, when I received a wireless message for him, I was to hide the money and camera in a safe place. His department would then inform their agent where to pick them up. If I did not hear from them regarding this agent, I could keep the money and use it for my own purposes.

Next day, in the company of von Grunen and Krauser, I was driven to the Lutetia, where a farewell luncheon was to be held in my honor. Colonel Gautier and two officers of his staff were present. Luncheon was served in Gautier's office, amid maps and official-looking documents. All the men I had met came in to say goodby, and the room was thronged with well-wishers. As they pressed my hand they nearly all managed to whisper:

"Now don't forget to mention me in Berlin. Tell them how I helped you."

The colonel made a short speech in which he acknowledged my services, and told the company that if my present mission succeeded it might have a profound effect on the war.

"It will also be a triumph for our Secret Service," he concluded.

The whole occasion seemed to me utterly unreal as I replied, thanking them for their kindness. Krauser alone remained silent during these orations. When my health and future success were toasted, he raised his glass but did not drink.

Now, were we really going? Yes, this time it was true! We were off! The last glimpse I had of the chiefs of the Lutetia was the group of them waving from the front steps as we drove away in the car.

◆　◆　◆

We spent that night in Brussels, and next morning went on to Utrecht. We were heavily armed, and had been warned to expect air attacks. The roads and rail centers along our route had been truly battered; wreckage of transport littered the countryside.

From the commandant at Utrecht we learned that the squadron which was to fly me was billeted at Den Helder. After many inquiries and false turnings, we tracked down its headquarters. These were in a large country house in the center of a wood, well camouflaged by the trees. Sunk in various parts of this wood were the petrol tanks, widely separated from each other and the outlying buildings. In the drive stood several high-powered cars belonging to the Luftwaffe staff. I was taken in to meet the major commanding the squadron. He was a tall, gray-haired, middle-aged man. He called in a lieutenant, a baby-faced youngster of twenty or so.

"This is the pilot who is flying you," he said. The machine and crew with which I was to make the trip had that day arrived from Berlin. The crew had been trained in night flying.

We walked out to our cars and drove off to view the plane. It was a Junkers machine, much like the one in which I had made my first flight, but more high-powered. A mechanic was working on the trap door. I inspected his work carefully, for I did not want to get stuck again in the hole as had happened on my first flight to England. I mentioned this to the major, and he agreed to have the hole enlarged as much as possible.

We went back to the mess, and I met the other two members of the crew. Both of them were young, between nineteen and twenty, and one of them was going on leave as soon as this trip was over. The idea of the journey did not seem to worry them much. Their main concern was how quickly they could do the job, so that their pal could get back and catch his leave train. All of them had flown at the Russian front.

The pilot was a shy young man, who sat quietly apart, saying little.

When I invited him to have a drink he apologized saying he was a teetotaller, and sipped a glass of milk instead.

We waited in a pleasant lounge, and had coffee. Weather reports and orders were continually being brought to the commandant. About an hour before midnight, he bade me come up to his office and get dressed for the flight. With von Grunen, I entered the room and stripped. I strapped my money belt around my shoulders. Then, climbing into my coveralls, I was ready to go.

We drove to the airport, where the roar of motors could be heard. On the way von Grunen told me that I would probably have no difficulty in getting through to London. The capital would be in a turmoil, for a heavy raid was to coincide with my landing in the eastern counties. I made a last-minute arrangement to send my first message three days after my arrival.

When we stepped out of the car my three flying companions came forward, saluted, shook hands and wished me a comfortable journey. One of them unpacked my parachute and pack, and strapped it on me.

Now the engines were roaring louder and flames shot from the exhausts. In the flickering light the plane looked like some hideous black vulture. A final handshake from von Grunen, who shouted *"Glück, viel Glück,"* and I clambered up the ladder to my appointed place.

The door slammed, and we moved off.

Three minutes later we were air-borne for England.

21

JOURNEY'S END

THE ROAD home was rough, and the plane swerved, dived and swooped up again like a mad bird. The whine of the engine and the violence of our movement added to the sensation of terrific speed.

As we left the ground, I had noticed that recognition lights shone on our wing tips, and as we flew we dropped recognition signals so that the German flak batteries should know who we were.

These were signs that the Germans were now intruders even in their own sky, and that the Allies had become the masters. My only fear was that this mastery would be so complete that the German plane which was carrying me home would be shot out of the sky by my countrymen before it reached the shores of England.

Our plan was to fly low over the North Sea and, when the coast was reached, to zoom up to a few thousand feet. This was in order to counteract the radio location devices.

Soon, we were scudding low over the sea. The wireless operator next to me continually tapped out messages. He looked at me and grinned. I smiled back—a sickly effort. I felt sick, anyway, with the continual slipping and swerving of the plane.

We flew past three ships, slowly steaming without lights toward the Channel. It was impossible for us to distinguish their nationality. Then I caught sight of searchlights waving frantically; there seemed to be hundreds of them. It was England! For some minutes we kept low and flew parallel to them. Then the pilot turned the plane and headed direct at the searchlights. "Hold fast," he shouted, as we screamed through the air. He went into a steep climb, which felt like going up in an extremely fast-moving elevator. As we climbed, we twisted and turned, always to avoid those inquisitive beams of the searchlights.

"Wir sind jetzt über England," boomed a triumphant voice in the

telephone, and again I heard the Stuka war cry.

When a searchlight cast its feeler in our direction (and it was often), the pilot would take us into a fast dive, turning around and around the beam like a corkscrew. This made me feel sick again, and I wanted desperately to vomit. Suddenly I saw a plane to my left, a couple of hundred feet away.

"Night fighter!" I shouted into the telephone.

"Where?" the wireless operator shouted back.

I pointed.

"No, no," he said coolly, "that is just an ordinary plane."

He then sat back and twiddled his thumbs. Sweat ran down my back. Then he stiffened in his seat.

"*Nacht-Jäger!*" he shouted.

I was suddenly aware of a black shape without lights, which was coming toward us at a terrific pace. It passed some hundred feet from our tail, apparently without noticing us.

A tap on the head—time to prepare for the jump. Off came my telephone, and on went the crash helmet. Another tap—it was time to go.

I pulled the lever, and the door beneath me dropped away. At that moment, something hit the plane—possibly stray flak from some battery far below. Through the hole I plunged, feet first, keeping my hands in front of my face to avoid hitting the instrument board. I dropped clear of the plane, which spun off into the darkness. A short drop—*zack*—my chute was open!

I swung in the empty sky, like a pendulum in a vast clock. It was too much for my rebellious stomach. I leaned over the side of my harness and spewed over England.

Slowly I came down. It was a perfect night, and the countryside was spread out below me. White wisps of clouds hid part of it from my view, but I caught sight of a clump of trees. Desperately, I kicked my legs in an attempt to steer clear of it. A gust of wind caught the parachute and carried me on. Then a hedge came into view. I dropped over this, right into the middle of a narrow country road. I made a hard landing, and was almost knocked out.

I lay there for full ten minutes, then picked myself up. My arm hurt, but it was not fractured. I undid my chute, and cut the pack free. I took off my coveralls and boots, replacing the latter by the shoes I had brought along. I cut away the sack from the briefcase, and started marching down the road. The briefcase was heavy, and the road long. Sometimes I carried it on my head, porter fashion, and frequently I changed it from arm to arm. Suddenly I heard footsteps, and I ducked behind a hedge. The footsteps hurried closer, and I knew that several people were approaching. Then I heard voices.

"The bastard must be somewhere near here," said one of them.

I realized that the hunt was on.

◆ ◆ ◆

I walked and crawled across fields. Everything was absolutely quiet. Occasionally a dog barked, and then I heard the welcome sound of freight cars moving. I saw a line of telegraph posts, decided which way London was, and made my way toward the track. I began to trudge along it toward London. Suddenly, to my right, I heard a car draw up, and a moment later a powerful spotlight was playing across the fields. I fell flat on my face beside the track. As I lay there, I realized that a general alarm was out and that distance was now the only thing that mattered.

The moment the car lights withdrew, I started pounding down the track, head down, clutching my heavy case, feeling absolutely fagged out but determined to put as many miles between me and my pursuers as I could. I ran and ran, and when I was near exhaustion I stopped for breath, got my wind back and ran on. Far away, at the end of the track, I could see a little one-horse station. I put out my last strength to reach it.

As I approached, I saw the inevitable searchlight probing the undergrowth. I realized what that meant, and decided to make a detour. I shot off to the left, fell into a ditch and buried myself in mud. I continued, still keeping my distance of the flashlights. I crawled over several walls, and went through several people's allotments. By this time, footprints were unimportant, besides being unidentifiable. I stumbled on, sometimes squatting on a wall for a breather. At length I found myself in a cemetery. I glanced at my watch—it was four o'clock,

I was cold and hungry and frightened. I found a vault with an iron gate, climbed over the top of it, got inside and looked around. It was empty, so I made a little fire of twigs, and camped down for the night. Here in the cemetery, life and confidence began to return to me....

◆ ◆ ◆

Six hours later, I found myself once again at Liverpool Street Station during the morning rush hour. The moment I set foot on the platform, I was aware of the curious tension that pervaded London. There was an air of expectancy about the hurrying crowds which made one feel that everyone's ears were cocked, even above the noise of shunting trains. Confidently this time, I made my way to the same buffet, and as I was munching my first breakfast sandwich I heard the sirens wail over London.

A silence seemed to descend upon the place, though everyone made a desperate effort to behave normally. Then, sure enough, came the distant rumble, growing to a full-throated roar. All the stories that I had heard of "Hitler's Toy" rushed back into my brain, and I felt a moment of near panic. Looking at the other faces, I saw the tremendous self-control that was being exercised. Teacups were grasped more tightly, knuckles were clenched white, and forced conversation was made. The English were refusing to acknowledge the existence of the doodlebug just above their heads.

The engine cut ... the silence was appalling ... I counted seven. There was a God-awful crash, and a little Cockney turned round to me and said, "That bleedin' 'Itler don't arf make a row."

I knew then that I was really back in London.

At this time the flying bombs were coming over thick and fast. The alerts merged into one another, so that there was no "all clear." I rented a room in Kensington. On the first night in my new abode, I heard the approaching note of another doodlebug, and waited for the engine to cut. It did so, apparently immediately overhead, and after the usual frightful pause I was blasted out of bed by a bomb. It had landed only fifty yards away.

I now set up my transmitter, and on the third day sent over my first message, simply saying:

"Safe. Will contact in seven days."

A week later I began to receive continual inquiries about the progress I was making in getting the U-boat radio location device. I kept telling them that I was trying to discover where this was being manufactured. One part of my mission was to find out about this detonating instrument which, on explosion, struck waves against the side of a submarine. The waves were measured, and gave the exact location of the U-boat.

I reported to the Germans that I thought I had located the factory which was manufacturing this device in Birmingham. However, as I was not quite certain that this was the gadget they wanted, I proposed carrying out a burglary there. If I was successful, I would send the plans through to Portugal by a seaman I had bribed. This seaman would not know the contents of the small package he carried. I intended to photostat everything with my camera, and simply send the film.

A few days later, I was obliged to send this message: "Have been unable to obtain detonator device plans."

I now began to have evidence that the wind had changed. The tone of the transmissions from Germany became completely different. One day I received the odd request that I should go to Warboys to report on the mustering of planes for the bombing of Germany.

I replied that this was impossible, and then received the message:

"Will you leave £1,000 and camera in suitable place and inform us where."

I replied:

"Need money for my work in England. Expense greater than expected."

When the fall of Paris was imminent, the Germans transferred my receiving station from there to Hamburg. Hamburg was at that time the headquarters of Himmler, chief of the S.S. This meant, of course, that I was more or less directly under his control.

I sent a message which ran:

"Rumor of gas main blowing up by mysterious explosions in London. Do you want me to investigate?"

To this there was no reply. It now almost seemed that the Germans were no longer interested in the messages I was sending, for their next request read:

"Report on divisions leaving England and place of embarkation."

Now this mission had never been discussed with me, and I took it that my masters were stalling. I immediately replied with an indignant refusal, saying that it formed no part of my contract. To this I got no direct reply. Instead, after a particularly heavy raid on Bremen, came the last message from Germany which I was to receive—a curious and rather touching one from von Grunen himself. It read:

"Regret delay in answering your messages but lost my house in bombing raid. Luck." It was signed "Stephan"—his first name.

This was my last personal communication with von Grunen, and I have never heard a word of him since. If ever he reads this, I am sure that he will understand....

[*Some further facts about Chapman's second return to England, censored by the War Office and reconstructed by George Voigt*]

CHAPMAN'S second return to England was no less hazardous than his first. His liaison with British Intelligence was waiting to be taken up again. There was no problem in that regard. But few people in England knew of this; and certainly none that he could contact immediately on landing. And now that he was deeply involved in intelligence work he was on his own. A captured agent is a deserted agent. It's only with difficulty that he can gain the aid of the intelligence organization with which he works. He couldn't go to the local police, identify himself and ask their aid in getting to London. He had to make his own way safely and undetected to London before he could re-establish his connection with MI5.

After his presence in the countryside became known, perhaps again through the watchful efforts of a local farmer on guard against parachutists, he had to escape the search net thrown out for him. There was no place he could turn to for help, no explanations that would be readily accepted if he was captured. And at this crucial stage in the war, he might not even have a chance to do any explaining if his hunters caught up with him.

The story of his return this time, of the pursuit and narrow escape, didn't suffer too much under the War Office censor's blue pencil. It could be told, providing he did not reveal that he was returning as a patriot and agent for his country. It was a badly shaken and thankful Eddie Chapman who finally reached London to re-establish the tenuous ties that made the difference between a traitor spying for the enemy and a patriotic double-agent in the service of his country.

Chapman had been gone from England a long time. It has never been revealed whether or not the War Office had been concerned over the length of his absence, or whether doubts had arisen in their minds over his trustworthiness while he was gone. We do not know whether he was ever suspected of desertion, of running out on his country to enjoy the fruits of the successful deception perpetrated for him by British Intelligence. Even though he retained some contact with British Intelligence during his months on the Continent and in Norway and was gathering information for the British all that time, some suspicion surely must have arisen during his absence of a year and a half.

Chapman's character and history were not the kind to inspire confidence or receive a high rating of trustworthiness in official circles. And some suspicions must have lingered even after Chapman reappeared in London and resumed his services with the British. After all, there was no guarantee that he had not been as cooperative and helpful to the Germans as he had been with the English. It is safe to presume that he was put through as lengthy and searching a series of grillings by the British on his return as he had received from the Germans when he returned to them after the De Havilland hoax. And he passed the test just as successfully as he had with the Nazis.

Any suspicions that might have been held against him dissolved in the flow of questions and answers with which the British intelligence officials probed every corner of his mind and checked every detail of his activities, from the day he left England aboard the Lisbon-bound freighter to the day of his return. Of course, he never planted the explosive coal to blow up that freighter. With the movement of ships shrouded in secrecy during the war, and with unidentified ships blowing up at sea regularly and frequently, there had been no way for the Germans to find out whether that freighter had exploded after steaming out of Lisbon. Finally, Chapman was allowed again to set up his transmitter and get in touch with the Germans. His first message reassured them about his return: "Safe. Will contact in seven days."

But the grilling continued. Efforts to determine whether Chapman was safe or suspect was only one reason for the long sessions of questions and answers. More important was information Chapman could give about the enemy. In his long travels about Europe, from Lisbon to Oslo, with freedom and privileges that few if any agents could enjoy, Chapman had soaked up a wealth of highly valuable secrets. And with the Allied armies pushing their attack on all fronts, every scrap of intelligence fitted a need somewhere. Under the expert guidance of his War Office overseers, Chapman drew from the jumbled mass of information in his head all the vital facts, the remembered and half-forgotten bits accumulated during his eighteen-month tour of Naziland. The questions he answered were many:

What are conditions in Berlin? How is the city carrying on under the bombings? How is the morale of the people? How strong is the will to resist in Norway? Who are the Quislings there, and who the patriots? How strongly will France support the Allied invasion armies? How close to the end will the Nazis be in control to prevent French aid to the Allies? Who are the Nazi intelligence agents in Lisbon, in Madrid, in Paris? What are the names, addresses and assignments of the new spies recruited to remain behind in Paris after the Germans evacuated it? What are the conditions of transport, food, supplies in Europe? What propaganda seems most effective? What military actions are most disturbing to the Germans? What German units are in what areas? How do their equipment and troops look and act? What seems of greatest concern to the Germans: some Allied military or propaganda tactic, or German troop morale and supply, or home front morale, or conditions in occupied countries where the Nazi hold is fast weakening?

To these and hundreds of other questions Chapman could contribute much in the way of answers. His sessions with German technical experts (discussing his assignments regarding radar and finding devices, rockets and remote-controlled aircraft) were most revealing. They showed what most concerned the Germans as well as how much fact and how much fancy went into their knowledge of the subjects. The German theory that Allied planes from certain bases in England always bombed specific targets in Germany was valuable knowledge for Britain, whether or not it was true. If the theory was true, the system could be changed; if untrue, it could be encouraged, thus upsetting German air defenses.

When the days of questioning were over and Chapman was once again drained of the last bit of information circulating in his brain, he once again set up his transmitter. The pattern of his work, like the pattern of his life, resumed exactly as it had been when he played the same role during his previous mission to England. Under the same restrictions, as before, he lived as normal a life as possible. He enjoyed himself as best he could with the stack of pounds given him by the Germans, and was careful not to meet too many people, being neither so active nor so secretive as to raise suspicions or attract attention. His value to British intelligence remained the same: he was again a vehicle for feeding misinformation to the enemy camp. Eddie Chapman turned over all his messages, and sent only those composed or approved by his overseers. But this time the value of his role was more immediately and dramatically measurable. It could be measured in lives and property saved, and in the frustration it brought to the Germans in their efforts to smash England with their new V-rockets.

As anxious as the Germans were for information on the Allied radar and sound detection devices, on rockets and remote-controlled aircraft, their prime concern remained the efficacy of their V-1 buzzbombs. To the German mind, the outcome of the war depended on this fantastic new terror weapon they had created. As they reeled back in defeat from the areas of their earlier conquests, the German High Command instituted a crash program for the V-rockets. Development and manufacture of the rockets received highest priority in the German defense effort as the buzzbomb assault on England was pushed to the greatest possible intensity. The Germans counted on it with desperate faith to swing the balance back in their favor and bring them victory at the eleventh hour. When the BBC continued to deprecate the effectiveness of the assault with nonchalant reports of minor damage and casualties, with no note of alarm, the German High Command screamed for true information on the rocket assault. British intelligence, through Eddie Chapman, gave them their "information."

The Germans were never completely satisfied about the accuracy of their new weapon. Rushed into service under a crash program, in almost frantic haste to stave off defeat, the V-1's did not have sufficient testing to provide all the data the Germans desired on the exact control of a launched rocket. In their ultra- thorough minds the fear of a margin of error in the accuracy of their firing devices always existed. And with every rocket available being thrown into the cross-Channel attack, the only source of such information was someone on the target scene. That someone was Eddie Chapman.

Chapman's job was to radio the Germans exact information on the landings of as many V-1 bombs as he could cover. He was to provide the exact location and the exact fraction of a second in which each rocket landed. Any other information he was told to send—was the rocket a dud, did it explode immediately on landing or was the explosion delayed, extent of damage it caused, amount of disruption, numbers killed—was strictly corollary. The Nazis wanted above all to know to the second when a bomb exploded, and where. From this information the Germans could deduce whether their calculations at the launching end were correct and whether the rockets were traveling accurately to their selected target. Chapman was expected to scout around London, with a stop watch, gathering this information. This would have been a tiresome, exacting and dangerous job. But it wasn't for Chapman. British intelligence did the work for him. And in doing so they pulled off another neat and brilliant coup that saved an inestimable number of lives and robbed the German buzzbomb assault of much of its force and effectiveness.

The Germans aimed for the heart of London: the heavily populated residential districts, which usually meant working-class districts; the congested old City of London where the business life is concentrated, the southeast dock areas, the western section where government and military planning were located. The reports that British intelligence gave Chapman to send systematically misreported the time and location of bomb landings, forcing the Germans to recalculate and readjust the aim of their launching devices, thus greatly widening their margin of error.

The intention of this deception was to move the Germans' center of fire away from the vital target areas they were aiming at. The misinformation had to be worked out carefully to the very fraction of a second. The reported times and locations of rocket explosions had to be off sufficiently to cause the Germans to change their sights. But they could not be so far off as to raise German suspicions. It was impossible to move the center of fire entirely out of London, into some uninhabited country area. That would have been ideal, but the Germans never would have believed the reports. The margin of error could not be great. But gradually, as the Germans accepted the reports and altered their aiming calculations, the center of fire moved into more sparsely populated outlying districts of London where the rockets killed fewer people and caused less property damage and disruption to the life of the city.

While this highly technical deception was in progress, and beginning to show results, Chapman received an expected but disheartening message. The V-1 attack was being interrupted and things would be quiet for a week or so, he was informed. He knew what that meant; so did his intelligence overseers. It meant the big switchover from V-1 to V-2 bombs was at hand. It would take at least a week to alter the launching devices to handle the V-2's and to replace the supply of rockets at the launching sites.

But the people of London, including even many highly placed persons in government, didn't know this. The silence of the days that followed, so ominous to those who knew that it would soon be broken by the increased fury of the new and much more destructive V-2's, was greeted by most Londoners with joyous enthusiasm. They saw the silence as a victory: the V-bomb attack had been broken.

In London pubs, in newspapers and even in government circles the victory was proclaimed and discussed. Whether the launching sites had been destroyed or captured, whether factories making the doodlebugs had been bombed out of operation, or whether London's anti-aircraft defenses had stopped the attack, nobody knew or cared. The fact was that the bombing had stopped. The skies no longer were filled with the terrible rumble and roar of the doodlebugs. Gone were the agonizing seconds of silence, the terrific, earth-shuddering explosions. There was no longer a constant day and night alert. Obviously, the Germans had shot their final bolt, and lost. Their highly touted secret terror weapon that was to bring Britain to her knees had fizzled. It was a major victory worth being happy about. That was the belief and attitude of most Londoners during the ominously silent interim. Then—came the V-2's.

The work of British Intelligence to move the center of fire away from the city's most vital areas didn't have to start from scratch with the V-2's. The effects of the deception already established with the V-1's carried over to the V-2's to some extent. But the new rockets presented certain new technical aspects to be taken into consideration, demanded a re-evaluation of the possible margin of error within which the times and locations of rocket landings could be misreported. But as the V-2's continued to rumble in from across the Channel, Chapman continued to send the carefully misleading reports on their landings.

The Germans continued to readjust their launching platforms and firing devices to bring the rockets more on target. And the rockets that the Germans thought were blasting away dock areas on the Thames and government buildings in Westminster were more and more frequently tearing up shrubbery in some lonely heath or dissipating their effect among the well-dispersed houses in outlying residential areas. Nobody could estimate how many lives were saved by this successful deception. But the vaunted V-bomb assault was not bringing Britain to her knees and the Germans continued to reel back in defeat on the Continent.

And Eddie Chapman again was having cause to worry. As the Germans were squeezed in on all sides into an ever-narrowing perimeter and the end was written in every dispatch from the war fronts, he saw his fortune withering away with the Wehrmacht. Fifty thousand pounds—more than two hundred thousand dollars by the exchange rates of the day—were slipping away from him with every mile the German army retreated, with every battle they lost. And there was nothing he could do about it.

It now was too late to get over to Europe once again and collect the debt. The Germans, those untrustworthy Nazis who'd broken so many contracts before, were now running out on his contract. It wasn't that Chapman honestly felt the money was due him for services performed. In fact, he was feeling increasing pride in the way he had deceived the Germans and at the same time served his country so well. Even a crook can be a patriot. But Chapman looked on it as sort of a gambling debt. He'd taken a gamble, a wild and dangerous one, for big stakes. He'd won. And a gambling debt is a debt of honor. There was no excuse for reneging on a debt of honor.

It was with considerable bitterness that Eddie Chapman received the order from British authorities to deliver up the thousand pounds he'd brought into England for another agent. Chapman refused to comply. He felt self-righteous, as only an accused criminal with an alibi can feel, when he haughtily turned down the Germans' request that he report on divisions embarking from England. When the end came, with the final message signed "Stephan," he did feel some pangs of regret, for he was honestly touched. His personal regard for von Grunen was real and sincere.

But the end left him bitter to his bowels. He felt deeply wronged, robbed, cheated. The Germans shouldn't have done it to Eddie Chapman. They shouldn't have let him down after all they'd been through together. In his bitterness, he turned around and entered into a long feud with the British War Office, a feud that continues to this day.

POSTSCRIPT

D ESPITE the deeply felt loss of a fifty-thousand-pound fortune, the war didn't really leave Eddie Chapman badly off. He had gained a great deal, in fact. Before the war he had been a master in his criminal trade. Now, if he chose to return to that trade after the war, he was even more accomplished and talented. He'd had an education at the best school in the world. He'd also learned a number of other useful trades: photography, how to navigate a boat through the tricky fjords of Norway, how to deal in international currency, and he was familiar with smuggling. Also, he was now an accomplished linguist: he knew French, German, Norwegian, and a smattering of Dutch. And his record at Scotland Yard was as clean as a choir boy's. If he was ever arrested again, he'd face the court as a first offender. It all added up to a considerable gain.

Chapman also had a story to tell and he soon learned that was an asset too. His war-time experiences were unparalleled. There would be published combat stories by the score, war memoirs by generals, diaries by war correspondents and long, learned treatises by military experts. But no one had a story like his own. Chapman realized this as soon as he began to circulate freely around his old London haunts. His underworld chums were amazed to see him walking about in the open, right past any Bobby or Scotland Yard detective with the innocent air of a man who had never seen a safe door pop open under pressure. But they were even more amazed when he told them how he had accomplished it.

Realizing he had a saleable commodity, and not being averse to having a few admirable and heroic facts known about himself, he decided to take up a literary career and write his war experiences. The story of Eddie Chapman, war hero, doubleagent, in the pay of the Germans but in the service of his country, was written. It appealed to him. But it appalled the War Office. It was then that his feud with the War Office opened. Chapman fired the first shot. He sold the story to a Paris newspaper, the *Etoile de Paris,* one of a rash of short-lived publishing ventures that sprang up and foundered in Paris immediately after the war. In a signed series of articles written in French, he told some of the details, a bare outline, of his story—

how he had duped the Germans while giving invaluable service to England, and indirectly to France.

The War Office jumped in immediately, and asked the *Etoile de Paris* to kill the story. When the editor refused, British officials made representations to the French government, asking help in getting the story stopped. But the French government, having no Official Secrets Act to wield, could not oblige. It had no legal basis for stopping publication of the story.

When the French articles were published, the news reached London and whetted the interest of publishers there. Eddie set himself up in the writing business. He contacted newspaper friends to help him sell the story to London newspapers. He also got an agent and some literary advisers, and proceeded to write a book—this book, which was eventually whipped into shape by Frank Owen. But more than eight years passed between the time he set out to write the story and the time the book was published in England. The War Office stepped in with the Official Secrets Act and balked at publication.

The first time this happened, Chapman was in conference at his Kensington flat. He was discussing with his agent and literary advisers some of the finer points of the writing business (such as how much money he might get out of his book)—and suddenly the War Office was there, represented by some very serious and businesslike men in plainclothes. They read the Official Secrets Act aloud to all present in the room, confiscated all the papers they were working on, informed Chapman he was under arrest and warned the others against publicizing any part of the story Chapman had told them or shown them. The basis of the government case against Chapman was the published series in the *Etoile de Paris*.

Chapman considered all this another dirty trick. He couldn't even tell what a hero he had been! First, he tried to brazen it out. He claimed he had never heard of the Official Secrets Act. The War Office coldly told him that he had—it had been read to him and he had signed an undertaking to observe it, as do all persons working for British Intelligence. Then he turned wily. He told the War Office quite plainly to go to hell, declaring he had never worked for British Intelligence and therefore was not bound by the Official Secrets Act. Actually, he had not been an agent in the true sense because he had never been on the British payroll and had never received a penny of compensation. How could anyone be considered an employee if he never was paid? The War Office had the answer: Chapman's compensation had been substantial. He had received several thousand pounds which, though provided by the Germans, he was allowed to keep by the grace of the British government; and he had had an extremely bad criminal record wiped from the books, saving him from a long prison term which he rightfully had coming.

The matter went to court. Because of the nature of the case it was heard in secret and none of the court testimony or argument offered by either side has ever been made public. Only the verdict is known: Chapman was found guilty of violating the Official Secrets Act. He was fined fifty pounds, plus twenty-five pounds court costs. Actually, he was lucky to get off so easily. When the guilty verdict was returned, he sweated through the agonizing moments that always pass between pronouncement of the verdict and the sentencing. The Officials Secrets Act is an ancient law unrevised from the day when the pound was a much more substantial sum of money than it is today. The maximum penalty on conviction under the Act is one hundred pounds' fine or seven years in prison. Chapman could have gotten the maximum prison term.

So ended, temporarily, the brief writing career of Eddie Chapman. But he never abandoned the intention to get his story published and his feud with the War Office continued, sometimes dying down for periods but eventually flaring up again. Chapman is not a person to be defeated by a mere War Office. He was to try and try again during the next several years.

In the meantime, deprived of a literary career, Chapman had to put some of his other talents to work. It was only a question of which ones to use. He didn't want to go back to the low criminal life—safecracker and common thief—that he had followed before the war. He was above all that now. So he cast about for other pursuits. In doing so he found he had another feud on his hands, with the police. Though he had no criminal record on the books, he still did in the long memories of the police. He found that in whatever business he undertook the police were always there looking over his shoulder.

Chapman went into the shipping business. He bought a war surplus landing craft and started running cargoes between Ireland and France, a suspect man on a suspect shipping route. The police suspected smuggling "Nonsense," said Chapman. "I'm a legitimate shipper. I ship wheat, fresh fruit, things like that. Nothing illegal." But there was a thriving black market along the route he traveled and the police persisted in their suspicions, keeping a close watch over him despite all his protestations.

They took to seeing him off at ports and greeting him on return. And they took all manner of liberties around his boat. They regularly searched his cabin, inspected his cargo and even his personal belongings. But they never caught him at anything illegal and he prospered in the shipping business. Chapman soon exchanged his landing craft for a two-hundred-and-fifty-ton steam vessel. He also bought a Beechcraft airplane "for business trips." He accumulated as much as forty-five thousand pounds. "I won it gambling," declared Chapman.

Soon after Chapman acquired his airplane, police noted that his business flights took him far beyond the bounds of his shipping interests and that his regular flight route was even more suspect than his shipping route. His destination was usually Tangier, that free and open port at the tip of Morocco, the paradise for smugglers, black-marketeers and currency jugglers. Police suspected that Chapman, with his talents, was probably putting the port to all of its possible uses. But try as they would, they couldn't catch him at anything.

At every airport between London and Tangier, whenever he landed he almost always had a police reception committee. He was asked embarrassing questions about his activities, and about the contents of his airplane and even of his pants pockets, especially the pocket he carried his billfold in. Sometimes he was held for hours at airport detention rooms while police questioned him and searched his plane from prop to tail.

Finally, in 1948, the police got him. On a flight back from Tangier he was caught with a thousand illegal dollars on his person. And the police just wouldn't believe his story that he had been paid in dollars on a business deal and planned to turn the money over to the Bank of England immediately on his return to London. He was sent to trial on a currency charge. That started a new page in the police record books. It went into the books as the first charge of law breaking to mar Chapman's clean post-war record.

At lie trial, Chapman got a surprise assist from the War Office. A senior official from the War Office voluntarily appeared as a character witness and testified to Chapman's considerable service during the war. Chapman, the official testified, "was one of the bravest men who served in the last war."

The testimony by the War Office official, helpful as it was to Chapman's case, was actually instrumental in reviving his feud with the War Office. It revived interest in Chapman's war exploits and encouraged him to make another attempt at defying the Official Secrets Act. Maybe now, he thought, he could resume his literary career. He was wrong. On that score the War Office had not budged. The Official Secrets Act would be invoked to the letter. Not a word of Chapman's intelligence activities would be allowed in print and anyone scorning the law would be prosecuted.

Chapman thought the more appropriate word would be *persecuted*. The fact that he had been tried and convicted under the Official Secrets Act was in itself proof that he had worked for British Intelligence. The fact that he was not in jail, either for pre-war criminal activities or war-time treason, was proof. The fact that a high War Office official would testify to his war service was further proof. But the War Office was adamant.

It did not matter how long after the fact it was, or how much circumstantial proof existed of a person's intelligence service, details of that service could not be revealed. The story could not be told. Newspapers that tried to tell the story, as some of them did, had their presses stopped and the printed copies confiscated. Despite such discouragements, Frank Owen set out to write Eddie Chapman's story for him and to get it published. Chapman went on to other endeavors.

The other endeavors took him far afield, geographically and professionally. One day in Tangier, where he was "just holidaying," a friend introduced him to a representative of the Gold Coast government. The Gold Coast, with its ambitious new government, had big plans for improving the country. The plans included extensive construction of housing, docks, roads, public buildings. Quick-witted Eddie saw at once that the Gold Coast was a land of opportunity. He convinced a Dutch construction firm that he, Eddie Chapman, was just the man to exploit this opportunity. In no time at all he was off for Accra, armed with an expense account from the Dutch construction company, with letters of introduction from the Gold Coast officials he'd met in Tangier, and with his usual built-in charm and savvy.

Chapman was a great success on the Gold Coast. His letters of introduction took him into homes that quickly fell under his spell. He worked hard cultivating the people and learning the country and its problems. He soon mastered Twi, the principal native language on the Gold Coast. He was an eminently satisfactory representative for any firm. His list of friends soon included almost everybody in the government, from Prime Minister Nkrumah down to the lowliest secretary. And he soon acquired other companies to represent, another Dutch firm and an English firm.

His income swelled and his companies got contracts. Chapman entertained lavishly, cemented his contacts with wine, and perhaps an occasional gift, as well as with charm. He once chartered an airplane and took thirty-five Gold Coast officials and newspapermen on a tour of Holland. He became so friendly with Prime Minister Nkrumah, a bachelor, that Mrs. Chapman, a highly decorative post-war acquisition, took over much of the work of running the Prime Minister's household, doing his shopping and supervising his menus. Chapman was so successful on the Gold Coast, in fact, that people began to talk.

There were those in Accra who whispered that Chapman spread money as liberally as wine and charm among his Gold Coast government friends.

Chapman ignored the whispers. But in the summer of 1953 he quietly packed his bags and left for a vacation in England. "I'd been down there about two years," he explained at the time. "It was time for a vacation at home." Shortly after he returned to London, the Gold Coast scandals broke. There were accusations of bribery of high government officials in construction contracts. Nkrumah himself was accused of accepting a forty-thousand-pound bribe, though the accusation was proved false at the subsequent Commission of Enquiry conducted by the British governor of the Gold Coast. Numerous other government officials were accused. Chapman was prominently and frequently mentioned. He was accused outright of passing bribes that brought him special favors.

Away from it all, in London, Chapman wasn't the least concerned. "If anybody asks me," he said, "I'm not guilty." And he added, rhetorically, "What's bribery anyway? You take a man to dinner, is that bribery? You buy a man a drink, or even maybe give him a small present, and is that bribery?"

In each individual accusation against him, the Enquiry found the evidence "inconclusive" or unsupported. He came out of the Enquiry with his reputation a bit besmirched by doubt but without an actionable charge standing against him. Nevertheless, he was through on the Gold Coast. He could not return. And so ended one more chapter in the fabulous career of Eddie Chapman. He began to think of new fields and new pursuits. It was a toss-up between moving to Tangier and taking up residence there, or Kuwait. "Lots of opportunity out there, there's a lot of construction and stuff going on out in Arabia," he said, and he had the old enterprising gleam in his eyes. He eventually chose Tangier. In partnership with Billy Hill, the Soho gambler and night-club operator, he bought a 112 foot ex-Navy launch, the *Flamingo*, with a cruising range of 3,500 miles. He operated the ship out of Tangier to various Continental ports. But within a few weeks he was ordered out of Tangier. Officials gave as their official reason for kicking him out fear that he and his gang (among which were some pre-war associates) intended to go back to their old occupation. Of course Chapman had outgrown such low-class peccadillos as safecracking and robbery.

The first time the *Flamingo* made the headlines was when, a few days before departing from Tangier, Chapman's hand-picked crew of ten ("they have no sailing experience, but we wanted them for a job that required other things besides sailing") fought a running battle from a bar back to the ship with about twenty Spaniards. "It all started over an insult to the Queen," says Eddie.

Chapman will not publicly divulge the exact nature of his operation, claiming that to do so would "set up a hundred other guys in the same business." So far he has been barred from Corsica and all French ports. But he does not seem to be very much concerned about this—despite the fact that the Italian police, too, are keeping a sharp eye on him. "We are not doing anything that anybody else is not doing in Tangier. I can't honestly say we're not smuggling, but it's all done on the high seas. We're not running arms. We have five .45's on board and 100 rounds of ammunition. But it's just to protect ourselves against hijackers. If anybody can hijack my ship, with my crew, they deserve the cargo and more."

But despite his Mediterranean operations, Chapman's war with the War Office has not ended. His story was still untold. While Chapman was down on the Gold Coast building a reputation as a five-percenter supreme, Frank Owen had finished the job of putting the Chapman story into finished manuscript form and had tried mightily to fight it past the War Office. But it wouldn't pass. Owen had hoped that with many details of the story having leaked out and circulating widely in press and semi-official circles like a hazy, inconsistent and only half-believed legend, the War Office would at last let the story be set down in all its fascinating details. But the hope was futile. The War Office would not ease its ban against the story and its censors sliced through the manuscript unmercifully, cutting out every single reference to Chapman's work for British Intelligence.

In the end Owen and Chapman agreed to patch together what was left and have it published, even though Chapman emerged in the book as a Nazi spy and traitor to his country. The true story still has not been published in England, or any place where the War Office can enforce its jurisdiction under the Official Secrets Act. Now it can be told in the United States. But Eddie Chapman still hasn't entirely abandoned the fight to tell the full story, some day, in his own country.